SOUTHERN HISTORY ON SCREEN

SOUTHERN HISTORY ON SCREEN

RACE AND RIGHTS, 1976–2016

Edited by Bryan M. Jack

UNIVERSITY PRESS OF KENTUCKY

Scholarly publisher for the Commonwealth,
serving Bellarmine University, Berea College, Centre
College of Kentucky, Eastern Kentucky University,
The Filson Historical Society, Georgetown College,
Kentucky Historical Society, Kentucky State University,
Morehead State University, Murray State University,
Northern Kentucky University, Transylvania University,
University of Kentucky, University of Louisville,
and Western Kentucky University.

Editorial and Sales Offices: The University Press of Kentucky
663 South Limestone Street, Lexington, Kentucky 40508-4008
www.kentuckypress.com

Library of Congress Cataloging-in-Publication Data
Names: Jack, Bryan M., 1969- editor.
Title: Southern history on screen : race and rights, 1976-2016 / edited by Bryan M. Jack.
Description: Lexington : University Press of Kentucky, 2019. | Includes index.
Identifiers: LCCN 2018025163| ISBN 9780813176444 (hardcover : alk. paper) | ISBN 9780813176468 (pdf) | ISBN 9780813176451 (epub)
Subjects: LCSH: Southern States—In motion pictures. | Historical films—United States—History and criticism. | Culture in motion pictures. | Race in motion pictures. | Race relations in motion pictures.
Classification: LCC PN1995.9.S66 S65 2019 | DDC 791.436/5875--dc23

This book is printed on acid-free paper meeting
the requirements of the American National Standard
for Permanence in Paper for Printed Library Materials.

Manufactured in the United States of America

ASSOCIATION of UNIVERSITY PRESSES

Member of the Association
of University Presses

Contents

Introduction

Bryan M. Jack

In 2017, as part of the continuing argument over history and memory in the United States, New Orleans, Saint Louis, Baltimore, and other cities questioned the appropriateness of Confederate statues in public spaces. These statues, erected in the late nineteenth and early twentieth centuries, are symbolic not only of the Civil War but also of the Lost Cause mythology that gained precedence for so many decades after the war. This myth, despite overwhelming evidence, held that secession was about states' rights rather than slavery and recast the war in terms of southern honor. Born in the years immediately following the war, by the early twentieth century this view was widely disseminated to the public through popular culture, for example, through the film *The Birth of a Nation* (1915), the novel (1936) and film *Gone with the Wind* (1939), vacation tourism to southern plantations, and advertisements.[1] For much of the twentieth century (and after), the Lost Cause myth was an attractive perspective for many in the United States because it allowed for a reconciliation that displaced slavery and racial questions to the margins of American history.

Film, with its ability to display iconic images to mass audiences, has been particularly powerful in creating the South in the American imagination. From the original *The Birth of a Nation* through *Remember the Titans* (2000), *The Help* (2011), and *12 Years a Slave* (2013), Hollywood has created indelible images that embed in American culture and influence public understanding of southern history and identity. From the earliest days of filmmaking, the historical South has been a frequent Hollywood subject, with hundreds of films set in the region. Because of this ubiquity, and since feature films reach such large audiences, films have profoundly shaped public discourse about southern history. Historian of the plantation South Catherine Clinton, speaks to this: "Millions of Americans have had their vision of the South, race relations, and even the entire panorama of our past shaped if not wholly defined by the movie business."[2]

However, history, especially as it relates to race, is contested terrain, and southern history especially so. People, particularly African Americans, have always challenged nostalgic views of the South, slavery, and the Civil War. The newly created NAACP launched protests against the Ku Klux Klan–celebrating *The Birth of a Nation* when it hit theaters, and activists during the civil rights movement of the 1950s and 1960s defied the legacies of slavery contained in the hegemony of Jim Crow segregation. Today, historians of the long civil rights movement connect the original sin of slavery with modern institutional racism. Nevertheless, the old views persist. Debates over the presence of Confederate monuments in public spaces, displays of the Confederate battle flag, and representation of slavery at historic sites are just three of the more recent examples of the continuing conflict. To many, the gains of the civil rights movement (including the election of President Barack Obama) were signs of unerring progress and the beginnings of a "postracial" America. Events in Charlottesville, Virginia; Ferguson, Missouri; New York City; Baltimore, Maryland; Sanford, Florida; Charlotte, North Carolina; and many other places, in addition to the rise and political power of the alt-right after the 2016 election repudiate this perspective and illustrate that the battle against racism is a continuing one.

In an era when political leaders and others tout the authority of "alternate facts," and label any criticism "fake news," it is vital to understand how our conceptions of the past shape and are shaped by our present. Various popular culture portrayals of the South often illustrate larger issues in American society, with the South serving as the canvas for their exploration. Societies, Michael Kammen argues, "reconstruct their pasts rather than faithfully record them, and . . . they do so with the needs of contemporary culture clearly in mind—manipulating the past in order to mold the present." This volume seeks to further our understanding of how the contemporary context affects filmic reconstructions of southern history and how those reconstructions affect the present.[3]

Using race as the primary, but not exclusive, lens and historical films as sources, this book studies the connections between contemporary historical films, southern history, and southern identity. Scholars do not universally agree on what constitutes "historical" films, but Jonathan Stubbs's most inclusive definition guides the selection of films for this volume: "films which engage with history or which in some way construct a relationship to the past . . . regardless of whether or not they purport to deal with 'real' people and events."[4] Some of the films explored in this collection deal with fictional subject matter, others with historical events. However, all construct relationships with and depictions of the southern past. The following questions are the volume's overarching framework, although every essay does not specifically deal with every question. What is the relationship between historical films, race, southern history, and identity? In the years since the civil rights movement, have the challenges to, and elimination of, codified Jim Crow segregation changed how historical films depict southern history? Specifically, how do films from the post–civil rights movement era portray the historical south and issues of race?

This volume builds on the strong body of literature exploring the connection between the South and popular culture but focuses on modern historical films, defined as Hollywood productions released after 1976, films underrepresented in the literature. In January 1977, the United States inaugurated a southerner as president and *Roots* introduced to a large mainstream audience a correction to the *Gone with the Wind* version of American slavery.[5] In his excellent study, *Southerners on Film: Essays on Hollywood Portrayals Since the 1970s,* Andrew Leiter writes "in conjunction with and subsequent to the civil rights and black pride movements of the next three decades that widespread revisionary representations of race relations would occur in popular American cinema."[6] This volume explores these revisionary representations in depictions of southern history, rather than depictions of the southern present, as explored in Leiter's volume. In their studies of constructions of southern identity, historians W. Fitzhugh Brundage, David Goldfield, and James C. Cobb argue to varying degrees that the passing of the civil rights movement offered an opportunity for the creation of a new southern identity, one moving beyond resistance to integration and support for repressive institutions. This volume explores how this new era affects filmic depictions of southern history.[7]

As with previous incarnations of southern identity, however, southerners are not the only ones doing the constructing. As Allison Graham in *Framing the South* and Karen L. Cox in *Dreaming of Dixie* argue about earlier time periods, popular culture from outside the South is often responsible for creating southern images, and southerners do not necessarily choose or control how people think about the South.[8] In the wake of the civil rights movement, popular culture is again creating southern identity. As in earlier eras, films are an integral component of this creation, but films of this era have been relatively unexamined in this context. Leiter's *Southerners on Film* is very valuable in understanding contemporary films that depict the South and southerners but does not focus on historical films or depictions of the southern past. The final chapter of Allison Graham's fine book begins to touch on post–civil rights movement films but does not focus on historical films. Earlier foundational works in southern film, including Edward D. C. Campbell's *The Celluloid South* (1981), Jack Temple Kirby's *Media-Made Dixie* (1981), Warren French's *The South and Film* (1981), and Karl Heider's edited volume *Images of the South* (1993) were all are written too long ago to examine more contemporary films.[9] Beginning in the wake of the national traumas of Watergate and the Vietnam War, the national celebration of the country's bicentennial, and the changes brought about by the civil rights movement, this project carries the exploration forward while focusing on films that depict the past.[10]

In *Reconstructing Dixie,* her invaluable study of southern identity, Tara McPherson echoes Benedict Anderson's work on imagined communities. She argues, "the South today is as much a fiction, a story we tell and are told, as it is a fixed geographic space below the Mason-Dixon line." The idea of the South as a created place beyond the bounds of geography is increasingly popular; McPherson is part of a growing community of scholars making similar arguments about the creation of southern identity in the American imagination. This exploration is part of a paradigm shift in southern studies, as scholars have steadily moved away from simply documenting southern distinctiveness. Instead, authors in numerous disciplines are investigating the sometimes contentious, sometimes complementary, but always dynamic relationship between the South and the rest of the United States and exploring the multilayered dimensions of southern identity.[11]

Because the South is more than just a geographic space—there are many "Souths" in the American imagination—it can be viewed simultaneously as a place of great beauty, culture, and refinement; as the site of incredible cruelty and violence and also as a place of nostalgia and simplicity in an increasingly complex and urbanized world. Various popular culture portrayals of the South are often illustrative of larger issues in American society, with the South serving as a canvas for exploring these issues. In short, American society has often portrayed the South and southern history to serve American society's ends and in so doing has created these many imagined Souths. Scholars, including Deborah Barker and Kathryn McKee in their edited volume *American Cinema and the Southern Imaginary,* are producing foundational work that examines this creation of the imagined South.[12]

James Cobb, one of the foremost voices in examining southern identity, argues that for most of US history, the South served as a "negative reference point" against which the North (and therefore the United States) created an identity of liberty, democracy, and the pursuit of equality. Cobb, Graham, and other scholars have argued that the rest of the United States conceptualized the South as the antithesis of the United States and used this creation of an oppositional South as a repository for American guilt, especially about the issue of race.[13] David Jansson, building on Edward Said's work, posits the idea of "internal orientalism," arguing that the United States built and sustained a privileged national identity by consigning both undesirable traits and "exotic" positive traits to the imagined place called the South.[14]

This subject resonates both personally and professionally for me, because I recognize how popular culture shaped my own thinking about the South. I grew up in the 1970s and 1980s as a history-loving kid with history-loving parents. We lived in a small town in southeast Kansas, a few miles from the Oklahoma and Missouri borders, and a short drive to Arkansas. As a ten-year-old, I had a subscription to *Civil War Times Illustrated*; my parents took my siblings and me to the few Civil War battlefields in the area; and on family road trips, rarely was there a historical marker that we passed without reading. My father even liked to stop at old cemeteries, and I was always on the lookout for markers noting the graves of Civil War veterans. When *Roots* premiered, my family sat in front of our console television, devouring every night of the miniseries and its depiction of slavery and the antebellum era. Although now I recognize and criticize the flaws in the miniseries, it was an important factor in teaching me (and many others) to question the dominant narratives of American history. Such is the power of popular culture in shaping how we think about the past.

In addition to these popular culture lessons, I learned through history classes, sports mascots, and place names that we Kansans we were on the "right" side of the war, fighting against slavery. John Brown, the Jayhawkers of Bleeding Kansas, and Kansas's identity as the "Free State" were all points of pride. I still vividly remember in my sixth-grade Kansas history class, discussing the Missouri bushwhacker William Quantrill's burning of Lawrence and finding out that this town's police uniforms bear a shoulder patch depicting the event. In Manichean fashion, learning this history and identity meant also learning of the opposition, an aberrant "South"—a South of slavery, racism, segregation, and backwardness. It was a perspective that allowed me and other northerners to ignore or downplay the racism and segregation in our own communities by displacing the guilt for American racism solely within the South.

Oddly enough, while popular culture was teaching us these lessons, it was also teaching us contradictory ones about the "aberrant" South. My nearly daily viewing of reruns of *The Andy Griffith Show* showed me a South not dissimilar from my own small town in Kansas—peaceful, friendly, and safe. Multiple viewings of *Gone with the Wind*—one of the first movies my family bought when home video players became popular—and its television descendants *The North and South* and *The Blue and the Gray* showed a historical South of southern belle and dashing cavalier, with slavery marginalized. My Mom's *Southern Living* magazine and vacation visits to plantations reinforced the vision of the historic South of splendor, hospitality, and refinement. However, it was also a South of unasked racial questions and minimized African American agency.

As an American studies graduate student and then as a professor teaching African American history, I questioned seriously the contradictions I first noticed as a child. Centered on race but multidirectional, my research explorations include African American views of Kansas and the Midwest (including racial segregation in the "free state" of Kansas, including my hometown), popular culture depictions of "black spaces" like East St. Louis, Illinois, and the subject of this book, the intersection of film, race, and southern history. Living first in Tuscaloosa, Alabama, and later in Winston-Salem, North Carolina, I realized that popular culture depictions shaped not only how my non-southern colleagues and I understood the South but also how many southerners did.

As a teacher, I am reminded regularly that many of my students, of all races and regions, have their views of history heavily influenced by films. When discussing the Civil War, slavery, or the civil rights movement, students often reference *Glory, Roots, 12 Years a Slave, The Help,* and *Selma.* For this reason, first at Winston-Salem State University, now at Southern Illinois University–Edwardsville, I designed and teach a class focusing on the long history of filmic depictions of the historical South. Thankfully, for years scholars from various disciplines have recognized the importance of the topic, producing a strong body of literature. However, in teaching the class, I found a lacuna in the scholarship regarding *contemporary* films about the *historical* South.[15] This volume does not completely remedy this situation. However, its intent is to begin to do so and add to the conversation about southern history.

The American South and southern history captures the attention of scholars both inside and outside of the South. Scholars from all regions recognize the South is not a niche topic but is a key to understanding the United

States. Studying the US South is important in Birmingham, England, as well as Birmingham, Alabama, even if there is not a "meat and three" restaurant in sight and sweet tea is not on the menu. At the British Association of American Studies conference in Birmingham, England, I was fortunate to sit with a room full of European colleagues discussing popular culture depictions of southern history. Together with the course I teach and a discussion with Leila Salisbury from the University Press of Kentucky, that conversation in England was the genesis for this volume. Compiling this volume, I believed it important to get as many perspectives as possible, including international and American scholars of various disciplines and stages of their academic careers.

Focusing on filmic depictions of the southern past, each of the ten essays of this volume features between one and three films and their contemporary representations of southern history. I chose the first, Oliver Gruner's "It's Now That Counts," to lead because Gruner skillfully outlines many themes present in the rest of the volume. In the heart of the essay, Gruner uses the films *Everybody's All-American* (1988) and *Get on Up* (2014) as the foundation to examine Hollywood's depiction of the 1960s South. Contextualizing these two films within a multitude of others, Gruner argues that in many ways the South itself has become a character in films set in the 1960s and discusses how films often depict the 1960s South as a struggle between continuity and change.

Thematically grouped, the following four chapters focus on films that feature slavery, the Civil War, and Reconstruction. In the second chapter, "History without a Capital H," Daniel Farrell examines *Django Unchained* (2012) to critique director Quentin Tarantino's erasure of African American agency. The third chapter, "You're Not the South," finds Bryan Jack using *The Outlaw Josey Wales* (1976) and *Ride with the Devil* (1999) to explore how Hollywood used nonslaveholding protagonists to show the Civil War from a southern perspective. In chapter 4, "Reconstruction on Film," Erik Alexander deploys *Free State of Jones* (2016) to discuss the missed opportunities in Hollywood depictions of the Reconstruction era. The final two chapters of this section, Caroline Schroeter's "From Griffith to Parker" and Todd Simpson's "*Roots* Reimagined" have scholars comparing updates and/or reclaiming of earlier works. Schroeter compares the original *The Birth of a Nation* by D. W. Griffith with the Nate Parker 2016 film of the same title but quite different subject matter. Next, Simpson completes a close comparison of the original *Roots* miniseries with the 2016 remake, examining how the intervening forty years changed interpretations of slavery and race in the United States.

The next section moves forward temporally as well as thematically, using sexuality, religion, generational conflicts, and personal reflections on "home" to expand our understanding of history and the South. In chapter 7, "The South as a Space/Place of Reclamation of Black Fe/Male Inheritance," Kwakiutl Dreher uses a personal, family story and the film *Down in the Delta* (1998) as a window into the migration of African Americans out of the South and the connections with the South and its history as home. Chapter 8, "Hollywood's Southern Strategy," has Megan Hunt examining *Ghosts of Mississippi* (1996), *Mississippi Burning* (1988), and *A Time to Kill* (1996), to demonstrate Hollywood's limited, one-dimensional portrayals of white, southern, religious responses to the African American civil rights struggle. In chapter 9, "Lesbian Invisibility Continued," Gene Kelly analyzes the films *Fried Green Tomatoes* (1991) and *The Color Purple* (1985) to explore southern womanhood through the lens of sexuality, particularly Hollywood's erasure of lesbian identity. In the final essay, "Intergenerational Struggle and Racial Progress in *The Help* and *The Butler*" Tatiana Prorokova surveys two recent civil rights films (2013) to examine relationships across generational and racial lines.

Notes

1. Karen L. Cox, *Dreaming of Dixie: How the South Was Created in American Popular Culture*, (Chapel Hill: University of North Carolina Press, 2011).

2. Catherine Clinton, *The Plantation Mistress: Woman's World in the Old South* (New York: Pantheon, 1982), 204.

3. Michael Kammen, *Mystic Chords of Memory: The Transformation of Tradition in American Culture* (New York: Vintage, 1993), 3.

4. Jonathan Stubbs, *Historical Film: A Critical Introduction* (New York: Bloomsbury, 2013), 19–20.

5. Matthew Frye Jacobson, *Roots Too: White Ethnic Revival in Post–Civil Rights America*, (Cambridge, MA: Harvard University Press, 2006), 43.

6. Andrew B. Leiter, *Southerners on Film: Essays on Hollywood Portrayals since the 1970s*, (Jefferson, NC: McFarland, 2011), 5.

7. W. Fitzhugh Brundage, *Where These Memories Grow: History, Memory, and Southern Identity* (Chapel Hill: University of North Carolina Press, 2000); W. Fitzhugh Brundage, *The Southern Past: A Clash of Race and Memory* (Cambridge, MA: Belknap Press of Harvard University Press, 2005); David Goldfield, *Still Fighting the Civil War: The American South and Southern History* (Baton Rouge: Louisiana State University Press, 2002); James C. Cobb, *Away Down South: A History of Southern Identity*, (New York: Oxford University Press, 2005), 222.

8. Allison Graham, *Framing the South: Hollywood, Television, and Race during the*

Civil Rights Struggle (Baltimore: Johns Hopkins University Press, 2001). Cox, *Dreaming of Dixie.*

9. Edward D. C. Campbell, Jr. *The Celluloid South: Hollywood and the Southern Myth,* (Knoxville: University of Tennessee Press, 1981); Warren French, *The South and Film*(Oxford: University of Mississippi Press, 1981); Karl G. Heider, ed., *Images of the South: Constructing a Regional Culture on Film and Video* (Athens: University of Georgia Press, 1993); Jack Temple Kirby, *Media-Made Dixie: The South in the American Imagination* (Athens: University of Georgia Press, 1986).

10. Leiter, *Southerners on Film.*

11. Tara McPherson, *Reconstructing Dixie: Race, Gender, and Nostalgia in the Imagined South* (Durham, NC: Duke University Press, 2003), 1.

12. Deborah E. Barker and Kathryn McKee, eds., *American Cinema and the Southern Imaginary* (Athens: University of Georgia Press, 2011).

13. Cobb, *Away Down South,* 3; Graham, *Framing the South.*

14. David R. Jansson, "'A Geography of Racism': Internal Orientalism and the Construction of American Identity in the Film *Mississippi Burning,*" *National Identities* 7 (September 2005): 265–70. For an example of this image creation on a state level, see Brent M. S. Campney, "'This Is Not Dixie': The Imagined South, the Kansas Free State Narrative, and the Rhetoric of Racist Violence," *Southern Spaces,* September 6, 2007, https://southernspaces.org/2007/not-dixie-imagined-south-kansas-free-state-narrative-and-rhetoric-racist-violence.

15. Excellent recent works for studying southern film that are not necessarily historical include Leiter's *Southerners on Film* and Barker and McKee's *American Cinema and the Southern Imaginary.*

1

"It's Now That Counts"

The South in Hollywood's Sixties Films

Oliver Gruner

Gulf Oil, Albertsons, Wendy's, Video Paradise—a chaotic arrangement of billboards punctures the landscape on all sides as Donnie (Timothy Hutton) and Leslie (Patricia Clarkson) make their first stop in Louisiana. "Here it is, the Old South, just the way you described it to me, Professor," Leslie quips, an advertisement for "old fashioned" hamburgers looming to her right. "Show a little reverence, will you," Donnie replies. "We're on hallowed ground here." And, gesturing toward a sign announcing a new tower block development, he informs her that this was where the Grey Ghost Inn used to stand. For Donnie, as for so many Louisianans in the sports-themed historical drama *Everybody's All American* (1988), the inn was both a memorial to football success and a testament to southern glories gone by. The establishment was once presided over by legendary running back Gavin Grey (known to all as "The Grey Ghost"); its demise is indicative of this hero's fading from the public imagination and the passing of an old way of life.

From the 1950s to the 1980s, *Everybody's All American* pits its main characters against the turbulent ebb and flow of late twentieth-century American history. As the civil rights movement stands up to official white supremacy in the South and shifting gender, family, and economic relationships bring a new way of thinking to the region, Donnie, Gavin, and their peers are forced to confront a changed world. The inn's demolition is but one act in a film replete with historical metaphors intended to evoke the South's sharp vicissitudes of fortune. *Everybody's All American* was part of a broader cycle of Hollywood historical films meditating on such issues. Indeed, when examining the South's role in conflicts of the recent past, cinematic representations have time and again evoked specters of "America's second Civil War." In particular, these films invest the 1960s with dramatic thrust and ideological resonance. Less a contained decade, 1960–69, than a loose collection of ideas and events spanning from the mid-1950s to the mid-1970s, this "long sixties" has established itself as a central piece of US public memory. Since the late 1970s, politicians and filmmakers alike have debated the legacy of the civil rights and feminist movements, the counterculture and Vietnam War. Such debates continue to echo in the twenty-first century.[1]

This essay examines Hollywood representations of the sixties South. If much has been written on filmic engagements with the civil rights movement as it appears in pictures such as *Mississippi Burning* (1988), *The Long Walk Home* (1990), and *The Help* (2011) among others, Hollywood's multifarious portrayals of the South at this time remains underexamined.[2] Whether taking the form of an explicit southern setting or simply evoking ideas and issues by way of southern characters transplanted to other parts of the United States, so pervasive is the region in cinematic portrayals that one might say it has become a character unto itself. I begin with a discussion of the emergence of the South as a politically charged trope in popular culture of the late 1960s, and its place in high-profile sixties commemoration in the 1970s and 1980s. While public remembrance often focuses on a region defined by brutal racism, one also detects what Tara McPherson has in another context called a "cultural schizophrenia about the South . . . at once the site of the trauma of slavery and also the mythic location of a vast nostalgia industry."[3] Using an analysis of *Everybody's All American* as a base from which to explore familiar characters and conventions of Hollywood's sixties South, I consider the ways cinema negotiates between these competing legacies. I conclude with a focus on twenty-first-century representations, in particular the James Brown biopic *Get on Up* (2014) and its engagement with the South as a political and cultural phenomenon.

"The Evil Was Down There": Hollywood's Sixties South

Many of the conventions that would come to define public memory of the sixties South were shaped during the 1960s themselves. Its status as "eye of the civil rights hurricane," argues Sharon Monteith, ensured the "'savage South" became a stand in "for larger social concerns, notably the nation's obsession with the fiction of racial purity."[4] At the time and in retrospect, through images of racist violence, state-sanctioned discrimination, and vicious law enforcement filmmakers used the region as historical shorthand for *all* of America's racial conflicts. As Deborah Barker and Kathryn McKee put it regarding the history of film portrayals, "the color line" is conspicuously placed "below the Mason-Dixon line."[5] On the streets of Montgomery, Greensboro, Birmingham, and Selma, a quasi-Manichean battle has unfolded on cinema screens. Paying little heed to the complexities of American race relations, the movies have offered a roll-call of unproblematic "heroes" and "villains." Central to this dichotomy is the status ascribed to black and white characters. "According to the movies," writes Allison Graham, "the southern problem has never been white people." Rather, it has "always been social class." If African Americans provided the civil rights movement's driving force, films, barring the occasional exception, tend to focus on the significant acts of white characters. Whether appearing as noble lawyers in works such as *To Kill a Mockingbird* (1962) and *Ghosts of Mississippi* (1996), "reborn lawmen" in *Mississippi Burning,* or politically and spiritually transformed women in *Heart of Dixie* (1989) and *Love Field* (1992), the upstanding white citizen is cast as a symbol of southern heroism.[6]

Such characters often find their nemeses in another prominent archetype. Crucial to the South's negative identity is the figure of the "cracker" or "redneck." Into this working-class, white, uneducated, and aggressively racist male is poured a nation's moral outrage. In this way, the blame for American racism is not laid at the feet of social and political institutions but leveled at the white working class. Graham notes the connections between the redneck and broader political conflicts over the Vietnam War. Hollywood liberals have frequently conflated aberrant racism with support for the war, charging the "uneducated rural white man" with being on the wrong side of history on both counts.[7] Thus are versions of the redneck found not only in civil rights dramas but also in films about the sixties counterculture and Vietnam War: the trigger-happy killers of Wyatt (Peter Fonda) and Billy (Dennis Hopper) in *Easy Rider* (1969), the rapists that haunt Joe Buck's (Jon Voight's) memories in *Midnight Cowboy* (1969), the misogynist country-and-western singers in *The Rose* (1979) and the war-loving, anti-counterculture "evil" Sergeant Barnes (Tom Berenger) of *Platoon* (1986), for example.

More generally, one might say that the South's racial conflicts have become entangled with a host of related issues and ideas pertaining to the sixties. In the vast literature of memoirs written by those involved in the era's political uprisings, the South serves as both political and moral battleground, and symbolic baptism of fire for a generation of young activists. In his 1988 memoir *Reunion*, cofounder of Students for a Democratic Society Tom Hayden described the "southern civil rights experience"—the marches, voter registration drives, and inevitable spells in prison—as "both a necessary moral act and a rite of passage into serious commitment."[8] Harrowing descriptions of violence in the early 1960s suggested, according to Annie Gottlieb, that "the evil was down there in the South" and encouraged a generation of young white liberals to join the movement.[9] In these texts, going South becomes both a moral imperative and an "adventure" for young men and women looking to leave their mark on the world. As in stories of the Wild West or the Civil War, the chaos and conflict of the South is a spur for a kind of generational bildungsroman, launching its protagonists on narratives of personal enlightenment. In many ways, it is the perceived "backwardness" of the South—"the region's image as not only 'behind' the rest of the nation but also reluctant to keep pace"—that has, conversely, enabled it to become so pervasive an icon in stories of sixties change and transformation.[10] Images of sunbaked landscapes, quaint rituals, and people stuck in the past have provided dramatic fodder for tales of the era's most significant conflicts: progress versus stasis, the past versus the future, and prejudice versus tolerance.

If the above-noted writers present the South as the crucible of their own coming-of-age, Hollywood representations often flip this on its head, transplanting "backward" southerners to the North and West and chronicling the sixties' impact on their lives. *Forrest Gump* (1994) is perhaps the most famous representation to derive its drama from a southern naïf's engagement with phenomena such as the counterculture and antiwar movement. It was, however, but one in a long line of similar portrayals. The same year as *Easy Rider* brought its murderous rednecks to the silver screen, two quintessential sixties representations introduced characters that prefigured this trend. *Medium Cool* and *Midnight Cowboy* (both 1969) were significant to the extent that they focused on migrant southerners affected by the political and cultural developments of the sixties. The former explores events surrounding the Democratic National Convention of 1968. John Cassellis (Robert Forster) is an ambitious, Chicago-based news cameraman swept up in both the political disarray of the period and in a relationship with West Virginian woman Eileen (Verna Bloom). While happy to talk journalistic ethics with fellow reporters, Cassellis remains detached from his subject matter. Little distinction is made between the real and the fictional; Eddie Adams's famous photograph *Saigon Execution* hangs on his apartment wall as if it were a poster; a large portrait of Jean Paul Belmondo, darling of the French New Wave, sits on the wall adjacent. When he first meets Eileen, he is quick to offer a tasteless impersonation of an Appalachian man unable to buy "tobacco on [food] stamps."

If Cassellis's actions suggest a man disconnected from the world around him, Eileen serves as *Medium Cool*'s symbol of authenticity. Leaving West Virginia after her husband is drafted, she joins the Appalachian community of uptown Chicago. The decrepit apartment blocks and dated interiors speak to the impoverishment of this part of the city. A stark counterpoint to Cassellis, with his comfortable, detached existence, Eileen is at the heart of Chicago's social strife. She has a poster of Robert F. Kennedy on her apartment wall, though by this stage in the film the senator's death has been announced. The presence of this sixties "martyr" only emphasizes her helplessness. Cassellis might fetishize the dramatic scenes of protestors fighting police on the city streets, but Eileen is dragged unwillingly into this political thunderstorm. This is manifested visually in *Medium Cool*'s famous footage of the protests outside the Democratic National Convention. In search of her son, Eileen wanders into the crowds of demonstrators and is caught up in the chaos. Eventually she locates Cassellis, and the two make it to his car, only to suffer a crash in which Eileen is killed. The very people the protestors should be helping—the poor and disenfranchised—continue to suffer on the streets of America just as they are dying on the battlefields of Vietnam. Eileen's death here becomes symbolic of an unfinished class struggle. Though events of 1968 made for good political theater, the clashes and protests did not necessarily translate into lasting social change.

Midnight Cowboy follows Joe Buck, a homespun fantasist from Texas, who travels to New York City to seek his fortune as a prostitute. His turbulent, and ultimately tragic, experiences symbolize the den of alienation that this film presents as modernity. In dress and mannerisms, Buck affects the trappings of a cowboy. He sees this mythic American archetype as an icon of virility and thus his meal ticket when he reaches New York. But Buck is no hard-bitten sentimentalist cut from the John Wayne cloth. Rather, he combines superficially identifiable western traits with a naïveté that this film associates with the South. The region emerges in different forms throughout *Midnight Cowboy*. Ghostly recollections of his grandmother singing him the traditional southern lullaby "Hush, Little Baby," scenes of Buck as a young boy undergoing immersion baptism, and images of rape at the hands of rednecks haunt his waking hours. These flashbacks are tinged with a surreal patina, thanks to the disconcerting cinematography: extreme low angles (as present in the baptism scenes) and dissolves (Buck's first recollection of his grandmother as he stares into a shop window). It is also notable that Buck ends the film in Florida. Like the antiheroes of *Easy Rider*, he and his partner in crime for much of the narrative, Enrico "Ratso" Rizzo (Dustin Hoffman), dream of relocating to the Sunshine State. Though Florida's diverse communities are, as Marlisa Santos points out, "not often characterized as Southern," in terms of typical understandings of the region's identity it is interesting the extent to which this, geographically one of the most southern states, appears as a narrative trope in sixties films.[11] Here and in later productions, it can serve as both the promise of a dream life and as the site of death and destruction. Appearing in Ratso's feverish hallucinations, images of Florida offer little more than a touristic trailer, complete with cloying jingle. Bingo and cocktails are the order of the day (the Florida of Ratso's imagination seems decidedly stuck in a 1950s time loop) as he and Buck cavort with wealthy pensioners. When the two finally arrive here, however, their circumstances have deteriorated. Buck immediately rids himself of the virile cowboy image he had spent so long cultivating. Ratso dies almost as soon as they enter the state. Buck returns to the South, only to find that the American Dream he had searched for throughout *Midnight Cowboy* is just that, a dream—as elusive as the promises of a glossy advertisement.

In many ways, *Midnight Cowboy*'s representation prefigured what Derek Nystrom has termed a "curious yoking of the South and West" in popular films throughout the 1970s.[12] Several scholars have explored the ways southern-set films drew on the Western as a means of revisiting American mythology, only presenting the South (not the West) as allegory for the nation's political, moral, and spiritual development. Warren French identifies 1969 as a key year, citing *Easy Rider* and the film's reversal of the traditional western trajectory whereby pioneers travel westward in search of a new world as a "watershed" in southern representations.[13] As America moved into the 1970s, transposing of western themes into a southern setting became increasingly pronounced. Films such as *Walking Tall* (1973) and *Smokey and the Bandit* (1977) are "adaptations of Western generic elements" where cowboys and horses are replaced with "good ole boys" and trucks. They tended to be set in rural landscapes and focused on the clashes between decent upstanding working-class men, whose rustic simplicity is presented in nostalgic terms, and "various functionaries of a corrupt 'System,' embodied by racist, vindictive policemen and organized crime."[14] The very fact that these films presented a "sunnier" version of southern white working class masculinity was indicative, argues Nystrom, of broader public debates of the 1970s.

The new decade witnessed a concerted attempt by southern politicians and businessmen to reinvent the South's public image. Such efforts ran in tandem with the emergence of the Sunbelt as an economic and political force.

Stretching from Florida and the Carolinas right across to the lower half of California, the Sunbelt was commonly discussed as symbol of a New South, "an attractive, renewed space for industrial and demographic growth."[15] If for much of the 1960s, the idea of the South was a "brutal paradigm for a racist and imperialist nation," the next decade suggested a shift "away from the hostile to a very friendly Dixie."[16] James C. Cobb has chronicled the attempts to transform the notion of a "backward, degenerate region" through promotional initiatives touting the South as a low-tax, resource-rich, air-conditioned paradise, ideal for corporate relocations. Political rhetoric endeavored to quell the flames of racial conflict, presenting a more reconciliatory image of the region—a South, to borrow Atlanta mayor William B. Hartsfield's famous description of his city, "too busy to hate."[17] The rise of Georgia native Jimmy Carter to the presidency in 1976 has been said to personify "the resurgence of the white South."[18]

At the same time, Hollywood's sixties films began to revisit and, to a degree, reinvent their southern archetypes, both male and female. Productions such as *The Rose* (1979), *Hair* (1979), and *Coal Miner's Daughter* (1980) presented "authentic" female artists and country boys transformed by the counterculture. Such characters bore similarities to *Medium Cool* and *Midnight Cowboy* while at the same time serving as vessels through which to reflect on the sixties' impact and legacy. *The Rose* follows Mary Rose Foster, a.k.a. "The Rose" (widely understood to be a stand-in for Janis Joplin, and played in the film by Bette Midler), on an odyssey of sex, drugs, and rock and roll circa 1969. That the filmmakers relocated the hometown of its Joplin character from Texas (Joplin's birth state) to Florida allows the latter to once again become a kind of hopeless dream for protagonists of the sixties. The film begins in the garage of Rose's childhood home. Photographs of dead icons—James Dean, Marilyn Monroe, John F. Kennedy—are splashed across the walls. This is a house of defeated rebels and martyrs. Rose, too, will ultimately die in Florida. Our introduction to Rose presents her as weary of success and the attendant pressures imposed on a pop-culture icon. Business interests have compromised her authenticity as an artist while incessant touring has wreaked havoc on her psyche. Rose comes to symbolize negative views toward the sixties counterculture more generally—its appropriation by big business and excessive indulgences. Desperate to escape this world, she begins a relationship with Houston Dyer (Fredric Forrest), a military man from Texas gone AWOL. Early drafts of the screenplay had actually presented Dyer as a freewheelin' hippie, a "25 year old dude with long black curly hair" very much in tune with the youth movements of the era.[19] By the time the film reached cinemas, however, all of these associations were cut and Dyer is more an inductee into than veteran of the counterculture scene. Interestingly, a similar rewriting occurred during the production of hippie-themed musical *Hair.* Released the same year as *The Rose, Hair* tells the story of country boy Claude Bukowski (John Savage) and his experiences of New York hippie lifestyles. The original stage musical presented Bukowski as a long-haired native of New York, whereas in the film he hails from Oklahoma. Leaving the farmlands of his youth behind, he arrives in the Big Apple a clean-cut country boy. The way is therefore left open for a narrative of personal and political transformation. In rewriting these central protagonists as "conservative" southerners, they become symbolic stand-ins for "ordinary" America and the changes (positive, as is the case with *Hair,* or negative, as in *The Rose*) that the sixties wrought on the nation.

Dyer is introduced as *The Rose*'s good ole boy just after the lead protagonist has encountered a less pleasant group of misogynist "redneck singers," led by Billy Ray (Harry Dean Stanton), and been bluntly propositioned by one of their entourage in the parking lot. Throughout the film, Dyer will play the role of gallant knight, rescuing his damsel in distress from the scrapes and conflicts in which she becomes embroiled (at one moment, he is shown to literally sweep her up into his arms and away from a grueling concert performance). Laconic, self-deprecating, and "real," Dyer offers Rose the promise of an escape from the excesses and egos of the sixties counterculture. The price he pays for his positive representation is the loss of much of his political agency. As well as the counterculture associations noted above, early draft scripts had Dyer making several statements against the Vietnam War.[20] These were also cut by the time *The Rose* reached cinema screens. The idea of a southern hippie or antiwar protestor seems to have ultimately proved anathema to those behind *The Rose,* and Dyer remains a politically a blank canvas onto which Rose projects her desires for a simpler life. However, unlike *Hair*'s Bukowski, who ends the film having absorbed and adopted principles of the counterculture—he escapes the draft and joins with fellow hippies in a last rendition of the iconic song "Let the Sunshine In"—Dyer becomes repulsed by its drugs and individualism. He abandons Rose to her own self-destruction. As with Ratso in *Midnight Cowboy,* Florida serves as the site of this protagonist's downfall. A final stage performance in her hometown sees Rose collapse from a drug overdose. The South once again provides an arena for a symbolic "death of the sixties." *The Rose, Midnight Cowboy,* and other films of the late 1960s and 1970s established common themes and motifs that would endure in later years. The site of political and social conflict, an arena for personal transformation, a symbol of "authenticity," a metaphor for sixties downfall—settings, characters and issues associated with the South became bound up with broader debates on the meaning of the era in the 1980s and beyond.

The Right Side of History: *Everybody's All American* and the Mythic South

On one level, *Everybody's All American*, adapted from Frank Deford's novel of the same name, is about political and cultural change in the sixties. On another, it is a rumination on history itself, the stories we tell each other about the past, and the mythic forms these stories take. One of its three central protagonists, Donnie—or, as his friends know him, "Cake"—ends up becoming a history professor. His thesis on Jeb Stuart, icon of the Confederacy, serves as an ongoing metaphor for the misplaced romance and rose-tinted nostalgia that can blind a community to the cracks lurking beneath. Links between the Civil War and the sixties are persistent throughout the film. After Donnie witnesses violent resistance to civil rights protestors in his hometown, he invokes Lost Cause rhetoric, declaring himself and his fellow white southerners to be "on the wrong side of history." Such words contained an especial resonance for late 1980s America. What and who were on the "wrong side of history" during the sixties was, by this time, a firmly established trope in US political and cultural discourse.[21] The election of President Ronald Reagan at the beginning of the decade had ratcheted up the intensity of debates about the sixties' enduring legacy. In a bluster of jeremiads against immoral hippies, weak liberal politicians, and spoilt activists, denizens of the political right charged the era with having irrevocably damaged the nation. And with the second half of the 1980s seeing an increased effort on the part of liberals to counter such charges, bitter altercations between the two camps abounded.[22] Hollywood cinema's contributions to this debate, though emerging from a broadly liberal perspective, were tentative in their political stance. When in 1986 Jack Temple Kirby suggested that the "emerging message about the South in the eighties" was "reconciliation within and without, between regions, races and sexes," he correctly predicted the route much Hollywood cinema would take over the coming years.[23] Building on the rehabilitation of the white South we observed occurring through the 1970s, *Everybody's All*

American turns the southerner into both sixties hero and symbol of national reunification. In fact, getting on the *right* side of history becomes the film's raison d'être, something that requires a unification of beliefs and peoples for so long at odds.

The film's opening sequence celebrates the Louisiana State University Tigers football team. Fading from faux newsreel footage of the Tigers winning the 1956 Sugar Bowl, the following image is of burning torches illuminating the night sky until, suddenly, the film cuts to a real tiger prowling in a cage. "Eat 'em up, Tigers, eat 'em up," goes the chant as the camera tilts upward to reveal a throng of young people decked out in LSU letter jackets. With the cage in tow, this excitable mob marches into downtown Baton Rouge. Even as celebratory cheers ring out in the city, visuals imbue the scene with a sense of foreboding. The torches, the flames rising into the night, the burning pyre around which they gather—in another context all of this could be the visual iconography of a Ku Klux Klan rally. A marching band makes its way down the state capitol's grand staircase, shot at extreme high and low angles. The cinematography here bears resemblance to the famous Odessa Steps sequence from *Battleship Potemkin* (1926), as if this performance is somehow heir to the military oppressors of Eisenstein's agitprop classic. "Don't wake up Governor Kingfish," bellows LSU's star blocker Lawrence (John Goodman) as he clambers upon the giant statue commemorating the subject of this nickname, Louisiana politician Huey Long. Remembered at times as a populist supporter of the working classes, Long has also been described as dictatorial and a "race baiter," happy to play to prejudice when it suited his aims.[24] Here, one might say that he, along with the grand buildings, marching band, and football team, becomes part of a broader display of southern pride. And yet, among all this is the caged tiger, a reminder that entrapment and suppression are integral to the display—albeit invisible at this stage. As *Everybody's All American* progresses, we bear witness to the metaphorical unshackling of chains as southern rituals and traditions come under assault.

In broad terms, the film reflects on the struggle between continuity and change. We follow the lives of superstar Gavin Grey (Dennis Quaid) and his friends, family, and acquaintances through thirty years of US history. From the glory days on the football field to a retirement beset with personal and financial struggles, Grey's life provides the film's emotional lynchpin. His words, deeds, hopes, and fears become symbols for a nation still struggling to reconcile age-old divides. Loaded with historical resonance, the "Grey Ghost" nickname is an allusion to another southern icon, famed Confederate cavalryman John Singleton Mosby. Grey's status as a folk hero echoes the manner in which Mosby's southern peers celebrated him.[25] Yet the parallel extends beyond hero worship, becoming a metaphorical bedrock to which Grey and Donnie's stories are anchored. Jeb Stuart and Mosby were, like the protagonists in *Everybody's All American*, close confidants who at different historical moments rallied to one another's aid. Though only a few months older than the latter, Stuart regarded Mosby as a "protégé," recruiting him as a scout in 1862, praising his endeavors and helping him to secure a promotion to major the following year.[26] "He made me all that I was in the war," Mosby would later write. "But for his friendship I would never have been heard of." Post–Civil War, these acts of kindness were reciprocated. Killed in battle in 1864, Stuart was not around to defend his legacy as a host of commentators attacked what they claimed were his failures during the Gettysburg campaign and, by extension, his calamitous role in the lost cause of the Confederacy. In the late nineteenth and early twentieth century Mosby wrote a series of impassioned defenses of Stuart's Gettysburg ride, seeking to reposition his old friend on the pantheon of Civil War heroes.[27] Such a narrative indeed finds its counterpart in *Everybody's All American*. As the nephew of Gavin Grey, Donnie enjoys privileges and respect among his peers simply because he is related to Louisiana State's greatest running back. When Grey first visits Donnie's dorm room, a crowd of awestruck freshmen gather outside. Through Grey, Donnie gains access to the university's elite: the parties, the local celebrities, and LSU's most desired belle, Babs Rogers (Jessica Lange). In these early days of gung-ho glory, Grey is Donnie's advocate and protector.

As the film progresses, however, the roles are reversed. A football career does not last forever, and with his star on the wane Grey turns to Donnie for assistance. "How would you like to write a bestseller," he asks of his old friend (now an established academic) toward the end of the film. "I talk it, you write it, we call it *The Grey Ghost*." Down on his luck, missing the veneration of old, Grey wants to become the next Jeb Stuart: "pride of the confederacy." And if Donnie is reluctant, here, to turn amanuensis, the moment nevertheless bristles with symbolic potency. Indeed, the persistence and fragility of myths is a central theme in *Everybody's All American*. Tossed about on the winds of change, "The Grey Ghost" serves as a palimpsest on which new stories, ideas, and ideologies are written and rewritten. As Grey leaves behind the carefree college days of the 1950s, his legacy is forged in a cauldron of political and social upheaval.

The sixties instigate a range of transformations pertaining to race and gender equality, business practices, and even typical notions of heroism. Some agents of change, such as the film's civil rights activist–turned–restaurant manager, Narvel Blue (Carl Lumbly), and successful businesswoman Babs Rogers Grey are presented in a positive light. Others, such as the seedy car salesman Bolling Kiely (Ray Baker) appear as little more than unscrupulous carpetbaggers, out to exploit the turbulent times for their own ends. Likewise, those characters more associated with continuity and tradition appear as both negative and positive archetypes. We have brief references to upholders of Jim Crow laws by way of angry mobs hurling abuse at Blue and others involved in lunch counter sit-ins. LSU blocker Lawrence is presented as an unreconstructed relic. Demonstrating an unwillingness to move with the times, he clings to his "golden days" like they were a game-winning pass. Grey, however, though very much an upholder of what this film presents as "traditional" southern values, is ultimately able to reconcile these with an embrace of changed social and political circumstances. These different mentalities become apparent during an early scene dealing with racial conflict. Narvel Blue, the one black character with whom we become acquainted throughout the narrative is introduced as a gifted ex-football player held back by a poor education. College boys Lawrence, Donnie, and Grey pay him a visit in the black community of Spanish Town. The subsequent race between Grey and Blue becomes a metaphorical treatment of antagonisms between whites and blacks. The colors in their respective surnames allude again to the Civil War while also being suggestive, perhaps, of a dull, dated past versus a vibrant future. Grey is better prepared and wins this race but, in a sign of things to come, only by a whisker.

It seems apt that Lawrence is the first official manager of Grey's business interest, the Grey Ghost Inn. Purchased after Grey turns professional, the bar and restaurant serves, in all its subsequent incarnations, as a kind of museum to the South of yore. Decked out with an array of sporting paraphernalia celebrating the 1956 Tigers, the inn freezes the past into a halcyon snapshot. Within its ornate interiors lies a South in stasis, visually and in terms of social relations. After hiring Blue to work in the kitchen, Lawrence reminds him not to enter or exit via the front door. He may be willing to extol Blue's football abilities, but in all other areas, Lawrence happily toes the Jim Crow line. It is no coincidence that he ends his life in the Grey Ghost Inn. Bad gambling debts catch up with him, and New Orleans gangsters come to claim their dues. A man so attached to his college years that he is unable to countenance

Cashing in on the Grey Ghost. *Everybody's All-American.*

even the slightest hint of social change, Lawrence expires surrounded by the inn's nostalgic bric-a-brac.

The Grey Ghost Inn maintains this relic status throughout the film. After Lawrence's death, revelations of financial irregularities mean the Greys find themselves on the verge of bankruptcy. They are forced to sell the inn to Bolling Kiely, who insists that Grey remain a fixture there, rolled out night after night to tell the same stories of football prowess. The key "innovation" will be to redecorate in what he and his wife proclaim to be an "Old South style." We are introduced to the new inn via a portrait of Kiely and Grey side by side clutching a football, a grim metaphor for the player's fall from grace.

If Grey had earlier described Kiely's business activities as "common," changed financial circumstances have left no room for moral outrage. The Grey Ghost is now little more than a commodity, perched amid other garish, vulgar accoutrements that form Kiely's vision of southern salubriousness. Babs now works at the establishment and emerges decked out in a belle's gown. "Can you believe what has happened to this place?" she asks of Donnie. "[It looks] exactly like a brothel." No longer a house of past glories but an empty pastiche of southern stereotypes, the Grey Ghost Inn is a manifestation of the heritage industry at its worst. Embodying the qualities critics such as Fredric Jameson and Jean Baudrillard have associated with "postmodern" culture, it evacuates the past of ideological meaning, creates its own reality out of recycled images, and flattens history into little more than a series of superficial vignettes.[28] This is not a house of memory but of forgetting.

From out of this spiritually dead establishment, however, emerge two individuals who come to symbolize the South's positive progress. Babs Grey and Blue are both employed at one time or another here; Babs endures Kiely's bullying, and Blue suffers Lawrence's belligerent racism. Both are also victims of broader social inequalities. If, as is often argued, cinema presents sport as "a powerful validation of American social mobility," the racial prejudice and economic pressures surrounding football in this film suggest a career dead-end for Blue.[29] He refuses Grey's offer of a trial with the Washington Redskins, turning instead to serious political commitment (he leads lunch counter sit-ins) and, subsequently, to a successful restaurant business. Similarly, Babs finds in football little more than a boys' club in which women become invisible. "They say the double standard was practically born in the South," Babs says to Donnie at one point, a reference to both her husband's philandering and the conventions governing the sexual behavior of men and women. References to gender of inequality persist throughout the film. In college, Babs gives up any dream of a career; "I'm majoring in Gavin [Grey] and me," she declares early on. When Gavin turns pro, she joins the group players' wives, women reduced to anonymous ornaments on the sideline. After an unpleasant apprenticeship with Kiely, she partners with Blue, and together they turn his local restaurant chain into a national empire.

That financial success is presented as the solution to race and gender inequalities is a problematic aspect of *Everybody's All American*. One hears little more of Blue's civil rights activism and whether he continued his protests beyond the early 1960s. Similarly, there is no great sense that Babs has changed as a woman and/or joined the feminist movement. Rather, her major transformation is the donning of a business suit. She is modern only in the sense that she has embraced corporate culture. By the film's conclusion, political oppression has been consigned to the past, just as is often argued to be the case with 1980s civil rights–themed films.[30] "It's now that counts," Donnie informs Babs as she prepares to witness her husband's last grand speech. "It's all that counts." The Grey Ghost is welcomed back onto a pantheon of legends not so much radically transformed as gently modified. He has learned by now that heroism is the product not of football success nor of becoming the next Jeb Stuart—who, as Donnie informed him, simply "embodied everything the

South wanted to believe about itself." Rather than speak about the games he has played, or the political changes to which he has borne witness, or the history he has experienced, Grey speaks about love. A room full of old friends and teammates look on as he provides a final homage to his wife, Babs. Tara McPherson has suggested the "southern lady" to have long served as "a central player in the aggrandizement of Dixie." In her stoicism, in her manners, in her carriage, in her purity she became part of a broader "celebration of the rebirth of a 'nation' defeated."[31] In a not dissimilar way, this appears to be the closing message of *Everybody's All American*. The old icons remain, even if the world they once inhabited has been defeated. Grey was the all-American hero—"the real deal"—and Babs his belle. Their innate authenticity enabled them to withstand thirty years of social and political change. A final flashback to them in their prime standing before the 1956 postgame celebrations provides one last suggestion that their rebirth as icons is down not so much to radical transformation as careful synthesis of the old and new. Nostalgia and progress rest seamlessly within these two figures as the second "Civil War" reaches its conciliatory denouement.

Conclusion: *Get on Up* and the New Sixties South

Flash forward twenty-six years, and a new southern hero struts onto cinema screens. Soul Brother Number One, the Hardest Working Man in Show Business, the Godfather of Soul—the James Brown biopic *Get on Up* (2014) explores these and many more of the man's multiple public personas. Not unlike its biographical subject, this film has a certain insouciance: its subversion of narrative conventions, its casual breaking down of the fourth wall, its playing with familiar iconography. Screenwriters Jez and John Butterworth and director Tate Taylor have atomized Brown's life into a series of short vignettes, mixed them up, flipped them around and—in a manner befitting Brown's own creative process—rebuilt them into a rhythmic and formally complex declaration. Indeed, with his frequent addressing of the camera, one almost gets the sense that it is Brown (played in the film by Chadwick Boseman) who is really in charge. Consider, for instance, a scene midway through the film. A caption informs us that we are in 1965. Brown meets his manager Ben Bart (Dan Ackroyd) in a café near Augusta, Georgia. "Compliments of Universal Attractions," declares Bart, gesturing toward a Cadillac parked outside. Record company executives have purchased Brown a car as a token of appreciation for all the money he has made them. As they sit down at a table

A new way of doing business: James Brown (Chadwick Boseman) in *Get on Up*.

outside the café, Bart continues in paternal vein, explaining to Brown how the record business "works." When Brown interjects with a suggestion on how to expand his music's reach, Bart quickly puts him in his place. "I understand your frustration, Jimmy, but you're entering a game here where the rules are already set." As the manager explains the music business's hierarchies, Brown gets up and enters the café. From here on in, Brown takes over. Directly addressing the camera (and by extension the audience), he explains to us *his* vision. By paying young DJs to promote his music and conscripting local people to help spread the word, he can circumvent the expensive old boys' network of established promoters. In this way, he will become king of his own music empire. Throughout Brown's speech, an advertisement emblazoned with the words "Old South" lurks prominently in the background.

Within a few minutes, past, present, and future collide in an ironic twist on southern history. His manager here serves as the symbol of white authority—the "boss" rewarding his black charge for loyalty. Earlier in the film, Brown was explicitly warned to stick to the music and leave financial operations alone. The split of *show* and *business* becomes a way of keeping Brown under control. As this scene unravels, however, Brown overturns these power structures. The "Old South" of white masters and black servitude is twisted into Brown's vision of a new (show) business in which he has absolute power. Symbolically, Brown "reclaims" the South for blacks. This scene is emblematic of *Get on Up*'s knowing, tongue-in-cheek approach to its historical themes. One can certainly note its relationship to other recent biopics and their turn toward formally complex narratives, playfulness, and "camp." [32] Films such as *I'm Not There* (2007), an account of Bob Dylan's many public personas, and *Love and Mercy* (2014), a time-shifting chronicle of Brian Wilson's Beach Boys heyday and later psychological problems, are but two of a wider cluster of biopics to push the boundaries of the genre.

More generally, one detects an increased self-consciousness on the part of Hollywood's sixties representations. After forty years of civil rights–, Vietnam War–, and counterculture-themed dramas, it is perhaps unsurprising that filmmakers are aware of the conventions and stereotypes that have coalesced around these films and, at times, seek to challenge them. For instance, the past fifteen years or so have witnessed a growth in productions that focus on a black central protagonist. If there had been a handful produced during the 1990s—*Malcolm X* (1992), *What's Love Got to Do with It?* (1993), and *Panther* (1995), for example—these have proliferated since 2000. In films about sports such as *Remember the Titans* (2000), *Ali* (2001), and *The Express* (2008); about musicians, as *Ray* (2004) and *Dreamgirls* (2006); and major political events, as Lee Daniels's *The Butler* (2013) and *Selma* (2014); black protagonists are central to the narratives, whereas once they walked on the peripheries. Some films endeavor to rethink the simplistic North-South divide with regard to US race relations. While tackling racism in the South, *The Butler* also evokes prejudices existing across the nation (even in the White House). As I have suggested elsewhere, the sports drama *Remember the Titans* disrupts standard regional and temporal distinctions and offers a more expansive view on the civil rights struggle.[33] *The Help,* also directed by Tate Taylor and set in Mississippi circa 1962, was subjected to some criticism for its promulgation of racial stereotypes (in particular, that of the African American mammy) and simplistic reconciliation of political tensions.[34] However, one might also suggest that Taylor did try to subvert some of the more familiar tropes associated with civil rights cinema. This film positioned a black narrator at the center of its diegesis and, rather than present the usual working-class redneck racists, focused on bigotry existing in "well-to-do" southern middle-class households. If Taylor was not always successful in his efforts, he was at least aware of, and made some attempt to challenge, the stereotypes of old.

Perhaps this is indicative of recent portrayals of the sixties South more generally. Filmmakers may well address and even critique the stereotypes, but they seem more comfortable doing so via playful, ironic allusions than with a serious political agenda. Some memorable scenes in *Get on Up* subvert the image of the South as America's "backward" region. Complex editing patterns counterpoint the vibrancy of southern musical culture and the more polished, stodgy offerings of mainstream entertainment emerging from the North and West. Sharp distinctions between a "wild" South and "tame" Californian cultural scene emerge during one sequence. From a shot of James Brown as a child, we jump to 1965 and a recording of Brown's anthem "I Got You (I Feel Good)" for the Frankie Avalon film *Ski Party* (1965). Dressed in corny argyle sweaters, Brown and his band provide a sanitized performance for their lily-white audience. "Oh, hell no. I'm in a honkey hoedown," laments Brown. Northern and western towns and cities are associated with a kind of regimented capitalism—the imposing record company building of Cincinnati, the pop-culture factory of California. In the sunlight bursting through dense forestry, the ribaldry, the vibrant musical culture, the South is conceived in line with freedom and authenticity. Brown's onstage histrionics (later to inspire performers such as Mick Jagger) are shown to have been influenced by a childhood meeting with a manic gospel preacher in Georgia. Brown's innovative syncopated beats are a legacy of his southern musical education. In this film, the South is not just savage counterpoint to sixties progress and transformation. The black communities of the region are also presented as a site of rich cultural expressiveness and energy—a modernizing force.

Of course, there are issues with such a representation. The extent to which *Get on Up* actually grapples with politics, racial or otherwise, is debatable. While Brown might mention his troubled relationship with the Black Panthers, this theme is not developed. We may hear a rendition of his anthem "Say It Loud—I'm Black and I'm Proud," but not of Brown's 1972 endorsement of President Richard Nixon. When, at the film's end, he informs longtime friend and collaborator Bobby Byrd (Nelsan Ellis), "We've come a long way . . . white people cleaning our pools," one might view such sentiments as rather too casual an extinguishing of ongoing racial inequalities. Once again, mainstream cinema's need for poignancy or narrative closure means a compromised political address. And yet, *Get on Up* does at least offer a refreshing portrayal bereft of white "saviors" and focuses on the region's turbulent relationship to black culture, past and present. In its formal and stylistic density and attempts to engage with alternative historical subject matter, there is perhaps the basis for a new sixties South in Hollywood film. In terms of historical representations, it is, to recall Donnie's words to Babs Grey, "Now, that counts."

Notes

I thank Bryan Jack for his advice and ideas on Civil War history as represented in *Everybody's All American.*

1. Daniel Marcus, *Happy Days and Wonder Years: The Fifties and the Sixties in Contemporary Cultural Politics* (New Brunswick, NJ: Rutgers University Press, 2004); Bernard Von Bothmer, *Framing the Sixties: The Use and Abuse of a Decade from Ronald Reagan to George W. Bush* (Amherst: University of Massachusetts Press, 2010).

2. Allison Graham, *Framing the South: Hollywood, Television, and Race during the Civil Rights Struggle* (Baltimore: Johns Hopkins University Press, 2001); Sharon Monteith, "The Movie-Made Movement: Civil Rites of Passage," in *Memory and Popular Film,* ed. Paul Grainge (Manchester: Manchester University Press, 2003), 120–43; Allison Graham, "'We Ain't Doin' Civil Rights': The Life and Times of a Genre, as Told in *The Help,*" *Southern Cultures* 20, no. 1 (2014): 51–64.

3. Tara McPherson, *Reconstructing Dixie: Race, Gender, and Nostalgia in the Imagined South* (Durham, NC: Duke University Press, 2003), 3.

4. Sharon Monteith, *American Culture in the 1960s* (Edinburgh: Edinburgh University Press, 2009), 22, 23, 25.

5. Deborah Barker and Kathryn McKee, introduction to *American Cinema and the Southern Imaginary,* ed. Deborah Barker and Kathryn McKee (Athens: University of Georgia Press, 2011), 3.

6. Graham, *Framing the South,* 193, 188; Monteith, "Movie-Made Movement."

7. Graham, *Framing the South,* 13, 14.

8. Tom Hayden, *Reunion: A Memoir* (New York: Random House, 1988), 70.

9. Annie Gottlieb, *Do You Believe in Magic? Bringing the 60s Back Home* (New York: Simon & Schuster, 1987), 34.

10. Andrew Leiter, introduction to *Southerners on Film: Essays on Hollywood Representations Since the 1970s,* ed. Andrew Leiter (Jefferson, NC: McFarland, 2011), 8.

11. Marlisa Santos, "Adaptation and Sunshine State: Nature and Nostalgia in Contemporary Florida Films," in Leiter, *Southerners on Film,* 175.

12. Derek Nystrom, *Hard Hats, Rednecks, and Macho Men: Class in 1970s American Cinema* (Oxford: Oxford University Press, 2009), 61.

13. Warren French, introduction to *The South and Film,* ed. Warren French (Jackson: University Press of Mississippi, 1981), 8.

14. Nystrom, *Hard Hats, Rednecks, and Macho Men,* 56.

15. Ibid., 71.

16. Jack Temple Kirby, *Media-Made Dixie: The South in the American Imagination,* rev. ed. (Athens: University of Georgia Press, 1986), 122, 141.

17. James C. Cobb, *The Selling of the South: The Southern Crusade for Industrial Development, 1936–1980* (Baton Rouge: Louisiana State University Press, 1982), 93, 97–121.

18. Kirby, *Media-Made Dixie,* 171.

19. Oliver Gruner, *Screening the Sixties: Hollywood Cinema and the Politics of Memory* (London: Palgrave Macmillan, 2016), 12–13.

20. Ibid., 11–37.

21. Eleanor Townsley, "'The Sixties' Trope," *Theory, Culture, and Society* 18, no. 6 (2001): 99–123.

22. Richard Maltby, *Hollywood Cinema: An Introduction* (Oxford: Blackwell, 1995), 385.

23. Kirby, *Media-Made Dixie,* 188.

24. Adam Fairclough, *Race and Democracy: The Civil Rights Struggle in Louisiana, 1915–1972* (Athens: University of Georgia Press, 2008), 22–23.

25. James M. McPherson, *Battle Cry of Freedom: The American Civil War* (Oxford: Oxford University Press, 1988), 738.

26. Daniel E. Sutherland, A *Savage Conflict: The Decisive Role of Guerillas in the American Civil War* (Chapel Hill: University of North Carolina Press, 2009), 165.

27. Eric Wittenberg and J. David Petruzzi, *Plenty of Blame to Go Around: Jeb Stuart's Controversial Ride to Gettysburg* (El Dorado Hills, CA: Savas Beatie, 2006), 219–20, 179–261.

28. Fredric Jameson, *Postmodernism, or, The Cultural Logic of Late Capitalism* (Durham, NC: Duke University Press, 1991); Jean Baudrillard, "The Precession of Simulacra," in *Cultural Theory and Popular Culture,* ed. John Storey (Harlow: Pearson, 2009), 409–15.

29. Bruce Babbington, *The Sports Film: Games People Play* (London: Wallflower, 2014), 27.

30. Monteith, "Movie-Made Movement," 137.

31. McPherson, *Reconstructing Dixie,* 19.

32. Carolyn Anderson and Jon Lupo, "Off Hollywood Lives: Irony and Its Discontents in the Contemporary Biopic," *Journal of Popular Film and Television* 36, no. 2 (2008): 102–11.

33. Oliver Gruner, "You're Only as Good as Your Last Game: *Remember the Titans* Remembers Civil Rights," in Leiter, *Southerners on Film,* 32–46.

34. On these criticisms, see Association of Black Women Historians, "An Open Statement to the Fans of *The Help,*" reprinted in *Southern Cultures* 20, no. 1 (2014): 32–33.

2

History without a Capital H

Violence, Commodification, and the Perpetuation of the Postmodern Condition in *Django Unchained*

Daniel Farrell

In 2012, Quentin Tarantino's *Django Unchained* was released to near-universal critical acclaim, receiving laudatory reviews from popular outlets such as the *New York Times,* the *Chicago Sun-Times,* and London's *Guardian.* These critics praised the film for its cinematic qualities, its acting, and, most importantly, its ability to portray a dark and disturbing aspect of American history: slavery. The film does so, according to several critics, by maintaining Tarantino's classic entertaining flair. A. O. Scott, writing for the *New York Times,* claims the film is "digressive, jokey, giddily brutal and ferociously profane" but "also a troubling and important movie about slavery and racism." He goes on: like "*Inglourious Basterds, Django Unchained* is crazily entertaining, brazenly irresponsible and also ethically serious in a way that is entirely consistent with its playfulness." As a film that artfully plays with genre and challenges traditional cinematic conventions, *Django Unchained* was positively received as a breakthrough in entertainment, as it successfully dealt with America's past while thoroughly entertaining its audience.[1]

Beyond these cinematic merits, not everyone was pleased with how Tarantino represented the institution of slavery. Detractors criticized his artistic choices, oversaturation of violence, and constant use of racial epithets. Spike Lee, for example, refused to see it, believing the depiction of slavery in a spaghetti Western was disrespectful to his ancestors. Jeffrey T. Kuhner, writing for the *Washington Times,* accused it of promoting reverse racism, writing that "anti-white bigotry has become embedded in our postmodern culture," claiming that the movie was nothing more than "anti-American propaganda masquerading as history."[2] For entirely different reasons, both saw the film's representation of history as problematic, raising broad, although not well-developed critiques of postmodern aesthetics. Lee, however, made headlines, as his comments prompted formal responses from Tarantino and several of the cast members. Tarantino believed Lee's charges "ridiculous," while Samuel L. Jackson asserted that these types of "stories must be told."[3] While no one involved in the film would later argue that *Django Unchained* embodied the qualities of a documentary, there was a persistent claim, in response to sharp criticism, that the movie offered a reasonably accurate depiction of American slavery.[4]

Lee never elaborated too deeply on his comments, and Jackson rightfully criticized him on this point. Yet, Lee's statements open an important debate. He questioned whether postmodern aesthetics were properly equipped to depict traumatic events and to foster an active relationship between the viewer and the historical past. On tragedy, Marxist literary critic Terry Eagleton is explicit in his doubts. He argues that, in a literary context, tragic works of art have "an ontological depth and high seriousness about the genre which grates on the postmodern sensibility, with its unbearable lightness of being."[5] He connects this back to a broader political point by castigating the postmodern left for its predilection toward historical relativism, contending that tragedy is not merely contextual but an immutable facet of the human condition. For Eagleton, to ignore this fact and instead fixate on the self-fashioned, destabilizing allure of postmodern theory creates fictional works oddly more in tune with capitalist commodification than with effecting any real change.[6]

Another Marxist literary theorist, Fredric Jameson, believes this phenomenon the result of postmodernism having achieved the status as a cultural dominant, a point altogether quite different than whether postmodernism retains any academic usefulness for the twenty-first century. He argues that, as an objective reality, the postmodern condition has become so thoroughly integrated into our commodity production that it has begun to dictate our "aesthetic innovation and experimentation." While he believes that not all cultural production is now postmodern, Jameson does claim, nonetheless, in a somewhat contradictory fashion, that we have completely lost our grip on the historical past. Arguing that even the most "realistic" forms of literature, including the historical novel, have fallen victim to the simulacra, Jameson condemns the genre as nothing more than a mere representation of historical stereotypes.[7]

It is under this basic framework that *Django Unchained* will be scrutinized, particularly about the movie's representation of slavery and southern history—not because the film depicts it but because Tarantino was adamant about the movie's historical authenticity. But as a commodity product of postmodernity, it will be shown that Tarantino often privileged aesthetic choices that made the film simultaneously more profitable and less historical. His use of violence played a prominent role in marketing the film, as genre tropes informed Tarantino's cinematography, forcing the movie to be divested of any tragic message, creating a pleasing, if not utopian, cinematic experience. And yet, this critique diverges from Jameson's in one critical area. There is no reason to believe that historical representations in art can never advance beyond an assortment of preconceptions and stereotypes. While a film can never fully represent the past, we can do better than the application of postmodern aesthetics, particularly since we have access to a vast body of historical scholarship. This fact becomes apparent when *Django Unchained* is contrasted with the 1975 Blaxploitation film *Mandingo,* especially since *Mandingo* served as one of Tarantino's chief inspirations.

Violence is then the centerpiece of Tarantino's film, and despite his lofty sentiments toward educating the public on slavery, the movie's artistic qualities erase much of what made slavery tragic in the first place. As a commodity production, *Django Unchained* ironically overlooks that slavery was a system of coerced labor and that African Americans actively attempted to resist their enslavement through a variety of means. As Tarantino has admitted, he drew inspiration from Westerns, plantation dramas, action films, and Blaxploitations to construct this work. He did this not to allow "a historical story to play out" but rather to "make it an exciting adventure."[8] As film critic Ed Guerrero has noted, violent action-adventure movies such as *Die Hard* (1988), *The Terminator* (1984), and *The Replacement Killers* (1998) are far more numerous and profitable than serious films "that try to historicize, comment on, or dramatize the psychic, moral, social, or political consequences of violence, like *Schindler's List* (1993), *Gandhi* (1982) . . . and *The Pawnbroker* (1965)."[9] For *Django Unchained* to first reach its intended audience, it had to satisfy the initial demands of its viewers, who expected to be treated to an intensely violent, hypersexualized visual experience.

Tarantino believed that what surrounded and contextualized this violence was his way of educating the public on America's past. Therefore, when one analyzes his work, what responsibility does he hold, and how should his purpose be reconciled with viewer-centric theories of literary criticism? To this point, film critics cannot overlook Tarantino's authorial intent because he advanced conflicting, often contradictory ideas about the historical representations. Specifically, he claims that pure historical accuracy was not necessary for his film—while adamantly advancing a strong truth claim about the nature of southern history, as well as Hollywood's failure to represent it. But unlike some of Tarantino's detractors, this chapter does not argue that he is a closeted racist or is deliberately advancing a damaging portrayal of African Americans. Mirroring the sentiments of film critic Joi Carr, this work acknowledges that "Tarantino's project [was intended] to challenge the pernicious imagery of black inferiority."[10] But when his statements and aesthetic choices are scrutinized, however, it becomes clear that Tarantino consistently privileged representations he believed the viewing public would view more positively. These decisions, however, reinforce damaging stereotypes about African Americans, particularly their supposed lack of agency within the plantation system. Although unintentionally, the film portrays African Americans as passive victims, incapable of asserting themselves or mobilizing themselves against injustice.[11]

Postmodernity has had much to do with this, as Tarantino's preconceived notions of the past limited his artistic choices on both a practical and conceptional level. In an illuminating interview with Henry Louis Gates Jr., Tarantino explained how he attempted to rectify the problem of accurately representing slavery while still making an entertaining film. An admirer of Sergio Corbucci, the director of the original *Django* (1966), Tarantino was impressed by Corbucci's ability to recreate the American West as a mechanism for commenting on Italian fascism. But in acknowledging that the Reconstruction-era West was not nearly as violent and depraved as Corbucci's version, Tarantino sought to find a historical period that would, in his own words, be "really . . . real." American slavery was the perfect fit but carried a certain realism that contradicted Tarantino's logic. Slavery was actually nothing like a Corbucci spaghetti Western, and therefore *Django Unchained* needed to incorporate more "entertainment value" to make it into "a thrilling adventure."[12]

Thus, Tarantino's conception of slavery appears to have been informed by a mixture of factors, some more legitimate than others, yet Tarantino preferred to emphasize the violence. Here, he has a correct, if somewhat vague, understanding that slavery was a brutal institution. But by surrounding trauma in genre play, especially spaghetti Western tropes, Tarantino loses much of the meaning behind the racialized violence to sustain some degree of entertainment. The film trivializes the lived experiences of African Americans and reduces their experiences to a series of profitable spectacles. Theorist Guy Debord believed, similar to Jean Baudrillard's conception of the simulacra, that such capitalist-driven representations could have the effect of essentially making these depictions seem to be an "objective reality," at least insofar as no other meaningful perceptions become possible.[13]

There were, however, other possible outcomes. Had Tarantino taken the time to be more open to historical interpretation, he would have discovered an enormous body of scholarship to work with. As he admitted, he straddled a line between wanting to recreate the southern past and making a "genre story."[14] Therefore many of his artistic choices were filtered through past cinematic experiences, creating a pastiche in which the image of slavery was disassembled through the lens of countless works of art and reassembled in such a way that was ironically pleasing to watch. Because Tarantino was unconcerned with "historians having a hissy fit," it can be inferred that he sees the institution of slavery as a literary text to be interpreted. He uses historical plausibility to pluck acts of violence and sadism from the past to enhance the viewer's later ability to release tension in order to derive pleasure from the more spectacular acts of fantasy violence that signify most of the film's end. By fixating on violence and genre play, *Django Unchained* privileges the existence of two different forms of violence under a shared postmodern language, since their relationship works together toward the creation of a more satisfying cinematic experience.

Tarantino explains how he situated these various kinds of violence within his undeniably violent film. In an interview with Jamaal Finkley, Tarantino stated that "two brands of violence" within the movie were intended to "deal with the true brutality of slavery." He characterized the Mandingo fight and D'Artagnan's death as "sobering" depictions of violence, while he described the final shootout as a "cathartic" representation of it.[15] These different images "play off each other" to create tension within the viewer that can only be released by *Django*'s blood-soaked conclusion. As film critic William Rothman notes, fantasy violence invites the viewer "to acknowledge that the world on film is separated from us" and thus not real, allowing us to enjoy it better.[16]

Rothman's observation is significant, as it brings clarity to Tarantino's argument that some forms of violence are intended to entertain, while others are not. The connection between the two, however, is intriguing. According to Mark Gallagher, postmodern violence aims to "present violence as a component of a spectacular visual style" that is intended "to thrill or excite rather than to shock."[17] Yet the "sobering" violence, as Tarantino puts it, works in tandem with the fantasy violence to create a narrative arc that the viewer can enjoy. In test markets, according to Tarantino, the original cut of the film included scenes deemed far too realistic and disturbing to make the final version. For the audience to have a "satisfying experience," these scenes needed to retreat from realism and create separation between the film's violence and the viewer, ensuring that the film maintained a strain of fantasy throughout.[18] Otherwise, Tarantino feared, audiences would be unable to enjoy the movie, hurting the film's performance at the box office.

In the few instances in which the onscreen conflict is meant to portray a traumatic element of the antebellum South, the sequence is brief, occurs offscreen, or stretches the imagination. While the Mandingo fight and D'Artagnan's death function as the film's primary moments of inhumanity, a few ancillary scenes allow the viewer to peer into the violent, everyday happenings of antebellum slave life. The first is when Django (Jamie Foxx) prevents one of the Brittle brothers from whipping a slave girl, while the other is a flashback in which Django recalls the physical punishment of his wife, Broomhilda (Kerry Washington). Both scenes, while profoundly disturbing, are relatively tame in comparison to the rest of the movie. In the first example, the whipping never occurs, while Broomhilda's scene is a short, bloodless affair. As historian Eugene D. Genovese has noted, slaves received the lash for "running away . . . stealing and poor work," and in both depicted cases, slave owners cruelly punish their slaves for these slight offenses.[19] But as a product of postmodernity, these tragic scenes are pushed to the margins and are made brief and palatable for an audience unprepared to confront real brutality during a light, playful, cinematic experience.

As the film's proclaimed sobering representations of violence move farther away from their historical roots, their representations increasingly become more graphic, fluidly shifting the images from the authentic to the fantasy. We see this progression begin during Django's trip to Candie Land, when Calvin Candie (Leonardo DiCaprio) executes D'Artagnan, a runaway slave, by having dogs tear him apart. By occupying a representational space that is simultaneously both plausible and unlikely, Tarantino can claim that this is an authentic representation of violence, even though economic considerations often prevented a master from purposefully killing a bondsman for running away. Employing a Western trope, Tarantino navigates this space by claiming he made the value of slaves unnaturally low since he "made it . . . obvious" that spaghetti Westerns often promoted the idea that life was cheap.[20] This use of genre mitigates the slave's lived experience by erasing the cruel reality that the lives of African Americans, at least to their slave owners, possessed much economic value, since their bodies belonged to a coercive labor system that exploited their work for profit.

Film critics should view D'Artagnan's murder as a historically plausible act of sadism, one that functions more as a horror scene than as social commentary, since the sequence sits uncomfortably between various cinematic tropes, historical accuracy, and the film's economic viability. That slave owners used dogs in the tracking and catching of runaway slaves is borne out in the historical record, as Genovese notes that it was the dogs themselves who often struck the most "terror into the slaves." The paternalist sentiment of the late antebellum era, however, began to force a reappraisal of this terrible exercise, as some slave owners saw the use of dogs as anathema to Christian values. Disagreeing, Judge Lumpkin, a member of the Georgia State Supreme Court, upheld the use of dogs in tracking runaways in 1855. He argued that the South had already lost more than sixty thousand slaves to the North and that southerners needed to utilize all available measures in reclaiming them. In revealing the cruel persistence of their use, Lumpkin reasoned that a dog's purpose was not to kill the runaway but rather to protect the economic investment of the slave owner.[21]

Readers should not assume that just because a slave owner could be seen as acting with some sense of self-fashioned kindness toward his slaves, this observation is a crude defense of the slave-owning pathos. Rather, it emphasizes a deeper tragedy about the situation, as masters routinely measured the physical well-being of their slaves against their earning potential. Slave owners sought to regulate the usage of dogs not out of kindness but as a way of reforming the institution as a means of protecting it. As Genovese has noted, southerners saw their way of life as superior and attempted to humanize slavery in order to defend it from criticism. One slave owner, Dr. John Wilson, observed that it was the "duty of all slaveowners . . . who are interested . . . in the perpetuation of the institution, to disclose its abuses . . . with a design of correcting those abuses and thus disarming our enemies." That Lumpkin supported the use of dogs against the wishes of some reformers reveals how these debates were framed around the question of how to best protect the institution of slavery as an economic system.[22]

Despite the existence of reform, however, flagrant abuse indeed existed, and Tarantino does touch on the salient point that as pieces of property slaves could be killed with impunity. But the scene does little to encapsulate the complexities of the antebellum South, as evident by both Candie's attitude toward the murder and as the way Tarantino shot the sequence. Initially, Candie bitterly complains that he will lose his $500 investment if D'Artagnan refuses to fight, but he quickly shifts his tone when he sacrifices D'Artagnan's life to test Django's resolve, rendering these economic concerns inconsequential. The scene is also an uneasy blend of restraint and horror, as Tarantino framed the shot in such a way as to address the complaints from his test audiences that the original killing was much too graphic. While the final cut remains fairly realistic, the violence had been toned down and was surrounded by illiterate, hollering backwoods southerners, giving the sequence a quality more similar to *Deliverance* (1972) or *The Texas Chainsaw Massacre* (1974). By treading a fine line between fantasy, plausibility, and marketability, Tarantino eschewed the possibility of adding depth to his film, ensuring that D'Artagnan's death remained a plot device to advance Django's revenge rather than function as a teaching moment for the audience.[23]

The Mandingo fight is the centerpiece of Tarantino's vision of authentic violence. The difficulty, however, is that no historian of the antebellum South supports the existence of such activity. Accordingly, then, the fight is qualitatively different from the other representations of "real" violence. As blood flows freely during the combatants' battle to the death, little is left to the imagination. The fight's fictitious construction is grounded not in historical sources but rather in the strong intertextual relationship between *Django Unchained* and *Mandingo,* a film that focused on Mede (Ken Norton), a slave purchased for breeding. Each movie contains a gladiatorial fight to the death, and both scenes are choreographed similarly, with elements, such as the eye gouging, having been recycled from *Mandingo* and interjected directly into *Django Unchained*. Highly referential to past cinematic aesthetics, the Mandingo fight is cloaked in the veneer of realism but is postmodern in its construction, as it more readily offers itself as a reference point to past cinematic developments of slavery rather than to slavery itself. Unlike the scenes too real to depict, this one sits comfortably within the movie's more ludicrous action sequences, as it functions as both entertainment and a meta-commentary on film genre rather than as substantive social commentary.[24]

It is not, however, meaningful to simply nitpick these scenes to ascertain their historical reality. Rather, this discussion helps demonstrate how marketability pushed Tarantino to privilege postmodern depictions of violence, no matter how "authentic" he claimed them. The historically plausible scenarios were altered to create anxiety within the viewers without scandalizing them. This tension is released as Django exacts his revenge in a series of joke-filled, comical shootouts that defy physics. Just as Eagleton was skeptical that the postmodern condition was not capable of addressing tragedy, it becomes apparent that *Django Unchained* shied away from traumatic events to prevent upsetting its viewers. The fictional Mandingo fight becomes the focal point of Tarantino's postmodern notion of authentic violence entirely because it is both false and falsifiable. It does not force the viewer to confront the past, and by insisting on its reality, it functions to rid the film of acknowledging the daily realities of slave life and punishment. As film critic Karen Johnston observed after watching the movie, her fellow audience members expressed how they found the film both "funny" and "entertaining" but never insightful.[25]

Having established that the violence in *Django Unchained* is postmodern in its construction, what, then, of the surrounding context that gives that violence its meaning? For Tarantino, the film's ostensible goal was to bring cultural awareness to the reality of southern history. And yet, when Jameson suggests that capitalism had been dictating postmodernism's "aesthetic innovation," he intends this as a totalizing feature of these cultural products, and this appears to have rung true for *Django Unchained*.[26] Slavery is therefore not a necessary precondition for Tarantino to produce a profitable cinematic experience. All of his films, save *Grindhouse* (2007), have been box office successes. But Tarantino did claim to have had a strong desire to confront America's past, as well as to take Hollywood to task for failing to deal with the actual harshness of slavery. Slavery, although undoubtedly a violent institution, was not violent in a way that translates well into entertainment. Therefore, to deal with the institution, and to produce a profit-driven cinematic experience, Tarantino surrounded his subject matter in "genre," thus making the film not about southern history or slavery per se, but rather a celebration of cinematic tropes.[27]

Beyond the violence, much of the movie's remaining historical reconstruction relies on its intertextual relationship with past works of art, not dissimilar to Jameson's argument that intertextuality can function as a means of displacing real history with that of a "history of aesthetic styles."[28] Thus, slavery and the antebellum South serve only as a backdrop to proliferate violent imagery for profit, as Tarantino develops his understanding of slavery primarily through cinematic stereotypes rather than from a close reading of history. Privy to general narrative structures, *Django Unchained* becomes utopian in its overall structure. Situated only "two years before the Civil War," the film is a tale of both revenge and the recuperation of one's agency that has been stolen by the institution of slavery. In Tarantino's reading of the past,

African American agency is only the product of freedom. Django derives his agency from Dr. King Schultz's (Christoph Waltz) benevolence; the rest of the enslaved need only to wait for the inevitable conflict between the North and South before earning their freedom.[29]

Tarantino based his artistic choices not on a malicious reading of history but rather on none at all. It can be difficult to pinpoint how Tarantino came to believe that slaves lacked agency, but he has left several clues. Rather than looking to history, Tarantino positions *Django Unchained* against previous films that have depicted slavery, providing evidence that the movie's final cut is the mostly the product of intertextuality rather than a close reading of historical sources. In an interview, Tarantino admitted that he wanted to correct a shortcoming endemic to the film industry, claiming that movies about slavery were rarely empowering toward African American audiences. His observation is poignant and largely correct. Even a cursory understanding of film history reveals that plantation dramas and other films about slavery rarely provide African Americans with an uplifting message. In many older movies, slaves are seen as happy and content and seldom express any agency. Tarantino corrects the mistake that slaves were content but sustains representations of black passivity. His handling of Jamie Foxx best illustrates this point, as Tarantino chastised Foxx for playing his role with too much "self-confidence and bravado." He identified this as a historically abnormal expression of slave agency and instructed Foxx to dial back his assertiveness to "express a lifetime lived on the plantation." The intervention is uncharacteristic of Tarantino's directing style, as he often encourages his actors to forge their own paths. Thus, Tarantino intervened into Foxx's acting method as a way to perpetuate an alleged historical truth. In Tarantino's understating of the antebellum South, slaves possess no agency and need to relearn it. Because Django is "exceptional," the implied meaning is that the clear majority of African American slaves were not, and thus Tarantino portrays them as downtrodden, silent victims who willingly submit to the slaveholding elite.[30]

Genre tropes help to reinforce this stereotype. In a panel discussion, Tarantino remarked that he was "opposed to doing a straight historical movie with a capital H," arguing that he could better portray the institution of slavery "if it was wrapped up in genre."[31] Therefore, his desire to blend Western imagery with southern slavery becomes problematic, as the highly personalized, masculine narratives of Westerns do not lend themselves well to telling stories about emancipation and southern slavery. Employing a plot device characteristic of Westerns, Shultz assumes the role of the "experienced gunslinger" who desires to help "the young cowpoke" on his mission.[32] Django's goal is to rescue his wife, Broomhilda, from the sadistic Candie, and because emancipation does not motivate Django, slavery's daily realities rarely present themselves within the film, relegating the surrounding black cast to the margins of Django's individualized tale of revenge.

A spatial issue further exasperates this point. Tarantino has also claimed that historically "many Westerns had taken place during slavery times" and that these films had "bent over backwards to avoid" addressing it.[33] While it is true that Hollywood has traditionally shied away from the subject of slavery as not to alienate a southern audience, Tarantino nonetheless constructs a straw-man argument. While many Westerns did take place during the 1840s and 1850s, slavery, as an embedded economic system, did not exist in the antebellum West. Rather, it existed as a contentious political abstraction that deadlocked US politics for over a decade. As a historian Daniel Crofts has noted, "the endlessly debated issue during the secession winter—and the years leading up to it—was slavery in the territories."[34] Issues over slavery's viability in the West were often at the heart of these debates. Stephen A. Douglas, for example, believed his doctrine of popular sovereignty was the perfect solution to these congressional deadlocks, as it allowed the territories to decide the status of slavery for themselves, thus keeping the peculiar institution out of national politics. Because Douglas believed the West inhospitable to plantation slavery, the problem, he reasoned, would naturally solve itself. And while it remains unclear whether slavery was truly incapable of spreading west, it would only have done so with the primary intention of enlarging the collective political and economic power of the South's slaveholding aristocracy. Increased southern power was a scenario many northerners had found intolerable.[35]

This analysis is not to suggest that Westerns accurately represent their subject matter or that slavery has no place in Western films. Rather, by surrounding *Django Unchained* in Western tropes and imagery, Tarantino creates a false impression that slavery, as a social system, was a defining characteristic of the antebellum West; it was not. This outcome is likely unintentional, as again, Tarantino primarily derived his knowledge of slavery through his understanding of film history. Because he actively resisted any engagement with historical sources, Tarantino can use genre to manufacture a false notion of slavery's very existence to tell a traditional Western tale out of both place and time. In doing so, the film erodes the reality that slavery existed only as an entrenched economic system within the South. It also overlooks that the West often served as a reference point for contesting the existence and spread of slavery, thus reducing emancipation to nothing more than a vague foretold consequence of the Civil War. By opening the film with a scene in which slaves trudge through the desert and by providing a textual clue that their emancipation is close at hand, Tarantino robs African Americans of their lived reality and their agency in obtaining freedom. That Tarantino depicts black slaves as entirely silent and powerless has no consequence for the film's progression, since the white Union army will soon be rescuing them. Slavery is only the sideshow to Django's quest to rescue his wife.

While many films share close intertextual relationships with *Django Unchained,* one movie in particular bears many similarities to Tarantino's. *Mandingo,* a 1970s Blaxploitation film about slavery, established many of the themes the two films hold in common, such as their violence and their portrayal of slave women as sexual objects. As a pioneering film for the era, *Mandingo* attempted to distance itself from the older plantation dramas by emphasizing slavery's tragic nature. In doing so, it often fell into its own problematic representations, such as the aforementioned Mandingo fight and a fixation on sexual objectification. Tarantino rightfully saw in *Mandingo* the terrible and arbitrary nature of slave ownership and adopted those themes in his own film. This was an admirable move. The difficulty, of course, is that Tarantino overlooked many of *Mandingo*'s nuanced themes, focusing only on the film's most sensationalist aspects, as those were also the most marketable. Without digging deeper into historical sources, *Mandingo* serves as just another text for Tarantino to reference, perpetuating Baudrillard's conception of the simulacra. But as historian and postmodern critic Richard Evans has noted, "the past is much more than a mere text, and to attempt to read it as a text is to capture only a small part of its reality."[36] As Baudrillard feared, the result of the simulacra is that images will no longer have any "relation to . . . reality whatsoever."[37] But we do not need to resign ourselves to this fate.

In fact, *Mandingo* is an illustrative example of how Tarantino could have improved upon the slave genre. Set during the 1840s, *Mandingo* depicts the drama of southern life at Falconhurst, a rundown Louisiana plantation. As Guerrero has described, the Blaxploitation formula "generally consisted of a black hero out of the ghetto underworld, violently challenging 'the Man' and triumphing over a corrupt, racist system."[38] Guerrero's description, however, is not entirely consistent with *Mandingo,* as the protagonist, Mede, is not easily identifiable as a hero, and the antagonist, Hammond Maxwell (Perry King), is not a clear villain. Their onscreen relationship is a complex and sophisticated look at the profound social contradictions created by racialized slavery. While Blaxploitation in name, *Mandingo* functions as an anti-plantation drama, deromanticizing the depiction of slavery and southern society found in such films as *Jezebel* (1938) and *Gone with the Wind* (1939). Thus, *Mandingo* utilizes some Blaxploitation tropes, such as violence and hypersexuality, to challenge these old plantation dramas. Like Tarantino, *Mandingo's* producer, Dino De Laurentiis, believed he had a calling "to reach beyond the sentimentalized South of other films with uncompromising honesty and realism to show the true brutalizing nature of slavery."[39] However, genre play is not the defining characteristic of *Mandingo* but is rather a subtle tool of protest. Problematic scenes exist but are reined in by the film's desire to remain reasonably accurate.

Instead of building off of its positive representations, *Django Unchained* is intensely referential to the most sensational aspects of *Mandingo,* particularly the way the film depicts Mandingo fighting, prostitution, and sexual exploitation. Additionally, like that of Candie Land, the operation of *Mandingo*'s plantation, Falconhurst, seems arbitrary to the viewer, with the slaves rarely depicted in economic activity. There is a certain subtlety, however, to Falconhurst's unproductive existence. It functions primarily as a breeding ground for human chattel, in which suitable males are then sold off to agricultural plantations. With no real sustained economic activity, Falconhurst is an old and decrepit plantation, lacking in the splendor and beauty of most Hollywood-produced plantations. Candie Land, in contrast, is a juxtaposition of magnificence and inactivity. Candie's plantation is completely devoid of cotton fields, as vast, open and empty space surrounds his mansion. Slaves exist only to cook meals, clean the mansion, engage in death sport, or make themselves sexually available to Candie. On Candie Land, and throughout the film in general, slaves rarely speak and willingly submit to authority without question. Tarantino continually portrays them as confused, dazed and downtrodden.

There is a profound difference, however, in the way the slaves of Falconhurst conduct themselves: these African Americans frequently speak, deny authority, and skillfully navigate the complex and oppressive realities of plantation life. For example, a rebellious slave, Cicero (Ji-Tu Cumbuka), is introduced in the film's opening scene as a troublemaker, distinguished by his physical branding as a convicted runaway. When Falconhurst's owner, Warren Maxwell (James Mason), presents Cicero to a potential buyer, to evaluate his physique, the slaver forces him to fetch a stick. Upon returning, Cicero defiantly throws it to the ground, in a subtle display of resistance. Later, Cicero conducts a secret meeting at night, where he teaches the other slaves how to read. He also instills in them an intense desire for freedom, asking them to contemplate their humanity. In a rousing monolog, he asks his fellow slaves if they think "that peckerwood [Hammond] don't know we as human as he is? Why you recon' he keep us from learning, religion, and reading? Cause they know! They fear deeps down that we is human!" Cicero's subplot of resistance crescendos into his final act, when he leads a failed slave rebellion, killing several whites before being apprehended. As the local white community prepares to hang him, for a final time he vocalizes the conundrum of slavery. He declares that whites were "oppressed in [their] own land, [and that] we was free and you brought us here, in chains," slyly suggesting that the South's problems transcend racial subjugation. The entire plantation system, with its vicious cycle of violence, exploitation, and class dominance, poisons southern society.[40]

Cicero's act of defiance is only one of several examples of black agency depicted throughout *Mandingo*. Mede may be the lead character, but these contextual subtleties, carried out by the surrounding cast, give the film its textual richness. In contrast, *Django Unchained* has few scenes of similar redemptive value. Rarely do slaves vocally question the plantation system, contemplate their humanity, or actively seek to rebel against slave society. From the opening scene until Django's triumphant victory, slaves, played by the supporting cast members, are characterized as silent, afraid, and confused, shuffling around in chains or cooperatively obeying their masters. Even Django is not the product of his own agency, nor does he seek freedom for its own merits. Shultz rescues him because he needs his assistance in assassinating the Brittle brothers. Once they complete the job, Shultz grooms Django to enact his revenge, and thus the driving motif of the film is to rescue Broomhilda. Consequently, Django rarely comments on the virtues of emancipation. For example, in one of the final scenes, he plucks Broomhilda's bill of sale off Shultz's corpse, perpetuating the document's legitimacy as an agent of freedom. In Django's world, freedom remains a condition defined by white power structures and perpetuates the idea that agency is only the product of one's legal freedom.

Furthermore, as the duo journeys across the South, the slaves they encounter are rarely shown in economic roles. The lone, brief exception is when Django and Shultz arrive at Spencer Bennett's (Don Johnson) Tennessee plantation, where several field hands stop working as they are mesmerized by

Django's fancy attire and horsemanship. As a ruse to identify and assassinate the Brittle brothers, Shultz convinces Bennett to have one of his slaves, Betina (Miriam F. Glover), escort Django around the grounds. Betina is confused over the conception of freedom and asks Django, "what you do fo yo master?" When Django reminds her he is a free man, Betina is incredulous. Kenneth Stampp argues that it is difficult to believe that slaves "had no understanding of freedom, and therefore accepted bondage as their natural condition. . . . All knew that some Negros had been emancipated [and they] knew that freedom was a *possible* condition for any of them."[41] The slaves of *Mandingo* intensely understood this, and the film actively portrays their desire for freedom. In contrast, the slaves of *Django Unchained* have a challenging time grasping this concept and acting accordingly.

There is also no indication that the slaves of Bennett's plantation resent their positions in life or are actively contemplating resistance. As Django interrogates Betina about the Brittle brothers, she tells him that one of the brothers is about to whip Little Jodie (Sharon Pierre-Louis), a house slave, relaying this information without any concern or empathy for Little Jodie's plight. As Django makes his way to the barn, he passes an enslaved woman riding on a swing, a strange juxtaposition between tragedy and complacency. Upon arrival, he kills John Brittle and asks the onlooking slaves "if they want to see something." Implying that they have no conception of their ability to resist plantation authority physically, he then kills the nearby Rodger Brittle. He does so in this manner not only to earn his bounty but also to introduce to the slaves to the idea of active resistance. It is a rare, fleeting moment in which Django seems to contextualize his position between the world of slavery and freedom. However, as Genovese once wrote, "the most impressive form of slave self-assertion has largely remained unsung . . . [as] a surprising number of slaves would not submit to the whip."[42] Historically, slaves would not have needed Django's lesson. That the slaves of Bennett's plantation are not even remotely concerned with Little Jodie's punishment, or cognizant of the possibility of active resistance, is an offensive removal of their collective plight.

As a highly referential, pastiche work, the remainder of *Django Unchained* continues to cannibalize the more sensationalist, commodifiable elements of *Mandingo*, while jettisoning most of its positive qualities. *Mandingo*'s greatest strength lies in its portrayal of human relations, as it serves as a commentary not only on antebellum race relations but also on the enervating effects of plantation life as well. This argument is particularly evident within the contradictory relationships that exist on Falconhurst. While Candie briefly reveals his vulnerability in an interaction with Stephen (Samuel L. Jackson), Warren's son Hammond continuously struggles over the morality of slavery. For example, when he takes on a concubine, Ellen (Brenda Sykes), he develops what appears to be a genuine relationship with her and impregnates her. When she pleads for the child's freedom, Hammond refuses emphatically. But when he sees how upset she has become, he changes course and promises her the child's freedom.

In a scene depicting the internal slave trade, the Maxwells have rounded up several slaves to bring to market. As the slaves prepare to leave Falconhurst, loved ones surround them in tears, visually upset at one of the most salient aspects of antebellum slave life: the splitting up of families. As Hammond gathers his bondsmen for sale, he's moved by one of his slaves' plea to keep her infant child. When he grants her request, his aging father chastises him. In fact, whenever Hammond indulges his slaves in any kindness, Warren is quick to criticize him. Warren was born during the 1700s; his attitude is reflective of the generational divide that often split the planter class. As historian Philip Morgan has argued, southern paternalism had its roots in the mid-eighteenth century but had become fully entrenched by the next century. As a product of the nineteenth century, Hammond's behavior conforms to Genovese's description of paternalism, claiming that it "grew out of the necessity to discipline and morally justify a system of exploitation. [While] it did encourage kindness and affection . . . it simultaneously encouraged cruelty and hatred."[43] Not only do these sequences help develop a rich, contextual setting for understanding the behaviors of the planter class in an unromanized way, but they also contribute to reinforcing the reality that slaves often negotiated the boundaries of their enslavement at every possible opportunity. Preying on Hammond's reformist sentiments, the slaves of Falconhurst seek any possible reprieves from the daily drudgery and pain of their predicament, a general point that Stampp emphasized in *The Peculiar Institution* (1956).[44]

Not beholden to genre tropes, Mede's experience on the plantation is fundamentally different from that of the rebellious Cicero. While his fellow slaves yearn intensely for freedom and self-expression, Mede forms a sincere friendship with Hammond, despite the other slaves warning him against this behavior. Shedding the stereotype of the underworld Blaxploitation hero, Mede is instead a tragic victim of Hammond's paternalism. He believes Hammond to be different from other slave owners, describing him as understanding, compassionate, and just. When Cicero initiates his uprising, it is Mede who ultimately catches him, resulting in Cicero's execution. Later, Hammond's wife, Blanche (Susan George), blackmails Mede into having a sexual relationship with her. When Hammond discovers the relationship, Mede convinces himself that Hammond will react calmly and acknowledge that Blanche had threatened him. However, Mede badly misinterprets Hammond's character and pays the ultimate price for his subservience.

Thus, in the final sequence, Hammond poisons Blanche for her sexual deviance, then seeks out Mede with the intention of killing him. Ellen tries to stop him, but Hammond forcefully shoves her to the ground. Despite their ostensibly loving relationship, Hammond reminds Ellen of her proper place, telling her to stop interfering because she "ain't anything but a nigger." Upon finding Mede, Hammond instructs him to boil a large kettle of water then, while his father, Warren, looks on, demands that Mede get into the scalding water. When Mede refuses, Hammond shoots Mede and shoves him into the kettle with a pitchfork. A nearby slave, Agamemnon (Richard Ward) grabs Hammond's rifle and pleads with him to stop. When Warren demands that Agamemnon drop the rifle, referring to him as a "crazy nigger," Agamemnon shoots Warren dead and flees the scene. Hammond cries out and clutches his father's dead body as the camera pans out to show the decaying Falconhurst one last time. While the building still stands, the plantation's inhabitants have been torn asunder by the terrible reality of southern slavery, with no clear resolution in sight.

In the end, both Hammond and Mede, ironically, possess the least agency as characters, as both navigate the antebellum landscape through the false assumption of paternalism and reciprocity. Failing to learn from Cicero's experience, Mede places his trust in Hammond, only to learn the hard truth that his life is ultimately at the whim of the planter class. On the opposite end of the spectrum, Hammond is incapable of escaping his racist mindset, despite having questioned the very foundation of racial subordination throughout the film. Both men born into a life that tolerates racial subjugation, their story imparts a powerful and haunting picture of the Old South: that the institution of slavery—with its perversion of social relations, its reliance on coercive labor, and its insistence on strict gender hierarchies—had ultimately limited their usable worldviews. *Mandingo* has far more to say than *Django Unchained* about the southern past, moving beyond slavery to paint a commentary on the entirety of antebellum southern culture.

As a film, *Mandingo* has its flaws. As a rare, big-budget production ostensibly of the Blaxploitation genre, it was still somewhat beholden to a public that demanded violence and sexually explicit material. The film shows slave fighting as an authentic experience of the antebellum South. Economic depictions of slave labor are deemphasized, while the movie glorifies crude sexual exploitation. And yet, *Mandingo* is anything but postmodern. It is not referential to any aesthetic past. It does not wrap a tragedy in genre to make it more palatable. It was, in part, a product of changing historical and intellectual trends that began challenging the romantic image of the Hollywood southern plantation. Its brutality was raw, and *Mandingo* rarely contrasted this conflict with fantasy violence. However, as Tarantino used *Mandingo* as a textual reference, the intertextual relationship between the two films was predicated on the crude profit-driven elements in *Mandingo*. In *Django Unchained*, gone are the intricate subtleties of slave life, agency, and resistance.

By *Mandingo's* end, the fate of Falconhurst, Hammond, and his slaves remains unknown, while the plantation system remains firmly in place. *Mandingo* deals with the actual tragedy of the situation—that even though its slaves are active and vocal resisters, their battle is continuous. *Django Unchained*, in contrast, is utopian. A single actor, driven by revenge and not freedom, destroys Candie Land and frees its slaves. The slaves do not require agency, as Django miraculously shows up to save the day for reasons that had nothing to do with their enslavement. As the film also points out, the Union army will valiantly finish the job two years later. As the credits roll, the viewer is left relieved that the racist plantation system is about to be overthrown.

Tarantino, of course, meant well. He also initiated a broad, however flawed, conversation that American society should be more proactive in discussing its past. Yet his desire to create a profitable, entertaining film led him to arrogantly dismiss the work of historians. As a product of postmodernity, *Django Unchained* fails to engage its viewer with the past and in many ways perpetuates damaging stereotypes of black passivity. Since entertainment is largely incompatible with tragedy, history becomes trivialized, commodified and repackaged in an agreeable fashion aimed at the largest audience possible. However, there is no insinuation that filmmakers are trapped in this predicament or that they should limit themselves to documentaries. No artist or historian can ever encapsulate the past exactly as it happened, but we can do better than postmodernism. There is a body of scholarship ripe for incorporation into fictional works, and *Mandingo* serves as an example of a film that attempted to do so. Film directors quickly abandoned the tradition established by *Mandingo* only to see the beginnings of its return in recent years, with such movies as Steve McQueen's *12 Years a Slave* (2013). More popular films like *Django Unchained*, however, continue to perpetuate the postmodern condition as a cultural dominant, but our acknowledgment of this condition is only the first step. Once we have done so, we can hopefully strive to escape it.

Notes

1. A. O. Scott, "The Black, the White and the Angry," *New York Times,* December 24, 2012, http://www.nytimes.com/2012/12/25/movies/quentin-tarantinos-django-unchained-stars-jamie-foxx.html?pagewanted=all; Robert Ebert, "Faster, Quentin! Thrill! Thrill!" *Chicago Sun-Times,* January 7, 2013, http://www.rogerebert.com/rogers-journal/faster-quentin-thrill-thrill; Peter Bradshaw, "Django Unchained: First Look," *Guardian,* December 12, 2012, http://www.theguardian.com/film/2012/dec/12/django-unchained-first-look-review.

2. Jeffery T. Kuhner, "Jamie Foxx and the Rise of Black Bigotry," *Washington Times,* December 12, 2012, http://www.washingtontimes.com/news/2012/dec/13/jamie-foxx-and-the-rise-of-black-bigotry/.

3. Stephen Rebello, "Playboy Interview: Samuel L. Jackson," *Playboy,* September 30, 2013, https://www.playboy.com/articles/samuel-l-jackson-playboy-interview.

4. Adelle Platon, "Spike Lee Slams Django Unchained: 'I'm Not Gonna See It,'" *Vibe,* December 21, 2012, http://www.vibe.com/article/spike-lee-slams-django-unchained-im-not-gonna-see-it.

5. Terry Eagleton, *Sweet Violence: The Idea of the Tragic* (Oxford: Blackwell, 2003), ix.

6. Rebello, "Playboy Interview"; Eagleton, *Sweet Violence,* xi.

7. Fredric Jameson, *Postmodernism; or, The Cultural Logic of Late Capitalism* (Durham, NC: Duke University Press, 1991), 6, 25. While Jameson is quick to point out that postmodernity, as a cultural dominant, is not necessarily hegemonic in an absolute sense, it functions nearly as such since most aesthetic production is forced to contend with it. And yet, when it comes to representing history, Jameson appears less flexible in what is possible.

8. Henry Louis Gates Jr., "Tarantino 'Unchained': *Django* Trilogy," in *Quentin Tarantino Interviews,* ed. Gerald Peary, rev. and updated (Jackson: University of Mississippi Press, 2013), 187.

9. Ed Guerrero, "Black Violence as Cinema: From Cheap Thrills to Historical Agonies," in *Violence and American Cinema,* ed. J. David Slocum (New York: Routledge, 2001), 213.

10. Joi Carr, "Introduction: *Django Unchained*-Disrupting Classical Hollywood Realism?" *Black Camera* 7 (Spring 2016): 38.

11. The classic text on a reader centric theory of literary criticism, which many film critics have adopted for their analyses, is Roland Barthes's foundational article, "The Death of the Author." Barthes argues that the way readers interact with the text is often more insightful then what the author ever intended. Recent scholarship on Tarantino's work, especially Adilifu Nama's *Race on the QT,* adopts this analytical framework. For our purposes, however, Nama takes a strong stance against critics who argue that Taran-

tino's work is the product of his racism, a sentiment this chapter shares. However, several scholars, such as Andrew Harrington and Karen A. Johnson, do continue to advance the position that Tarantino's underlying racism is to blame for the film's shortcomings. But as a product of postmodernity, it is more convincing to see Tarantino's artistic choices stemming from his misconceptions rather than cultural appropriation. What he depicts on screen is what he believes happened. It is perhaps a subtle difference, but it reorients our analysis away from kneejerk reactions into something hopefully more insightful. See Roland Barthes, "The Death of the Author," in *Image-Music-Text,* trans. Stephen Heath (New York: Hill & Wang, 1977), 142–48; Adilifu Nama, *Race on the QT: Blackness and the Films of Quentin Tarantino* (Austin: University of Texas Press, 2015), 2, 10; Andrew Harrington, "Is Quentin Tarantino Calvin Candie? The Essence of Exploitation in *Django Unchained,*" *Black Camera* 7 (Spring 2016): 79–87; Karen A. Johnston, "*Django Unchained*: An Analysis," in *From Uncle Tom's Cabin to the Help: Critical Perspectives on White-Authored Narratives of Black Life,* ed. Claire Oberon Garcia, Vershawn Ashanti Young, and Charise Pimentel (New York: Palgrave Macmillan, 2014), 211–26; Gates, "Tarantino 'Unchained,'" 191–92.

12. Henry Louis Gates Jr., "An Unfathomable Place," *Transition* 112 (2013): 60.

13. Guy Debord, *The Society of the Spectacle* (Berkeley: Bureau of Public Secrets, 2014) 2.

14. Gates, "Tarantino 'Unchained,'"187.

15. "Quentin Tarantino on Violence, the 'N' Word, and Django Unchained," YouTube video, 6:04, posted by Black Tree TV, December 18, 2012, https://www.youtube.com/watch?v=fCPTDQkKe3I.

16. William Rothman, "Violence and Film," in *Violence and American Cinema,* ed. J. David Slocum (New York: Routledge, 2001), 44.

17. Mark Gallagher, "I Married Rambo: Spectacle and Melodrama in the Hollywood Action Film," in *Mythologies of Violence in Postmodern Media,* ed. Christopher Sharrett (Detroit: Wayne State University Press, 1999), 201. Although critics often characterized *Django Unchained* as an homage to Westerns and Blaxploitation, it does bear many similarities to action films of the 1980s and 1990s that often relied on hypermasculinity, implausible scenarios, and cartoonish levels of violence for entertainment. Therefore, as action films privilege the pleasure derived from watching violence within a safe space, so too does *Django Unchained.* This overlooked connection should receive increased attention.

18. "Quentin Tarantino on Violence."

19. Eugene D. Genovese, *Roll, Jordan, Roll: The World Slaves Made* (New York: Vintage, 1976), 65.

20. Gates, "Tarantino 'Unchained,'" 192.

21. Genovese, *Roll, Jordan, Roll,* 651, 652.

22. Wilson quoted in ibid., 56. For an excellent discussion on reformist ideology among slave owners, see 49–70.

23. "Quentin Tarantino on Violence." It is also of note that Gallagher has argued that postmodern violence privileges "comic, stylized, or otherwise exaggerated treatments of violence in action films [to] repress screen violence's [most] obvious meaning: that hor-

rific pain and suffering should repulse the viewer." D'Artagnan's murder is somewhat different, as it does not fully conform to Gallagher's notion of comic violence. However, the way the scene uses horror tropes helps to stylize it and give it a comic element, as to ease its traumatic nature. See Gallagher, "I Married Rambo," 205.

24. Aisha Harris, "Was There Really 'Mandingo Fighting,' Like in *Django Unchained?*" *Slate,* December, 24, 2012, http://www.slate.com/blogs/browbeat/2012/12/24/django_unchained_mandingo_fighting_were_any_slaves_really_forced_to_fight.html; Erica L. Ball, "Response: 'Goodbye Miss Lara!' or What's Slavery Got to Do with It? Regeneration through Violence in *Django Unchained?*" *Safundi: The Journal of South African and American Studies* 16, no. 3 (2015): 315.

25. Johnston, "*Django Unchained,*" 212; Eagleton, *Sweet Violence,* ix.

26. Jameson, *Postmodernism,* 5.

27. "Meet the Press, *Django Unchained,*" YouTube video, 39:39, posted by Movie Maniacs, January 1, 2013, https://www.youtube.com/watch?v=-1QpScB-HJg.

28. Jameson, *Postmodernism,* 20.

29. *Django Unchained,* directed by Quentin Tarantino (New York: Weinstein Company, Columbia Pictures, 2012), Blu-ray.

30. Gates, "Tarantino 'Unchained,'" 185–86.

31. "Meet the Press, Django Unchained."

32. Gates, "Unfathomable Place," 60.

33. "Meet the Press, Django Unchained."

34. Daniel Crofts, *Lincoln and the Politics of Slavery: The Other Thirteenth Amendment and the Struggle to Save the Union* (Chapel Hill: University of North Carolina Press, 2016), 10.

35. Larry Langman and David Ebner, *Hollywood's Image of the South: A Century of Southern Films* (Westport, CT: Greenwood, 2001), 11; Crofts, *Lincoln and the Politics of Slavery,* 4, 8, 10–11.

36. Richard J. Evans, *In Defense of History* (New York: Norton, 2000) 95

37. Jean Baudrillard, *Simulacra and Simulation* (Ann Arbor: University of Michigan Press, 1994), 6.

38. Guerrero, "Black Violence as Cinema," 214.

39. Quoted in Andrew DeVos, "'Expect the Truth': Exploiting History with *Mandingo,*" *American Studies* 52 no. 2 (2013): 9; Ed Guerrero, *Framing Blackness: The African American Image in Film* (Philadelphia: Temple University Press, 1993), 31–42.

40. *Mandingo,* directed by Richard Fleischer (1975; Los Angeles: Paramount Pictures, 2010), Blu-ray.

41. Kenneth M. Stampp, *The Peculiar Institution: Slavery in the Ante-Bellum South* (1956; repr. New York: Vintage, 1989), 88.

42. Genovese, *Roll, Jordan, Roll,* 619.

43. Ibid., 4.

44. Philip D. Morgan, *Slave Counterpoint: Black Culture in the Eighteenth-Century Chesapeake and Lowcountry* (Chapel Hill: University of North Carolina Press, 1998),

284. It should be noted that the historiography of American slavery is quite rich and that this article has intentionally referred to older works, such as Stampp's and Genovese's, to reinforce the point that historians have long accepted the historical reality that slaves expressed agency. In other words, these are not new ideas.

3

You're Not the South

The Outlaw Josey Wales, Ride with the Devil, and Confederate Guerrillas in Modern Films

Bryan M. Jack

This chapter uses the films *The Outlaw Josey Wales* (1976) and *Ride with the Devil* (1999) as starting points to explore the intersection between race, class, and depictions of white southern identity. Since the end of the civil rights movement, films showing the Civil War from the point of view of common Confederate soldiers attempt to separate the issue of slavery from the Civil War by either minimizing its impact or avoiding it altogether. Minimizing slavery as an issue allows films to capitalize on the popularity of the Civil War as a subject without stigmatizing the South for the institution or raising uncomfortable racial questions for the rest of the nation. Meanwhile, featuring nonslaveholding Confederate soldiers as protagonists, these films use class to separate the Confederacy from the institution of slavery. Most importantly, unlike previous periods, when the creation of white southern identity relied on overt opposition to blackness, the displacement of slavery from Civil War depictions allows for a white southern identity created in the apparent absence of blackness. However, the absence is illusory, for, even when unacknowledged, race and slavery continue to shape how we remember the southern past.[1]

The two films discussed in this chapter both minimize slavery's connection with the Civil War by featuring Confederate guerrillas as protagonists. However, they are different in their aspirations, perspectives, and approaches to the connections between race, the Civil War, and identity. *Josey Wales* ignores slavery as an issue and silences African Americans, using personal interactions between white and Native American characters to camouflage a reactionary perspective. *Ride with the Devil,* while more directly and effectively confronting racial slavery and racism, still works to distance white southern identity from the institution. Scholars argue the imagined South has multiple meanings and is often, paradoxically, both a "romantic and disavowed space." These films, unlike many earlier Civil War films, do not romanticize the South. However, they also do not necessarily reject the institution that was the foundation for southern society. Despite this, they are still able to create worlds where modern audiences relate to Confederate soldiers.[2]

In one sense, these films demonstrate Hollywood embracing a bottom-up version of history by focusing on individual Confederate soldiers who are neither officers nor wealthy. Paul Haspel argues that films' portrayals of individual Confederate soldiers have long provided an effective lens for understanding the level of sympathy or criticism of the South, and his formulation provides a good framework to follow. Discussing recent films, Haspel states, "Films with Civil War subject matter made since the end of the Vietnam War . . . tend to avoid passing judgment on the individual Confederate soldier, presenting him as a military adversary of the Unionists but not necessarily as a political enemy of human rights." The two films featured in this chapter fall under this description both temporally and thematically. By sympathetically universalizing the soldiers' experiences, the films obscure the Civil War's political causes beneath a layer of common humanity. This concealment allows audiences to identify with the protagonists but not with the Confederacy or slaveholders, thus maintaining a view of the war as a tragic mistake rather than a war of union and emancipation.[3]

To create distance from slavery, the filmmakers craft protagonists who are reluctant warriors, geographically and socially liminal characters not connected to the Deep South or plantation life. With the war embodied in two Missouri bushwhackers, the geographic, economic, and social marginality of the primary characters differs markedly from many previous film representations of the Confederacy but has many commonalities with non–Civil War films released in the wake of the civil rights movement. The themes of challenging government authority, the white working class as rebellious heroes upholding traditional American values, and mobility (represented through cars, tractor trailers, as well as horses) were consistently celebrated in these films, as well as in other forms of popular culture. I turn next to the popular culture context of the era immediately following the civil rights movement.

To combat the negative images of the South produced during the civil rights era, the years following the era saw popular culture rehabilitating the South. The 1970s witnessed this in country music's growing popularity, television shows like *The Waltons* and *Hee Haw*, Jimmy Carter's campaign, down-home advertising, and the redneck-and-car film genre. In this last, illustrated best by the *Smokey and the Bandit* films (1977, 1980, and 1983) and *Dukes of Hazzard* television show (1979–1985), the terrifying, brutal, murderous southern lawmen of civil rights movement experience become buffoons incapable of catching anyone, especially the white, southern, working-class heroes, comic versions of their filmic Civil War contemporaries.[4]

This rehabilitation, and the celebration of white, working-class, southern males that accompanied it, was part of a larger geographic and political shift in American society as southern and western conservatism gained power. In reaction to the social upheavals of the civil rights movement, the Watergate scandal, and the Vietnam War, antigovernment sentiment increased. These disruptions to the existing order, as Joseph Lowndes reminds us, had represented a challenge in which "white Americans, and white men in particular, faced a challenge to their authority and primacy as the unquestioned representatives of American national identity. The South, representing white victimhood, was a strong metaphor for such feelings." *The Outlaw Josey Wales* represents a time that "begins to mark a shift in American politics from liberal and left distrust of government . . . toward a more right-wing antigovernment sentiment. It does so by simultaneously depending on and erasing the reality of black subjugation in the U.S."[5]

Concurrent with this political shift, the white middle class embraced the idea of rebellion and celebrated the individualism of "outsiders." This rebellion also celebrated the white rural South as the place to find the "real America" represented by "country music and Lynyrd Skynyrd, barbecue and NASCAR, political conservatism, God and guns, the code of masculinity" and a distrust of government. In her analysis of this movement, Grace Elizabeth Hale argues, "At the level of imagination and identification, the romance of the outsider reconciled incompatible yearnings for self-determination and emotional and social connection" for members of the white middle class, as they "displaced these contradictions onto their fantasies of outsiders and remade themselves through identification with these figures." Although Hale does not cite many films as illustrations of this and carries the argument far beyond white working-class "outsiders," there are myriad examples of post–civil rights movement films contributing to white middle-class identification with white working-class rebels. Two examples especially demonstrate this point. Influenced by the song *Convoy* (1975) and its namesake film (1978), the *Smokey and the Bandit* films, and the supposed romance of the open-road lives of diesel truck drivers, a citizens band radio craze in the 1970s saw members of the white middle-class copying the language of truckers. Shortly after, the film *Urban Cowboy* (1980) sparked a trend of white middle-class men across the country dressing in blue jeans, cowboy boots, and hats like the Texas refinery worker featured in the film. The two films discussed in this chapter contain features of this shift in identification, but *The Outlaw Josey Wales* most embodies it.[6]

Modern films that rehabilitate the South employ various approaches—some show a contemporary, racism-free South, some a contemporary South where race is absent, some a historical South where racist individuals are defeated or redeemed, and others a historical South where race is ignored. Allison Graham argues that after the 1954 *Brown v. Board* decision, there was "an accelerating tendency in Hollywood films to chasten and reform the recalcitrant Southern white man." I agree but question whether this remained the case after the civil rights era ended. Carrying the question forward temporally, I ask why modern Civil War films have largely avoided the opportunity to explore the complex relationship between race and southern identity, even though the Civil War provides a potent canvas for such an exploration. Produced twenty-three years apart, from the end of the civil rights movement into the end of the twentieth century, the two films featured in this chapter are products of this era of missed opportunity. Of course, earlier eras also depicted the Civil War without seriously questioning slavery and the South. Following is a brief discussion of this history of filmmaking about the Civil War.[7]

From Hollywood's beginnings, the Civil War has been a popular subject for filmmakers; the over seven hundred films produced on the era are nearly three times the number produced about World War II, making the Civil War the most frequently depicted historical event in American history. These films have been instrumental in creating powerful images of the American South in the American imagination. As Catherine Clinton, historian of the plantation South, states, "millions of Americans have had their vision of the South, race relations, and even the entire panorama of our past shaped if not wholly defined by the movie business." In discussing *Gone with the Wind's* influence on the public's understanding of the war, Civil War historian Gary Gallagher writes that the iconic film "has shaped what people think about the Civil War probably more than everything we've written put together, or put together and squared." Even Margaret Mitchell lamented film's influence on historical memory: "Southerners could write the truth about the ante-bellum South," but "everyone would go on believing the Hollywood version." Although the romanticized depictions of the plantation South have largely disappeared from contemporary film, they are still deeply engrained in

American cultural consciousness. Film's disproportionate influence on the public's understanding of historical events is not ideal; preferably, everyone would embrace an understanding of history grounded in academic historical scholarship. However, despite the extraordinary body of academic work on the antebellum South and the Civil War, it is undeniable that many people discover the war through popular culture, and it is imperative that historians engage these texts and do so in productive ways.[8]

Modern Civil War films are part of a long tradition of finding meaning in the Civil War and using the war as a canvas for exploring contemporary issues. Considering the devastation and deep division the war caused, it may seem surprising that consistent themes have been national unity and American identity. However, this is not so extraordinary when we consider that popular culture often shows people the history they want to believe. As Trevor McCrisken and Andrew Pepper observe, "the Civil War has traditionally occupied a hallowed place in the benign meta-narrative of American history, one in which the bloody divisions between North and South are incorporated into a larger story of nation in which the sacrifice, suffering, and bravery of both sides are equally celebrated." Likewise, maintenance of this narrative requires the elimination of potentially disruptive regional and ethnic differences. Before the modern civil rights movement, overt white supremacy often provided the means for eliminating these regional differences. As Karen Cox argues, from the end of the war through World War II, the theme of "Anglo-Saxon brotherhood" was used to bring "together white people in the cause of destroying a common enemy—black southerners." In the post–civil rights movement era, "Anglo-Saxon brotherhood" has ostensibly given way to more universal themes in Civil War films. However, by illustrating these themes in the absence of blackness, these films often use whiteness to represent a synthesis of all the attributes of humanity.[9]

The Civil War, like the American South as a whole, has been a site of both reflection and creation of American identity, a funhouse mirror of sorts, contested terrain offering multiple images depending on changing perspectives. Issues of race are central to the contested politics of Civil War memory, because race is central to southern and American society. This results in both individuals and social groups seeking to, as Alice Fahs and Joan Waugh argue, "legitimize claims, and even to redefine what is American, by evoking selective memories of the war. Such evocations have been—and continue to be—a powerful means of claiming membership in the nation as well as denying others' claims to such membership." Films that depict a Civil War absent of slavery overlook African American involvement in the defining moment of American history and contested arena of American identity. Such films potentially discount African American claims to full membership in the nation.[10]

This propensity to discount the importance of African American connection to the war is nothing new. David Blight contends that initially there were three overall visions of Civil War memory: reconciliation, white supremacist vision, and emancipationist (demonstrated in African Americans' conception of liberation and reinvention of the nation). In the years after the war, reconciliation between North and South combined with white supremacy in historical memory and restoring national unity took precedence over achieving racial justice. According to Blight, race was so "deeply at the root of the war's causes and consequences, and so powerful a source of division in American social psychology, that it served as the antithesis of a culture of reconciliation." Consequently, reconciliation necessitated erasing slavery as the fundamental cause of the war and "delivered the country a segregated memory of the Civil War on Southern terms," while "the inexorable drive for reunion both used and trumped race." This understanding of the war, in which devotion to cause made everyone right and no one wrong, developed in the popular culture of the late nineteenth century. Many northerners, anxious about modernity, industrialization, and urbanization, and seeking a simpler time, accepted and even perpetuated these myths in the newly emerging mass culture. In the twentieth century, these myths achieved their most widespread influence through film.[11]

From the war's end, former Confederates and their allies used Lost Cause ideology to justify secession and shape the thinking about the war and its aftermath. There are several recurring themes in Lost Cause arguments. Foremost is the argument that slavery was unimportant to the cause of secession. The slavery of Lost Cause films presents a paternalistic relationship between slave owners and enslaved, with the enslaved expressing loyalty to their owners. The Lost Cause argument also maintains that Confederates were the rightful heirs to the founders and defenders of constitutional principles who were simply advocating states' rights, not slavery. Additionally, it was argued that despite the gallantry and heroism of the individual Confederate soldier, the honor and genius of the southern gentleman embodied by Robert E. Lee, and the stalwart nature of the southern belle, the Confederacy's admirable struggle was doomed in the face of the industrial North's overwhelming resources. Professional historians have contested this view for decades, their conclusions resting "upon the notion that slavery was the core cause of the Civil War and the Confederate experience" emerging as "the dominant force of inquiry in Southern history in the last thirty years." Non-academics have strongly criticized these conclusions, resisting "any claim that slavery caused secession, that the Confederacy was devoted to human bondage, or that Lee defended the enslavement of African-Americans" and accusing historians of "political correctness." This dispute plays out in many arenas—historic sites and statues, the use of the Confederate flag, public recognition of Confederate figures, and various other mediums, including the films *Gettysburg* (1993) and *Gods and Generals* (2003).[12]

An important characteristic of Lost Cause ideology is the image of an innocent South victimized by the aggressive, invading North. Non-southerners accepted and even promoted this view through popular culture; notably, early twentieth-century American silent films' treatment of the beginning of the war illustrates this. Although, historically, the South's shelling of Fort Sumter began the war, this does not fit the narrative of an innocent South. Therefore, the majority of silent Civil War films begin not with the shelling but with Abraham Lincoln's call up of troops in response to the shelling, thus absolving the South of blame for the subsequent bloodshed. This remained such a staple of chronology that *Ride with the Devil* and *The Outlaw Josey Wales,* made long after the silent films, follow a similar pattern by beginning with Union murders of and arson against innocent southerners, thus telling the stories from the southern, aggrieved perspective.[13]

In 1915, D. W. Griffith released *The Birth of a Nation,* America's first full-length feature film and a textbook example of Lost Cause mythology. Despite protests from African Americans and the newly formed NAACP, *The Birth of a Nation* was enormously popular. Released and rereleased numerous times, the $110,000 film earned over $50 million from its release through 1949. Its cultural reach was staggering; in the first thirty-five years of its life, 200 million people viewed the film and its message of an America reunited under the banner of white supremacy.[14]

In 1939, *Gone with the Wind* built on this legacy, to become arguably the most successful film of all time, reinforcing in American culture an image of an antebellum South peopled by southern belles, dashing cavaliers, and loyal slaves.[15] The film was part of a larger trend; an estimated seventy-five films produced between *The Birth of a Nation* and World War II featured antebellum southern plantations. Although images of a gothic and decadent contemporary South gained currency in the years following *Gone with the Wind,* the antebellum South and Civil War of that film continued to be the dominant image of the nineteenth-century South. Unlike in more modern films, the common Confederate soldier is not central to the South of *Gone with the Wind,* where the South is a land of natural aristocracy, with the common Confederate soldier part of a faceless, voiceless mass. White working-class people are rather nonexistent; symbolizing the Confederacy are southern belles Melanie Wilkes and Scarlett O'Hara, and the noble Ashley Wilkes, who abhors the war.[16]

In contrast, in *The Outlaw Josey Wales* and *Ride with the Devil,* bushwhackers, irregular soldiers fighting a guerrilla war far from famous battlefields, represent the Confederacy. Although the bushwhacker character can show common southerners and present the Civil War from a personal, nonslaveholding point of view, not all bushwhackers serve this purpose. William Quantrill, real-life bushwhacker and leader of the raid on Lawrence, Kansas, that killed approximately 150 men, appears as a character in numerous films, but not as the hero. Instead, his brutality often serves as contrast to the common southern farmer whom villainous Yankees have turned bushwhacker. The film *Dark Command* (1940) illustrates this when victims of a raid by William Cantrell (Walter Pidgeon) shout at him, "You're not the South!" *Ride with the Devil,* produced nearly sixty years later, follows this pattern by depicting Quantrill leading the raid on Lawrence, but showing its hero, Jake "Dutchy" Roedel (Tobey Maguire), protecting Lawrence citizens rather than participating in the mayhem. The novel that introduced Josey Wales as a character includes the attack on Lawrence, but Quantrill and Lawrence are absent from the film version. When examined through the lens of race, the recent portrayals of bushwhackers in *The Outlaw Josey Wales* and *Ride with the Devil* offer a unique opportunity to analyze how we think about the southern past.[17]

Josey Wales

Of the two films featured in this chapter, *The Outlaw Josey Wales* is perhaps the more problematic racially, and this stems in part from its source material. Based on a novel written by an avowed white supremacist, it vividly demonstrates the racial unease many white Americans felt in the wake of the civil rights movement. Directed by and starring Clint Eastwood, one of Hollywood's most popular stars, the film was successful on its release, ranking in the top twenty most popular films of 1976.[18] Nearly forty years after its theatrical release, the film remains regularly featured on television, and its cultural impact outweighs its initial box office position. In 1996, it was included in the National Film Registry at the Library of Congress, which recognizes culturally, historically, or aesthetically significant films. After years of leaving it understudied, academic critics are now effectively examining *Josey Wales;* however, there is still much to learn in questioning the film's relationship with race and southern identity. It is in this capacity that the film's adherence to, and departure from, its source material becomes most important.[19]

The character of Josey Wales originally appeared in the 1973 novel *The Rebel Outlaw: Josey Wales,* authored by Forrest [Asa Earl] Carter. Carter was a notorious segregationist, Ku Klux Klan leader, and speechwriter for Alabama governor George Wallace. In this last position, he penned the governor's infamous inaugural address promising "segregation now . . . segregation tomorrow . . . segregation forever." While offering a full-throated advocacy of segregation, Wallace often described the conflict in terms that went beyond region or race. His arguments painted segregation as a constitutional issue, pitting states' rights against a federal government determined to "destroy the rights and freedom and liberty of the people of this country." Wallace's mix of white populism and antigovernment sentiment would later prove to be a powerful combination nationally. After Wallace received strong support from outside the South in the 1968 campaign, NBC's Douglas Kiker reported that Wallace had something of an epiphany, realizing that when it came to racial issues, "the whole United States is *Southern!*" Historian Dan Carter argues that Wallace utilized "soft-porn racism" in the North, not explicitly mentioning race but cultivating fear and hatred among white voters in reaction to the issues including school desegregation, fair housing, and race riots.[20]

In addition to working for Wallace, Carter had a long history as a segregationist, and, like Wallace, his resistance to integration and dedication to white supremacy carried beyond the South. As the founder and coeditor of the *Southerner,* an ardently racist magazine, Carter "ranted against the threat of integration in everything from education to rock and roll, and warned of communist conspiracies in both the Republican and Democratic parties." Foreshadowing Wallace's appeal to white northern voters, Carter's words often dramatized the plight of white workers in northern cities who, he believed, were suffering because of racial liberalism. Carter backed his words with violence against African Americans. Thinking the Ku Klux Klan and White Citizens Councils were too soft, he organized a paramilitary group, the Original Ku Klux Klan of the Confederacy, which numbered approximately a hundred men. Over a two-year period in 1956–1957, his followers attacked singer Nat "King" Cole during a concert, kidnapped and castrated a mentally challenged African American man as a warning against civil rights activists, and viciously assaulted with knives and chains Reverend Fred and Ruby Shuttlesworth for trying to enroll their children in a segregated school. During this time, Carter helped instigate race riots on two occasions—in Clinton, Tennessee, after one of his speeches, and at the University of Alabama to protest the enrollment of Autherine Lucy. Carter even turned violent toward other Klansmen; when two of his followers challenged his leadership, he shot and seriously wounded them.[21]

By 1970, with Carter's commitment to segregation unchanged and Wallace recognizing the political realities of changing voting demographics, the two men had a falling out. Accusing Wallace of selling out to African Americans and communists, Carter ran against Wallace for governor. After badly losing the primary, Carter abandoned Alabama, moved west, and fabricated a Cherokee ancestry. Reinventing himself as an author, Carter produced four books before his death. In addition to the two Josey Wales novels, Carter also wrote a fictionalized biography of Geronimo, and, most famously, *The Education of Little Tree,* a "memoir" of his Cherokee childhood. Eventually revealed as a fraud, *The Education of Little Tree* remains popular, though now listed as fiction rather than nonfiction. Other scholars have documented and analyzed Asa Carter's invented self-identification as Cherokee; while a fascinating story, it is not the focus of this work. However, the following analysis does explore how Eastwood's film depicts the Native American characters from Carter's novel, in particular framing their use in the absence of African American characters.[22]

Carter created Josey Wales as codified segregation was ending and used the character to redeem his Confederate heroes and criticize what he believed was a too-powerful federal government. In taking the pen name "Forrest," Carter honored the Confederate general and Ku Klux Klan founder Nathan Bedford Forrest. In 1956, Carter had spoken of his hero as "the only redneck in the army," a soldier who did not accept southern defeat but "tried to figure out how to keep on fightin'." His character Josey Wales would closely follow this script, refusing to surrender at the end of the Civil War and continuing to fight, most notably against the federal government. Years after Carter's proclamation of admiration for Nathan Bedford Forrest, and after his successful reinvention as a novelist, a reporter told him that "his Wales novels were an attempt to win back the values on a mythical level that the Confederacy lost on the battlefield." Carter replied, "The values of a civilization never die so long as they're kept alive in legend." Setting the novel in the Reconstruction era, Carter carried the conflict beyond the Civil War, to an era in which Confederate outlaws and the Ku Klux Klan violently opposed political and social advances made by African Americans. By setting his novel in the West, rather than his home state of Alabama, he could mute questions about slavery and disregard African American characters. To Carter, the Civil War and opposition to civil rights were the same long, continuing struggle, whether waged at Antietam or Cold Harbor, the governor's mansion or the streets of Birmingham, the pages of his novels or on the screens of a thousand movie theaters.[23]

After Carter sent his novel to Clint Eastwood's production company, Eastwood agreed to produce the film, hiring Sonia Chernus to write the script. Eventually, Eastwood hired Philip Kaufman to rework the script and direct the film. Years later, Kaufman spoke about his initial reaction to Carter's *The Rebel Outlaw: Josey Wales*: "Fascist is an overworked word, but the first time I looked at that book that's what I thought: this was written by a crude fascist. It was nutty. The man's hatred of government was insane." Although Kaufman stripped a great deal of the book's political ideology from the script, he kept the strong pro-South, anti-North viewpoint as well as an antigovernment perspective. When Kaufman and Eastwood had a falling out during filming, Eastwood fired Kaufman and took over as director. In an interview included on the DVD version of the film, Eastwood says he sees the film as a statement against the destructiveness and futility of war, not just for the combatants but also for all involved. Consequently, Eastwood's film emphasizes reconciliation more than the novel does. While he is careful about not drawing a parallel between the Civil War and the Vietnam War, he does state that the film speaks to "the dissatisfaction that people were having with the war in Vietnam." This reading of the film has its strengths; there is a strong antiwar sentiment in the film. However, despite Eastwood's antiwar interpretation, the film's antigovernment and white supremacist currents are strong as well. By having the federal government be the aggressor, destroying southern families and relentlessly pursuing Josey Wales, and showing the Confederate hero build a multicultural "family," absent of African Americans, the film offers a white South that is not responsible for slavery and is the defender rather than enemy of civil rights. Within this framework, it is an early post–civil rights movement attempt to recast the white South through white victimization. As Joseph Lowndes argues, drawing from both left and right, the film "preserves the regenerative role of frontier violence while upholding old forms of racial domination."[24]

In *The Outlaw Josey Wales,* the conflict between Confederate soldier and federal government carries beyond the official dates of the Civil War into an era and a geography that allows Carter to frame the conflict on his own terms and to advocate white supremacy without the questions raised by the inclusion of African American characters. Consequently, I position *Josey Wales* as a Civil War film, although the majority of the story takes place in the American West, and after the war, providing a setting and time where the film can ignore slavery. As Shari M. Huhndorf asserts, "by rearticulating the conflict of the 1950s and 1960s in the historical context of the postbellum South, an era which saw white supremacy reaffirmed, Carter fantasized a similar resolution to the challenges posed by contemporary civil rights activists. His novels provide such visions of white social regeneration and the reestablishment of white political power, although these visions are less explicit and are thus more widely acceptable than his Klan activism was."[25]

Although the film generally follows the plot of the novel, there are some differences. The film's plot is relatively simple. During the Civil War, Josey Wales (Clint Eastwood) and his family are living on a small farm in Missouri. One day, a group of Kansas Red Legs, an antislavery militia, attacks his farm and, when he tries to defend his home and family, knocks Wales unconscious. When he awakens, his family is murdered and his farm destroyed. Vowing revenge, Wales joins Missouri bushwhackers and begins fighting against the federal government. At the war's end, Josey refuses to surrender and heads to Texas, with the Red Legs and his craven former commander in pursuit. There are many narrow escapes along the way, as Wales flees across the Missouri, Oklahoma, Arkansas, and Texas frontier. During his journey, Wales allies himself with two Native Americans, a man and a woman, and eventually saves a family of antislavery white Kansans from attack by Comancheros, a racially diverse band of ruffians. By the story's end, Wales has achieved his revenge over the Red Legs by killing their commander. He, the Native Americans, the Kansans, and others have formed a new family, peacefully living on a Texas ranch near a neighboring tribe of Comanche.

Both the book and the film allow Wales to have it both ways—to symbolize white southern resentment against government power in the wake of the civil rights movement while simultaneously becoming part of growing multiculturalism. However, created on the white man's terms, this multiculturalism results in Wales as the head of the new family, with white supremacy unchallenged. Combining multiculturalism themes familiar to those on the left, the right's antigovernment individualistic hero, and a good story, the

Josey Wales (Clint Eastwood), burying his family members after they are murdered by Kansas ruffians. *The Outlaw Josey Wales.*

film became a hit. To do so, though, it made slavery and African Americans invisible. Otherwise, the viewer would have to consider that the story's hero was fighting not just against an authoritarian government but also for an oppressive society.[26]

From the beginning of the film, *The Outlaw Josey Wales* establishes Wales as a small farmer who has avoided the war. It opens with Wales and his young, blonde son plowing their small farm. It is a far from idyllic life—Wales is a poor dirt farmer, earning his living from the land and the sweat of his own brow. Clearly, Wales and his family are not involved in politics, nor are they slaveholders. To the viewer, the attack on Wales's family is committed without any context. The film does not discuss the conflict over slavery that led to violence between Kansans and Missourians in the years preceding the war. Although violence between Kansans and Missourians frames the action and is continually referred to, neither the book nor the film mentions slavery, the issue that caused the violence between Kansans and Missourians.[27]

The framing of the opening scene at the Wales farm also helps the viewer identify with Wales and his cause. The film frames Wales as the victim of a random attack carried out by quasi-government agents. In the words of one historian, the attack scene "evokes nothing so much as the image of marauding Klansmen on a night ride, except that the victims here are not Southern blacks but Southern whites." With much of the scene shot in point of view, the viewer sees the burning of his house and the attack on his wife from Wales's perspective. After Wales is knocked down, the viewer sees the Red Legs from the bottom up, primarily identifiable not by their faces but by their paramilitary uniforms. After the attack, literally taking his gun from the ashes, Wales transforms himself from a farmer into a warrior, and the war becomes one of southern vengeance against northern aggression.[28]

Underscoring this point is the group of bushwhackers that Wales joins; they are primarily middle-aged family men also seeking revenge for northern transgressions. Led by "Bloody Bill" Anderson (John Russell), a historical figure, the bushwhackers come on Wales sitting at his family's graves. Seeing the burned farm and fresh graves, Anderson, says, "Red Legs? You'll find 'em up in Kansas. They're with the Union, and we're going up there and set things right." Historically, and illustrated much more realistically by *Ride with the Devil,* bushwhackers were usually young men in their teens and twenties, rather than middle-aged family men. However, by making Josey Wales and his compatriots older men who fight for revenge rather than young men fighting for adventure, the film absolves them of any blame for the resulting violence.[29]

After the murder of his family, Wales fights out of revenge and a hatred of the federal government rather than a commitment to slavery or the Confederacy. After Wales joins the bushwhackers, the film's title montage, shot in blue and gray tones, shows the more traditional Civil War, with uniformed troops, cannons, cavalry charges, and set battles interspersed with burning barns and lynched Red Legs. This montage connects the bushwhackers with the war while still keeping some distance between them and the Confederacy.

After the title montage, Fletcher (John Vernon), the new bushwhacker leader, tells his band that the war is over. They are the last group left, and every one else has surrendered. Looking at his men, he says that if they "go into the Union camp" and surrender, they are free to "go home." Although Wales does not say anything, it is clear from his reaction that he has no home to go to and that he will continue to fight. When the bushwhackers surrender, Wales refuses to join them. After turning in their weapons, they recite a loyalty oath to the federal government, when Union soldiers gun them down in cold blood. Wales rides into the massacre, rescuing Jamie (Sam Bottoms), a young bushwhacker, who is mortally wounded during their escape. The scene is not in the novel—by adding it to the film, Eastwood reinforces both the evilness of the federal government and Wales's independence.

At this point, the film becomes a chase film, with Wales (and the doomed Jamie) running from the pursuing Red Legs, who have allied with the turncoat Fletcher. Chased through Arkansas and into the Indian Territory of Oklahoma, Wales heads toward Texas and freedom. With a bounty on his head and a growing reputation for violence, Wales has many adventures

Josey Wales, mild-mannered farmer turned warrior, fights against Captain Terrill (Bill McKinney), representative of the corrupt federal government. *The Outlaw Josey Wales.*

during the chase. Continuing to fight, hounded by an unforgiving government bent on destroying him, Wales avoids capture by hillbillies, mocks (and spits on) a northern carpetbagger, and finds southern allies who support his escape. Perhaps most importantly, in Indian Territory, he meets Lone Watie, an elderly Cherokee ally.

While Asa Carter would later invent a Cherokee ancestry and publish the "memoir" *The Education of Little Tree,* he also published a fictionalized biography of Geronimo, and Native Americans figured prominently in his writing. As scholar Mark McGurl notes, "In the South after *Brown v. Board of Education,* the Native American becomes, for Carter, an imaginary ally of the white Southern segregationist victimized by the 'tyrannical' power of the coercively assimilative Federal government." In Lone Watie, Carter creates a Cherokee character victimized by the federal government, who finds common cause with Josey Wales. Cherokees had, of course, kept African Americans enslaved, and supported the Confederacy. In an obvious acknowledgement of this connection, Lone Watie shares a name with Stand Watie, the historical Cherokee brigadier general of the Confederacy and the last Confederate general to surrender. Through his alliance with Josey Wales, Lone Watie reinforces Wales's antigovernment stance while also providing multicultural cover for a white supremacist perspective.[30]

Another Native American character becomes Wales's ally during his escape, which, when contrasted with Wales's interactions with white characters, reinforces this perspective. Entering a trading post, Wales is aware of two white bounty hunters raping a Native American woman. He pointedly ignores the ongoing rape and only kills the men when they try to capture him. To Wales, the Native American woman, a Navajo named Little Moonlight (Geraldine Keams), is not worthy of saving. However, because he had killed her attackers, she feels indebted to him and joins him and Lone Watie in their travels. Despite Wales's hypermasculinity, Little Moonlight's status as a Native American supersedes her status as a woman, so he does not feel a responsibility to offer her protection from rape.

In contrast, when Wales happens on a group of white settlers under attack from a multiracial (white, Native American, and Mexican) group of Comancheros, he attacks the Comancheros to keep them from raping two white women, the elderly Grandma Sarah (Paula Trueman) and her granddaughter, Laura Lee (Sondra Locke). The settlers are antislavery Kansas Jayhawkers, heading to a Texas ranch owned by Grandma Sarah's son, killed in the war fighting for the Union. White womanhood now saved from defilement, the settlers join Wales, Little Moonlight, and Lone Watie, forming a new family, with Wales in charge. Contrasted with the Comancheros' multiculturalism, which is a threat to white chastity—this new multicultural family provides Wales with a white love interest and is multiculturalism on his terms. Although Grandma Sarah believes she was right regarding slavery, and Wales was wrong, she is willing to form a family with Wales, thus reuniting North and South, with the South in charge. As the father figure and, in the film's view, in his rightful place as the head of a new family, Josey Wales is able to create a new home.[31]

Home, and the threat that government plays against home, is a recurring theme. Wales, Lone Watie, even the antislavery Kansans who lost a family member to an avoidable, by the film's logic, war have all suffered and lost their homes because of the federal government. By the end of the film, Wales has created a new home at the Crooked River Ranch and has a new family consisting of "a whore and a barkeep, a Latino man and two Kansas Jayhawkers, a Navajo woman and a Cherokee man" in addition to Wales, the Missouri bushwhacker. However, this diverse and inclusive community is possible only because its members have moved beyond the reach of government. Additionally, for such a multicultural community, the absence of any African Americans is notable, but not surprising. Including a single African American in the film would "call into question the heroism of a protagonist who fought not just against an oppressive government that had indiscriminately wronged his family, but also for a society that was defined by its devotion to slavery." Consequently, Wales would no longer be a symbol of American independence and frontier justice, but of white supremacy.[32]

Ride with the Devil

Like *The Outlaw Josey Wales, Ride with the Devil* focuses on a Missouri bushwhacker reluctantly drawn into war. Based on Daniel Woodrell's extraordinary novel *Woe to Live On* (1987) and directed by Ang Lee, the film offers a more complicated depiction of the war, race, and slavery than *The Outlaw Josey Wales*. However, like the earlier film, it provides a sympathetic portrayal of Confederates as victims of northern aggression. By showing brutality on both sides of the conflict, it provides more balance than *The Outlaw Josey Wales*. In making a modern, sympathetic film about Confederates, Ang Lee attempts to "explore a proslavery society that nearly destroyed the United States without alienating critics and much of his potential audience." To do this, he shows brutality committed by both sides of the conflict. He also creates "a violent tapestry in which the principle characters stand aloof from politics and ideology, dealing in human terms with disruptive events and manifesting enlightened attitudes about slavery and race." Very few scenes in the film address the Confederacy, although the bushwhackers do talk about protecting the "southern" way of life. At no time does anyone adequately explain the meaning of that phrase, nor does anyone explain their connection with the Confederacy.[33]

The violence in *Ride with the Devil* begins with an attack by Kansas Jayhawkers against peaceful Missourians. After witnessing the destruction of his friend Jack Bull Chiles (Skeet Ulrich)'s family farm, the protagonist, Jake "Dutchy" Roedel, joins a band of young, Confederate guerrilla bushwhackers. Defying his pro-Union German immigrant father, Roedel is a capable and brave fighter but is something of an outsider among the rebels. Roedel's fellow bushwhackers dislike him because of his German ancestry, and they are not

Missouri bushwhackers before the raid on Lawrence, Kansas, in *Ride with the Devil.*

convinced of his dedication to "The Cause." He is a liminal character, caught "between North and South, between Kansas and Missouri, and between his father's pro-Unionist immigrant community and Jack Bull's Southern heritage."[34]

The bushwhackers are also distrustful of Roedel's growing friendship with Holt (Jeffrey Wright), an African American compatriot who fights alongside the white rebels. Through both Roedel's status as an immigrant and Holt's marginality as an African American fighting for the Confederacy, both the novel and the film explore issues of identity and race, but slavery is a lesser concern. Although Holt is described as character George Clyde (Simon Baker)'s "man," his status is unclear; presumably, he is formerly enslaved. Clyde insists that he does not own Holt, and Holt asserts his independence in various ways. In fact, in some respects, the relationship between Holt and Clyde parallels the relationship between Roedel and his best friend, Jack Bull Chiles, who serves as sort of a big brother. In an interview, Woodrell states, "Holt and Jake Roedel are loyal to individuals who happen to be on the Southern side. Their personal loyalties supersede any political notion." Although Jake Roedel's parents are unionists, his friendship with Jack Bull Chiles and relationship with the Chiles family make Roedel "as southern as they come." Thus, southern identity is not a function of geography or family but of personal loyalty. This focus on the personal allows the viewer to relate to Roedel

Jake "Dutchy" Roedel (Tobey Maguire) and Holt (Jeffrey Wright). *Ride with the Devil.*

and separate his actions from their larger racial consequences and, in the words of Woodrell, "supersede any political notion."[35]

Woodrell based Holt on a historical figure, an African American bushwhacker named Nolan, but African American bushwhackers were extremely rare. Of an African American riding with southern bushwhackers, Woodrell states, "the uniqueness of that began to bring it into focus for me." Holt's significance in the book and film is important, because after Chiles and Clyde die, Roedel and Holt grow in affection and trust toward one another. This relationship with Holt provides the opportunity for Roedel to achieve a level of release from responsibility for southern racism. Additionally, Roedel's ethnicity creates a marginality that allows him to identify with the African American character. The film tries to differentiate Chiles, Clyde, Roedel, and Holt, the "good" Confederates from the "bad," especially around issues of race. They all participate in violence and bloodshed, and Roedel even murders a German noncombatant to show his loyalty to the cause. However, the four main characters have more modern attitudes about race than their fellow Confederates, who openly express racist ideas and celebrate atrocities against African Americans. As Gary Gallagher notes, "one of the bad guerrillas casually mentions that some units are 'scalping every nigger they can find,' glances at Holt, and adds, 'except of course, our own.'"[36]

As the film progresses, Holt and Roedel's friendship deepens and Holt's racial identity grows. By the end, we learn that Holt's first name is Daniel, an important step in his asserting his humanity. After Clyde dies and he feels increasingly threatened by the other bushwhackers, Holt decides to leave. In one of the film's few, although oblique, references to slavery, Holt sets out to track down his long-lost mother. Finally free of both the institution of slavery and personal ties to those on the Confederate side, Holt vows to "be nobody's nigger" ever again.[37]

As his friendship with Holt and disillusionment with the war grows, Roedel matures and gains a sense of independence. He eventually forms a family with Chiles's partner, Sue Lee (Jewel Kilcher) and her infant child, and they leave the bushwhackers and the war behind. Striking out for the west in a wagon, the family is a familiar sight, American pioneers creating a new life. However, like Josey Wales, Jake Roedel heads West not in an "expansive, confident desire to settle the frontier" but "simply because there is nowhere left for him to go, and heading either North or South is no longer a viable option."[38]

Conclusion

As white, nonslaveholding characters depicted in a world where slavery is nearly invisible, Jake Roedel and Josey Wales allow filmmakers to continue to use the Civil War as a subject without grappling with the questions of racial equality raised by the civil rights movement. Although their source material, and thus their perspectives differ greatly, they both use economic class as a way to separate their protagonists (and thus the Confederacy) from the issue of slavery. Similar to *Cold Mountain* (2003), a later film sharing similar characteristics, by displacing or eliding slavery, these films allow audiences to identify with Confederate soldiers on a personal level without questioning the war's larger issues.

Notes

1. Grace Elizabeth Hale, *Making Whiteness: The Culture of Segregation in the South, 1890–1940* (New York: Vintage, 1999).

2. Gina Caison, "Claiming the Unclaimable: Forrest Carter, *The Education of Little Tree*, and Land Claim in the Native South," *Mississippi Quarterly* 64, no. 4 (2011): 585–86.

3. Paul Haspel, "From Hero to Villain to Unknown Other: The Confederate Soldier in American Film," *Studies in Popular Culture* 19, no. 2 (1996): 131–32; Reinhard Isensee, "Fictions of Reconstruction: Narratives of the Civil War in American Literature," *Amer-*

ican Studies Journal 53 (2009): http://www.asjournal.org/53-2009/narratives-of-the-civil-war-in-american-literature/.

4. Amy Corbin, "Multiculturalism and Melodrama: Southern White Heroines of the 1980s," in *Southerners on Film: Essays on Hollywood Portrayals since the 1970s,* ed. Andrew Leiter (Jefferson, NC: McFarland, 2011): 15; Deborah Barker and Kathryn McKee, *American Cinema and the Southern Imaginary* (Athens: University of Georgia Press, 2011): 10; Allison Graham, *Framing the South: Hollywood, Television, and Race during the Civil Rights Struggle* (Baltimore: Johns Hopkins University Press, 2001), 184.

5. Richard J. Meagher, "Backlash: Race, Sexuality, and American Conservatism," *Polity* 41 (April 2009): 260; Joseph E. Lowndes, *From the New Deal to the New Right: Race and the Southern Origins of Modern Conservatism* (New Haven: Yale University Press, 2008), 140–43, 149; Joseph. E Lowndes, "Unstable Antistatism: The Left, the Right, and *The Outlaw Josey Wales,*" *International Journal of Politics, Culture, and Society* 16, no. 2 (2002): 243.

6. George Packer, "Southern Discomfort," *New Yorker,* January 21, 2013, 19; Grace Elizabeth Hale, *A Nation of Outsiders: How the White Middle Class Fell in Love with Rebellion in Postwar America* (New York: Oxford University Press, 2011), 6. To illustrate this connection using a personal example—my father, a middle-class salesman from Kansas, used the name "Outlaw," taken from the film, as his CB handle when traveling highways in the 1970s.

7. Graham, *Framing the South,* 135.

8. Bruce Chadwick, *The Reel Civil War: Mythmaking in American Film* (New York: Knopf, 2001), 12; Catherine Clinton, *The Plantation Mistress: Woman's World in the Old South* (New York: Pantheon, 1982): 204; Gary Gallagher, quoted in Bob Thompson, "Civil War, Take 2: Hollywood Captured the Blood of Battle But Shrank Away From Slavery's Reality," *Washington Post,* December 24, 2003; Margaret Mitchell, quoted in Karen L. Cox, *Dreaming of Dixie: How the South Was Created in American Popular Culture* (Chapel Hill: University of North Carolina Press, 2011), 93; Andrew B. Leiter, introduction to Leiter, *Southerners on Film,* 1.

9. Trevor McCrisken and Andrew Pepper, *American History and Contemporary Hollywood Film* (New Brunswick, NJ: Rutgers University Press, 2005): 64; Barker and McKee, *American Cinema and the Southern Imaginary,* 5; Cox, *Dreaming of Dixie,* 3; Robert Burgoyne "Race and Nation in *Glory,*" in *The War Film,* ed. Robert Eberwein (New Brunswick, NJ: Rutgers University Press, 2006), 66.

10. Graham, *Framing the South,* 4. David Blight, *Race and Reunion: The Civil War in American Memory* (Cambridge, MA: Belknap Press of Harvard University Press, 2001), 4. Alice Fahs and Joan Waugh, introduction to *The Memory of the Civil War in American Culture,* ed. Alice Fahs and Joan Waugh (Chapel Hill: University of North Carolina Press, 2004), 1.

11. Blight, *Race and Reunion,* 2–4; James Cobb, *Away Down South: A History of Southern Identity* (New York: Oxford University Press, 2005), 80; Cox, *Dreaming of Dixie,* 1; Robert M. Myers, "'It's What People Say We're Fighting For': Representing the Lost Cause in *Cold Mountain*" in Why *We Fought: America's Wars in Film and History,* ed.

Peter C. Rollins and John E. O'Connor (Lexington: University Press of Kentucky, 2008), 122; Chadwick, *Reel Civil War,* 14.

12. Joan Waugh and Gary Gallagher, *Wars within a War: Controversy and Conflict over the American Civil War* (Chapel Hill: University of North Carolina Press, 2009), 157–58; Myers, "'It's What People Say We're Fighting For,'" 122; Gary W. Gallagher, *Causes Won, Lost, and Forgotten: How Hollywood and Popular Art Shape What We Know about the Civil War* (Chapel Hill: University of North Carolina Press, 2008), 2; Peter S. Carmichael, "Truth Is Mighty and Will Eventually Prevail," *Southern Cultures* 7 (Spring 2001): 9–10.

13. Chadwick, *Reel Civil War,* 70.

14. Ibid., 104, 132; James M. McPherson, "Klieg Lights and Magnolias," *New York Times,* September 30, 2001; Godfrey Cheshire, "'Personal in My Memory:' The South in Popular Film," *Southern Cultures* 17 (Fall 2011): 29; D. W. Griffith, *The Birth of a Nation* (Hollywood, CA, David W. Griffith Corp., distributed by Epoch Co. 1915), YouTube video, 3:13:15, posted by A cinema history, July 10, 2014, www.youtube.com/watch?v=13k-mVgQHIEY.

15. Adjusted for inflation (2018), *Gone with the Wind* has made $1.854 billion. "Domestic Grosses: Adjusted for Ticket Price Inflation," *All Time Box Office,* accessed March 22, 2018, www.boxofficemojo.com/alltime/adjusted.htm (accessed March 22, 2018).

16. Cox, *Dreaming of Dixie,* 86. Leiter, introduction, 5.

17. Chadwick, *Reel Civil War,* 240–41.

18. *The Outlaw Josey Wales* earned $31.8 million, the sixteenth most popular movie of 1976. "*The Outlaw Josey Wales,*" *Box Office Mojo,* accessed February 13, 2018, http://boxofficemojo.com/movies/?id=outlawjoseywales.htm.

19. Robert C. Sickles, "Clint Eastwood's *The Outlaw Josey Wales,*" *Journal of Popular Film and Television* 30 (Winter 2003): 220.

20. Lowndes, *From the New Deal,* 141–43; Lowndes, "Unstable Antistatism," 239; James C. Cobb, *Redefining Southern Culture: Mind and Identity in the Modern South* (Athens: University of Georgia Press, 1999): 79; Dan T. Carter, *From George Wallace to Newt Gingrich: Race in the Conservative Counterrevolution, 1963–1994* (Baton Rouge: Louisiana State University Press, 1996), 4–9.

21. Paul Haspel, "Studies in Outlawry: The Strange Career of Josey Wales," *Quarterly Review of Film and Video* 22, no. 2 (2005): 156; Dan T. Carter, "The Transformation of a Klansman," *New York Times,* October 4, 1991; Carter, *From George Wallace to Newt Gingrich, 2.*

22. Carter, "Transformation of a Klansman." For an analysis of Carter's appropriation of Native American identity, see Shari M. Huhndorf, *Going Native: Indians in the American Cultural Imagination* (Ithaca, NY: Cornell University Press, 2001).

23. Mark McGurl, "Learning from *Little Tree*: The Political Education of the Counterculture," *Yale Journal of Criticism* 18 (Fall 2005): 250; Allen Barra, "The Education of Little Fraud," *Salon,* September 20, 2001, accessed March 22, 2018, www.salon.com/2001/12/20/carter_6/; Huhndorf, *Going Native,* 138.

24. Barra, "Education of Little Fraud"; *The Outlaw Josey Wales*, directed by Clint Eastwood (1976; Warner Hove Video: 2010) DVD; Lowndes, "Unstable Antistatism," 243.

25. Haspel, "Studies in Outlawry," 159; Huhndorf, *Going Native*, 39.

26. Lowndes, "Unstable Antistatism," 243–49; McGurl, "Learning from *Little Tree*," 243–67.

27. Haspel, "Studies in Outlawry," 162–65.

28. Lowndes, "Unstable Antistatism," 243.

29. Michael Fellman, *Inside War: The Guerrilla Conflict in Missouri during the American Civil War*, (Oxford: Oxford University Press, 1988), 133.

30. McGurl, "Learning from *Little Tree*," 253.

31. Lowndes, "Unstable Antistatism," 247; Haspel, "Studies in Outlawry," 165.

32. Sickles, "Clint Eastwood's *The Outlaw Josey Wales*," 226; Lowndes "Unstable Antistatism," 249.

33. Waugh and Gallagher, *Wars Within*, 167–68; Gallagher, *Causes Won, Lost, and Forgotten*, 72.

34. McCrisken and Pepper, *American History*, 80.

35. Daniel Woodrell, Kay Bonetti, and Jo Sapp, "An Interview with Daniel Woodrell," *Missouri Review* 22, no. 3 (1999): 85; Gallagher, *Causes Won, Lost, and Forgotten*, 69.

36. Woodrell, Bonetti, and Sapp, "Interview with Daniel Woodrell," 84; Gallagher, *Causes Won, Lost, and Forgotten*, 70.

37. Gallagher, *Causes Won, Lost, and Forgotten*, 72.

38. Woodrell, Bonetti, and Sapp, "Interview with Daniel Woodrell," 89–90. Ang Lee, *Ride with the Devil*, directed by Ang Lee (1999; New York: Criterion Collection, 2000), DVD; McCrisken and Pepper, *American History*, 84.

4

Reconstruction on Film

Free State of Jones and the Historical Memory of Reconstruction

Erik B. Alexander

Within the broader genre of films about the historical South, the 2016 *Free State of Jones* is unique. *Free State of Jones* tells the story of a poor white farmer and Confederate medic named Newton Knight, who deserted the army and led an interracial uprising against the Confederate government in Jones County, Mississippi. Not only is *Free State of Jones* the rare modern film that actually depicts the drama of Reconstruction in the South, including the aftermath of the war and the end of slavery, but it is also a Civil War film. In that regard, *Free State of Jones* is particularly distinctive in the ways it connects the history of the war to what came afterward. Further, it is what the film has to say about what came afterward that makes it truly noteworthy. While the bulk of the film does focus on the Civil War, in its portrayal of the postwar years, *Free State of Jones* provides the first cinematic view of Reconstruction that aligns with modern historical scholarship. This chapter attempts to demonstrate the significance of that achievement by analyzing *Free State of Jones* against the backdrop of some of the different ways both historical scholarship and films have depicted Reconstruction.

Part of the explanation for what makes *Free State of Jones* unique is that Americans, white and black, have long had a complicated relationship with their understanding and memory of the history of Reconstruction. The turbulent period of violence, social change, and political conflict following the Civil War as the United States adjusted to the end of slavery has never quite had the same grasp on the public imagination as the war that preceded it. To wit, in the last half century, a broad consensus has emerged in both the scholarly and public views of the Civil War, which recognizes the primacy that the institution of African American slavery played in that conflict, in terms of both explaining its causes and understanding the war's purpose and outcome. By contrast, since the 1960s, Americans' understanding and memory of the postwar years has generally remained out of step with the views of professional historians. During the 2016 presidential campaign, for example, candidate Hillary Clinton equivocated Reconstruction with the subsequent era of Jim Crow and segregation—two very different periods with very different goals.[1] As Eric Foner, the most influential scholar of Reconstruction, stated recently "people know next to nothing about Reconstruction. And what they do know is just not correct."[2]

One can readily view this disparity in a variety of ways. From 2011 to 2015, Americans celebrated the sesquicentennial of the Civil War, and the opportunities for study, reflection, and commemoration were practically unlimited. Historians published an endless array of books and articles on virtually every aspect of the war's history. There were countless symposia, panels, conferences, special issues of scholarly journals, op-eds, and public memorials. The public's historical appetite for all things Civil War, insatiable enough as it is, seemed unquenchable. Yet, as that sesquicentennial celebration has ended, there has been, with a few exceptions, a deafening silence for any kind of corresponding commemoration of Reconstruction.

This imbalance in interest between the Civil War and Reconstruction is certainly not new. Americans, of course, have long viewed the Civil War as the nation's Iliad—its grand sweeping epic. Moreover, in the last generation the war has also become a hallmark in the story of American progress—collectively we have come to celebrate the story of emancipation and destruction of slavery. Many Americans, however, have usually viewed Reconstruction as a tragic failure, though for varying reasons. For nearly a century, white Americans saw Reconstruction as a failure because the United States had even attempted it in the first place. Later, white Americans came to view Reconstruction in the same way many African Americans had since the end of the nineteenth century: as a failure for what it did not accomplish: civil, economic, and political rights for 4 million newly freed African Americans in the South. Either way, when comparing these broad interpretations of the Civil War and Reconstruction—one as a story of uplift and progress versus the other as a story of failure—one can begin to comprehend the gulf between the two periods in public memory and understanding.

As Edward L. Ayers has recently pointed out, the Civil War also benefits from the fact that it lends so easily to narrative. It has a story, with a recognizable beginning, Fort Sumter, and end, Appomattox; turning points in the middle, Gettysburg and the Emancipation Proclamation; clear heroes and villains, North vs. South, Union vs. Confederate, free vs. slave; and elements of victory and tragedy, freedom for 4 million set against Lincoln's assassination and 750,000 dead.[3] At the same time, Ayers notes, Reconstruction is complicated. It defies generalizations and characterization. There are few easily identifiable heroes and villains, and insofar as there is a story, it ends with disappointment: racism, violence, and segregation for freedpeople in the Jim Crow South. Of course, this is not how scholars have come to view the era. Academic historians have long grappled with the complexities of both the war and Reconstruction, and scholars increasingly emphasize the connection between the two, rather than seeing them as distinctly separate eras.[4] Nevertheless, the public's understanding has failed to keep pace.

Cultural productions mirror the contrast in enthusiasm between the Civil War and Reconstruction as well, particularly in the history of film. There have been literally hundreds of films made about the Civil War since the early twentieth century, ranging in quality from exceptional films like *Glory* (1989) and *Lincoln* (2012) to the problematic, *Gettysburg* (1993); plodding, *Gods and Generals* (2003); and truly awful, *Abraham Lincoln: Vampire Hunter* (2012).[5] Yet, despite the overwhelming number of Civil War films and their range in quality, for the most part, the interpretation those films have presented reflects the basic evolution of how historians and Americans have interpreted the war. *Glory* and *Lincoln*, for example, reflect the consensus of the late twentieth and early twenty-first centuries on the importance of slavery and emancipation in understanding the war's causes, purpose, and outcome.

By contrast, the number of films that exist about the Civil War dwarf the number that focus solely on Reconstruction. More important, the interpretations of Reconstruction presented in the films that do exist have generally lagged well behind the consensus of academic historians. Indeed, modern historians writing in the last half-century have come to focus on the impact of the postwar years on the South and the lives of the 4 million African Americans who navigated the end of slavery. Nevertheless, most films about Reconstruction have continued to propagate the view of Reconstruction as lamentable, with federal policies driven by vindictive and corrupt Republicans at the expense of subdued and conciliatory white southerners, undeserving of such treatment. No wonder, then, that Americans' understandings of Reconstruction remain so cloudy and convoluted!

We may finally be witnessing a shift in the dearth of public understanding of Reconstruction, however. While public interest in Reconstruction history may never approach the fanfare and spectacle witnessed during the Civil War sesquicentennial, the end of that celebration has prompted several national conversations about the public memory of the postwar years. In Memphis, for example, a fervent debate recently emerged over how best to commemorate the riots of 1866—among the worst racial riots in American history, which ended in dozens of African American deaths at the hands of the city's white citizens.[6] Ultimately, that public conversation produced a historical marker acknowledging the "1866 Memphis Massacre" and a scholarly symposium on the University of Memphis campus in the summer of 2016 exploring the history of the massacre and the legacies of slavery in the African American community. In addition, the recent efforts of several prominent historians to begin a national conversation about commemorating Reconstruction culminated in President Obama's January 2017 announcement of the first national memorial dedicated to Reconstruction, to be located in Beaufort, South Carolina.[7] Similarly, the National Park Service continues to expand its educational offerings on Reconstruction, recently releasing a theme study entitled "The Era of Reconstruction, 1861–1900."[8]

Against this backdrop, the 2016 film *Free State of Jones* has provided a significant contribution to the ongoing revival of Americans' understanding of Reconstruction. Indeed, within the realm of film, *Free State of Jones* stands alone as a singular depiction of the period, the first modern film to offer an interpretation of the postwar years that matches what has been the scholarly consensus for at least thirty years. While not perfect, *Free State of Jones* ultimately presents an interpretation of Reconstruction that emphasizes the complexities of race and class in the South during the Civil War and Reconstruction and the importance of African American agency to that narrative. Further, it also demonstrates the duality of Reconstruction through the contrast of the promise and optimism of the postwar experiment that ultimately ended with the tragedy of failed opportunities. The remainder of this chapter will explore the film *Free State of Jones,* focusing on how it portrays race and class in the history of the Civil War and Reconstruction, and attempt to place the film within the broader context of Reconstruction historiography and previous films depicting Reconstruction.

"Based on true events," *Free State of Jones* tells the story of Newton Knight, a poor white farmer from Jones County, Mississippi. Knight has always been a historical figure of some note for Civil War buffs. Historians have previously told his story several times, perhaps most notably in Victoria E. Bynum's 2003 *The Free State of Jones: Mississippi's Longest Civil War,* which arguably provided much of the source material for the film (Bynum is listed in the credits as one of the film's historical consultants).[9] The film opens in October 1862, with Newton Knight (Matthew McConaughey) serving as a medic in the Confederate army. His experience at the 1862 Battle of Corinth disillusions him with the war, and following the death of his (fictional) nephew Daniel (Jacob Lofland), Knight deserts the army in order to take Daniel's body home. After returning home to Jones County, Knight becomes even more disenchanted with the Confederate cause, as he witnesses Confederate officers' conscription efforts to seize crops and livestock from the poor white farmers of Jones County.

After learning of Confederate attempts to seize property from a family of poor women, Knight helps the mother and her three young girls resist by turning away the cavalry officers at gunpoint. To avoid capture and punishment, Knight is forced to hide out in nearby swamps after being chased and injured by slave-patrol dogs; subsequently he receives aid from an enslaved woman named Rachel (Gugu Mbatha-Raw). (In an earlier scene, Rachel had provided medical care and helped Knight's infant son recover from a life-threatening illness. In response, a grateful Knight had offered a piece of gold jewelry as payment, which the film indicates was clearly outside the expectations and norms of white-black relationships in Civil War Mississippi.) Rachel then helps lead Knight to a hideout used by runaway slaves deep in the swamps and provides medical care for his leg, badly injured when he was bitten by the slavecatchers' dogs.

While hiding out and recovering in the swamps, Knight's character begins his transcendence of the color line, which also becomes the overarching theme of the film. Newton becomes romantically interested in Rachel, the enslaved woman, and his legal wife leaves him out of frustration at his apparent need to help others, black or white, rather than caring for his own family. Knight gradually develops a sense of camaraderie with the enslaved men, seeing more unity with the runaways along lines of class than divisions along lines of race. In particular, he develops a close friendship with the central African American character, Moses Washington (Mahershala Ali), a black man who serves as the film's representative for the thoughts and beliefs of all black men.

Gradually, more and more of the white farmers of Jones County become angry and disillusioned with the Confederate cause, and Knight slowly builds a sizeable following, including increasing numbers of Confederate deserters like himself. By the summer of 1863, Knight has enough men, arms, and supplies to stage a full-on revolt against the Confederacy. Using guerilla tactics,

Knight and his men continue to resist Confederate efforts to seize supplies and property, as he becomes a kind of Mississippian version of Robin Hood. After Confederate troops capture and hang four of Knight's followers (including two young boys), Knight and his men surprise Confederate forces at the funeral for the hanged men. As the rebellion comes to a climax with a battle at the funeral, Knight strangles a Confederate major to death in a church and declares Jones County the "Free State of Jones," pulling down the Confederate flag and replacing it with the United States' flag. After gaining control of Jones County, Knight and his men successfully seize two other neighboring counties. They are rebuffed by requests for assistance from the Union and General William T. Sherman but manage to hold their "Free State of Jones" until the end of the war.

The third act of *Free State of Jones* begins with the end of the war in April 1865 and follows the course of Reconstruction and the aftermath of the end of slavery. If the war years had provided Newton Knight with the opportunity to build a class-based rebellion fueled in part by unity among whites and blacks, the film shows how any hopes of a postwar society inclusive of interracial harmony collapsed in the chaos of Reconstruction. As opposed to the first two-thirds of the film, which follow a relatively straightforward and linear narrative, the final third on Reconstruction consists of a series of vignettes. Newton enters into an interracial common-law marriage with Rachel, resulting in the birth of at least one son. While Newton builds a farm, Rachel teaches at the local school set up through the Freedman's Bureau.

The real power in the film's portrayal of Reconstruction, however, is in the centering of its narrative on the black experience during the postwar years, and it clearly demonstrates the confusion and chaos of Reconstruction on the ground in the South. The film's depiction of Reconstruction begins with the ratification of the Thirteenth Amendment ending slavery, the reuniting of black families, and widespread hopes among freedpeople that they might receive William T. Sherman's promise of "40 acres and a mule."[10] Those hopes are quickly shattered, however, as under the administration of Andrew Johnson, the federal government rescinds any promises of land redistribution and restores southern land to whites on the basis of loyalty oaths. The film then shows the efforts of former slaveholders to restore prewar conditions of labor under the infamous Black Codes, and Knight fights to free Moses Washington's son from working in the fields under a "lawful apprenticeship," which in practice was slavery in all but name.

The film then fast-forwards through the years of Radical Reconstruction.

Here, we see the role of Union Leagues in the South empowering black men to take advantage of the Fifteenth Amendment, which, on its ratification in 1870, granted all men the right to vote. The film mirrors the Union Leagues and their efforts to organize political rights for black men with the simultaneous rise of the Ku Klux Klan and use of racial terrorism to achieve the exact opposite. Ultimately, *Free State of Jones* depicts the corruption and violence inherent to redemption in the South—the process by which conservative white Southern Democratic regimes regained control of southern state governments, largely using racial violence and intimidation to prevent black men from voting. After actively trying to register freedmen to vote, Moses Washington is attacked and lynched by white vigilantes. In response, Newton Knight leads a group of several dozen black men to defiantly cast their ballots for the Republicans in an 1875 election in Jones County; however, the final vote tally lists 419 votes for Democrats and only 2 for Republicans. The film closes with a brief coda, indicating that though they were never able to legally marry, Newton and Rachel Knight lived together for the remainder of their lives.

The central argument of the film is that class trumps race. It attempts to show, through the actions and beliefs of the character of Newton Knight, that poor whites and blacks had more in common based on class than divided them based on race—according to the film, whites were victims too, especially during the war years. Throughout the film's portrayal of the Civil War, the language of class is constant. Early on, Confederate soldiers lament the Confederacy's "Twenty Negro Law," part of the Second Conscription Act of 1862, wherein white men on plantations with twenty or more slaves could be exempted from military service.[11] Before Knight's nephew dies in battle, we learn that he had enlisted because the Confederate government had seized his family's crops and farm, making it impossible for him to sustain a living. Indeed, the villains in this film, at least during the war years, are "big government" and the wealthy elite, here represented by the wealthiest of slaveholders, usually in the background. In other words, in *Free State of Jones* the real enemies of white Confederate soldiers were not the Union army but the wealthy slaveholders who were to blame for the onset of the war. This is the Civil War, then, seen through the lens of our own modern economic critiques of income inequality—Newton Knight may as well be channeling recent jeremiads against the so-called 1 percent.

To be sure, there are elements of truth to this portrayal of the war. The film demonstrates the tenuous balance of Confederate ideologies and how quickly the war could test the strength of those ideologies.[12] Class tension was very real in the South during the war, no better demonstrated than in the widespread bread riots across the South in 1863. White women on the Confederate home front experienced severe shortages of food, clothing, iron, and other necessities and exercised their frustration in a series of riots in southern cities, most notably in Richmond, Virginia, in March and April 1863.[13] Confederate conscription efforts challenged the ideological basis of their government and forced white southerners to face the irony of protesting a government that was taking some of the same actions that had prompted them to form that government in the first place.

Nevertheless, there is also an inherent danger in succumbing to this interpretation of the Confederacy during the Civil War. Class tensions in the South during the war did exist, but casting the Jones County rebellion as the white South writ large presumes that the only people in the Confederacy who benefitted from or maintained a vested interest in sustaining slavery—and therefore by extension benefitted from the war effort—were the smallest minority of slaveholders. This assumption belies the degree to which slavery served as the cornerstone of the Confederacy and ignores the commitment that many white southerners—slaveholders and nonslaveholders alike—shared in preserving slavery, not to mention the varying ways they benefitted from the institution. Of course, such an interpretation is tempting, as it provides one way to explain the motivations of the vast majority of Confederate soldiers who owned no slaves at all. Yet, it ignores the realities of a slave society in which only approximately 25 percent of southern white households owned slaves.

Furthermore, the film's emphasis on class tensions and division among white Confederates adheres to an older narrative that the Confederacy collapsed from within, in part because it suffered from a depletion of morale. Such an interpretation ignores the recent work of historians who have identified the widespread and frequently stunning commitment among white southerners to Confederate nationalism, particularly among white women. Indeed, what is often most surprising is just how unshakeable that commitment was, even in the desperate late years of the war. As the historian Gary W. Gallagher has observed, "Far from being a loosely knit collection of individuals whose primary allegiance lay with their states, a substantial portion of the Confederate people identified strongly with their southern republic."[14]

Ultimately, the film's focus on class tensions serves to define the motivations of its central character, Newton Knight. Because Knight views the Civil

War as a form of class warfare, he primarily sees the economic commonalities shared by poor whites and blacks rather than the divisions created by their race. This is almost immediately clear when the film first introduces Rachel as she cares for Knight's sick child and Newton treats her as a social equal. Indeed, later on, as Confederate officers pursue Knight for his efforts in helping other families resist conscription, Newton's white first wife is at great pains to point out that the slave-patrol dogs are about to chase him, as if to imply that Knight shares the same fate as enslaved African Americans. The subsequent scenes as Newton hides out in the swamps reinforce this message. After seeing the hideout of the runaway slaves, Newton turns to Rachel and exclaims, "They're runaways!" to which Rachel responds, "Ain't you?" suggesting that their cause is one in the same.

As Knight builds his rebellion, shared sacrifice among his white and black followers is a central theme, and he maintains an ideal of interracial harmony based on class. Not all of Knight's white supporters share his beliefs. Following a successful raid of Confederate forces, several of Knight's white followers refuse to let the black men join in the celebratory feast, followed by Knight stepping in to defend the black men, commenting, "They [black men] just picked cotton for them [slaveholders], you, you was willing to die for them." Later, when the same white man questions, "Are we gonna start killin' rich people?" Newton responds, "We're all out there dyin' so they can stay rich." After announcing the establishment of their "Free State of Jones," Knight proclaims its guiding principles: "1) No man oughta stay poor so another man can get rich; 2) No man oughta tell another man what he's gotta live for, or what he's gotta die for; 3) What you put in the ground is yours to tend and harvest, and ain't no man oughta be able to take that away from you; 4) Every man's a man—you walk on two legs, you a man." Thus, according to the film, Newton Knight's independent "Free State of Jones" sets up a society built on class interests undergirded by a dream of interracial harmony.

One of the strengths of *Free State of Jones* is the ways it links the developments of the Civil War to the aftermath of Reconstruction through the lens of race, reflecting a burgeoning trend among scholars highlighting the connections between the two periods, rather than viewing them as distinctly separate eras.[15] Along these lines, if the film uses the Civil War to build up a utopian ideal of interracial harmony in Jones County, it uses Reconstruction to demonstrate how that ideal collapsed and fell apart. If the film advances the argument that blacks and whites shared common economic interests during the war, it also argues that the subsequent struggle over black voting rights during Reconstruction undercut and destroyed those interests. Thus, *Free State of Jones* is really two films in one. Furthermore, its representation of the Civil War and Reconstruction are very different. While its portrayal of and conclusions about the Civil War are problematic, simply put, its depiction of Reconstruction offers one of the best portraits of the complexities and tragedies of the postwar years that we now have on film. Moreover, whereas the film's interpretation of the Civil War is at odds with much of the prevailing scholarship on the war, part of what makes the film's portrait of Reconstruction so compelling is its echoing of the scholarly consensus on the period.

For nearly a century after the end of the Civil War and Reconstruction, the consensus among white scholars was that Reconstruction was a tragic failure that the United States should have never attempted. According to this view, vindictive northerners unduly punished humble white southerners who had been prepared to move on from the war, grant freedom to the freedpeople, and reenter the Union. Radical Republicans, motivated by nothing other than the desire to consolidate power and cement their political ascendancy, installed corrupt governments in the South through the unjust disfranchisement of former Confederates while empowering illiterate and uneducated freedmen unprepared to handle the responsibilities commensurate with democracy and freedom. Indeed, central to this interpretation of Reconstruction was a virulent racism in which whites saw African Americans as inherently inferior, undeserving, and incapable of exercising the responsibilities of freedom. This view originated with former Confederates and was a natural extension of the mythology of the Lost Cause that surrounded the war, its causes and aftermath, and pervaded every aspect of white southern culture. By the early twentieth century, the best-known academic scholars writing on Reconstruction had embraced this interpretation, which came to be known as the Dunning school, typified by the work of historian William A. Dunning and his students at Columbia University. The Dunning school's interpretation remained the prevailing understanding of Reconstruction for the next half-century.[16]

A wide range of film portrayals also reinforced this view of Reconstruction, most notably in two of the most important films of the twentieth century: *The Birth of a Nation* (1915), and *Gone with the Wind* (1939). These two films need little introduction as two of the most culturally significant and widely viewed films in American history, and both offered portrayals of Reconstruction that matched the prevailing scholarly consensus of the time. In each film, Reconstruction is depicted as a tragic era, dominated by corruption as white southerners find themselves trapped under the boot heel of the recalcitrant North. In *Gone with the Wind,* for example, Scarlett O'Hara is unable to pay the unreasonable taxes levied on her plantation under the Republicans' Reconstruction government. *The Birth of a Nation* was perhaps the film that most closely mirrored the scholarly view of Reconstruction, as it depicts the aftermath of the Civil War when supposedly savage freedmen, emboldened by their wartime service in the Union army, roamed the countryside and lusted after white women. In one of the film's most famous scenes, a chaste southern white woman attempts suicide by hurtling herself from the top of a cliff rather than submit to the sexual advances of a black Union veteran. In this version of Reconstruction, the Ku Klux Klan serves as conquering heroes, quite literally riding in to save the day and rescue the white South from Republican rule and restore proper order to the racial hierarchy.

Other twentieth-century films, including the 1942 biopic *Tennessee Johnson* —a sympathetic treatment of the life of Andrew Johnson—offered similar portrayals of Reconstruction. Where it dealt with Reconstruction, *Tennessee Johnson* depicted Johnson (Van Heflin) valiantly resisting the corruption and tyrannical rule of the Radical Republicans. (At one point, black servants carry Radical Republican senator Thaddeus Stevens [Lionel Barrymore] into the Senate chamber on a litter). The film culminates with Johnson's impeachment trial, and in the film's most outrageous scene, Johnson descends to the impeachment proceedings in the Senate to give a speech in his own defense (an event that never took place), persuading just enough of the Radical Republicans to vote to acquit him.

Of course, these views of Reconstruction in scholarship and film during the first half of the twentieth century reflect the Lost Cause and the white southern view of the so-called Tragic Era.[17] At the same time, however, there was a wide range of black voices that pushed back against this view of the postwar years, many of which were among the first academically trained African American scholars. The most famous example of these scholars was W. E. B. Du Bois, who published the monumental *Black Reconstruction in America* in 1935.[18] Du Bois, perhaps the most influential black thinker and scholar of the twentieth century, countered the prevailing white views of the postwar years, as he "portrayed Reconstruction as an idealistic effort to construct a democratic, interracial political order from the ashes of slavery."[19] While it did not receive mainstream acceptance at the time, Du Bois's work would influence much of the revisionist and post-revisionist scholarship on Reconstruction of the 1960s and 1970s, discussed below.

Du Bois was certainly not alone, either. Other black scholars and historians, including Alrutheus A. Taylor and Carter Woodson, published work that challenged the Dunning interpretation of Reconstruction by refuting many of its myths, while simultaneously presenting Reconstruction as a noble effort that ultimately fell short of securing the fruits of democracy for freedpeople in the South.[20] Outside of the academy, Afrocentric cultural productions also challenged the views presented in films like *The Birth of a Nation,* including, most notably, the 1920 *Within Our Gates,* written, produced, and directed by the African American filmmaker Oscar Micheaux and often viewed as a direct response to *The Birth of a Nation. Within Our Gates* showed the realities of racial violence and lynching in the South in the late nineteenth and early twentieth centuries.

While these African American voices marked dissenting views in the early twentieth century, by the 1960s, other scholars of Reconstruction began to follow suit and dramatically revise the earlier interpretations of the Dunning school. Inspired by the civil rights movement as well as earlier scholars like Du Bois, many historians turned what was still the traditional Reconstruction narrative on its head: they still viewed Reconstruction as a failure, but for what it had failed to achieve rather than what it had attempted to accomplish. In this vein, the central problem of Reconstruction became the failure to secure civil, political, and economic rights for freedpeople in the South. So-called revisionist and post-revisionist historians writing in the 1960s and 1970s redeemed the reputation of the Radical Republicans and rightfully overturned the racist idea that blacks in the South had been unfit for freedom.[21] Synthesizing the previous generation of scholarship in 1988, Eric Foner labeled Reconstruction "America's Unfinished Revolution" in what remains the seminal account of the period. Most important, Foner emphasized the myriad achievements of black communities in the South and in doing so restored a sense of optimism to the postwar years.[22]

Yet, despite these advances in our scholarly understanding of Reconstruction, a corresponding revision in cinematic portrayals of the period never took place. On film, Reconstruction remained trapped in the interpretations of the Dunning school and *The Birth of a Nation.* There have been a few notable exceptions—including the 1974 *The Autobiography of Miss Jane Pittman* (based on a 1971 novel of the same name by Ernest J. Gaines)—which have portrayed the struggles of freedpeople after the war, but these accounts unfortunately remained outside of the mainstream views of Reconstruction in American culture.

This is what makes *Free State of Jones* such a powerful depiction of Reconstruction: essentially, it is the first Fonerian version of Reconstruction to appear on film. Thus, like Eric Foner thirty years ago, the film insists that the central struggle of Reconstruction was over the power of black men voting. *Free State of Jones* follows very carefully the experience of freedmen as they fight to embrace the right to vote through grassroots organizing in Union Leagues and individual efforts to register black men to vote. Moreover, unlike older views of Reconstruction, the Ku Klux Klan appears in *Free State of Jones* as it was: a terrorist organization designed to intimidate and prevent blacks from voting. In this way, *Free State of Jones* is the first film to provide a concrete sense of what the political stakes were during Reconstruction for black men and women in the South.

The film's account of Reconstruction is not perfect, however. In particular, many reviews have criticized *Free State of Jones* for casting Newton Knight in the typical "white savior" role so central to many Hollywood films about race and history.[23] There is some truth to this critique: for example, it is Knight who steps in to rescue Moses Washington's son from a "lawful apprenticeship" during the early years of Reconstruction, and it is Knight who leads a group of black men to exercise their right to vote in the film's penultimate scene. Moreover, the film's central argument, advanced by Knight's character, that class trumps race, is deeply problematic. Such an argument ignores the stark realities of race, slavery, and the nineteenth-century South and is equally problematic if intended as a lesson for contemporary America.

That said, dismissing *Free State of Jones* as just another example of Hollywood's "white savior" trope underestimates much of what the film has to say. Black agency is not altogether absent. *Free State of Jones* provides the best (and quite possibly the only) representation of black political mobilization after the war, whether through its depiction of political organization in the form of Union Leagues, or Moses Washington's efforts to canvas and register black men to vote, ultimately at the cost of his own life. In the first half of the film, we see black men and women resisting the institution of slavery in a variety of ways, through the examples of runaway slaves, and Rachel stealing supplies from the plantation to aid the men hiding out in the swamp. Moreover, much of Knight's survival early in the film depends on help from black characters. He would not have escaped Confederate capture nor would he have recovered from serious injuries were it not for the enslaved men and women who helped him hide out in the swamps or provided medical care for his injuries. Finally, because much of the film is based on true events—Newton Knight was a real person, and he did lead a revolt against the Confederacy that included both black and white followers—critiquing Knight's character as just another "white savior" does not do justice to the nuances of race and politics presented in the film.

In the final analysis, *Free State of Jones* is not a perfect film, but it represents a step in the right direction, particularly in its interpretation of Reconstruction. While the film's central argument about race and class is problematic, its honest and authentic account of the struggles of the postwar years provides us with a cinematic version of Reconstruction for the twenty-first century. By giving audiences a vision of Reconstruction that matches much of the best historical scholarship on the period, *Free State of Jones* can help move the public understanding of the postwar years beyond the older portrait of Reconstruction, which continues to persist, even 150 years later. With the end of the Civil War sesquicentennial and public attention on Reconstruction increasing, perhaps more films like *Free State of Jones* will finally improve Americans' understanding of the most contentious and misunderstood period of American history.

Notes

For assistance with this essay, the author wishes to thank Gary Gallagher, Bryan Jack, and readers for the University Press of Kentucky.

1. Ta-Nehisi Coates, "Hillary Clinton Goes Back to the Dunning School," *Atlantic,* January 26, 2016, https://www.theatlantic.com/politics/archive/2016/01/hillary-clinton-reconstruction/427095/.

2. Eric Foner, "'People Know Next to Nothing about Reconstruction': The Pernicious Civil War Revisionism Poisoning American History Students," *Salon,* August 20, 2015,

http://www.salon.com/2015/08/20/people_know_next_to_nothing_about_reconstruction_the_pernicious_civil_war_revisionism_poisoning_american_history_students_partner/

3. Edward L. Ayers, "How the Enemies of Reconstruction Created Reconstruction," 2, paper presented at the Jepson Colloquium: Reconstruction and the Arc of Racial (In) Justice, session 3, University of Richmond, September 16, 2016. See also Edward L. Ayers, *The Thin Light of Freedom: The Civil War and Emancipation in the Heart of America* (New York: Norton, 2017).

4. On periodization and emphasizing the connections between the Civil War and Reconstruction as opposed to treating them as completely separate and distinct eras, Gregory P. Downs has recently made the case for the idea of a "long war," in Gregory P. Downs, *After Appomattox: Military Occupation and the Ends of War* (Cambridge, MA: Harvard University Press, 2015). Along these lines, thirty years ago Eric Foner began his magiste-

rial history of Reconstruction in 1863, not 1865. See Eric Foner, *Reconstruction: America's Unfinished Revolution, 1863–1877* (New York: Harper & Row, 1988).

5. Calculating the total number of Civil War films ever made remains a difficult task, in part because it depends on how one defines what constitutes a Civil War film. For example, in 1961, the Library of Congress published a comprehensive bibliography that counted 608 Civil War films, with many coming from the silent-film era. See Paul C. Spehr, *The Civil War in Motion Pictures: A Bibliography of Films Produced in the United States since 1897* (Washington, DC: Library of Congress, 1961). By contrast, in 1996 Roy Kinnard identified approximately one hundred Civil War films. See Roy Kinnard, *The Blue and the Gray on the Silver Screen: More than Eighty Years of Civil War Movies* (Secaucus, NJ: Birch Lane Press, 1996). To take a modern example, is the 2003 film *Gangs of New York*—a historical epic about immigration and violence in nineteenth-century New York City—a Civil War film because it overlaps with the New York City draft riots of 1863? For a focus on the Civil War in film largely since the Vietnam War, see Gary W. Gallagher, *Causes Won, Lost, and Forgotten: How Hollywood and Popular Art Shape What We Know about the Civil War* (Chapel Hill: University of North Carolina Press, 2008).

6. On the Memphis race riots of 1866, see Foner, *Reconstruction,* 261–62.

7. Gregory P. Downs, Eric Foner, and Kate Masur, "Why We Need a National Monument to Reconstruction," *New York Times,* December 14, 2016; "President Obama Designates First National Monument Dedicated to Reconstruction," *New York Times,* January 12, 2017.

8. See Gregory P. Downs and Kate Masur, "The Era of Reconstruction: 1861–1900," National Parks Service, U.S. Department of the Interior, National Historic Landmarks Program Web site, 2017, https://www.nps.gov/nhl/learn/themes/Reconstruction.pdf.

9. See Victoria E. Bynum, *The Free State of Jones: Mississippi's Longest Civil War* (Chapel Hill: University of North Carolina Press, 2003).

10. On William T. Sherman's famous Special Field Orders, No. 15, which allocated lands in coastal areas of South Carolina for the use of freedmen in 1865 and served as the genesis for black expectations of "forty acres and a mule" after the war, see Foner, *Reconstruction,* 70–71, 104–5. See also James M. McPherson, *Battle Cry of Freedom: The Civil War Era* (New York: Oxford University Press, 1988), 840–41.

11. On Confederate conscription efforts generally, and slave impressment efforts in particular, see Jaime Amanda Martinez, *Confederate Slave Impressment in the Upper South* (Chapel Hill: University of North Carolina Press, 2013), 20, 43.

12. Ibid., 1–17.

13. On the 1863 riots across the South, see McPherson, *Battle Cry of Freedom,* 617–19.

14. Gary W. Gallagher, *The Confederate War: How Popular Will, Nationalism, and Military Strategy Could Not Stave Off Defeat* (Cambridge, MA: Harvard University Press, 1997), 7. See also Aaron Sheehan-Dean, *Why Confederates Fought: Family and Nation in Civil War Virginia* (Chapel Hill: University of North Carolina Press, 2007).

15. On this point, see, again, Downs, *After Appomattox.*

16. See William Archibald Dunning, *Reconstruction: Political and Economic, 1865–*

1877 (New York: Harper & Brothers, 1907). On the Dunning school generally, see Foner, *Reconstruction*, xvii–xxv. See also *The Dunning School: Historians, Race, and the Meaning of Reconstruction*, ed. John David Smith and J. Vincent Lowery (Lexington: University Press of Kentucky, 2013).

17. Claude G. Bowers, *The Tragic Era: The Revolution after Lincoln* (New York: Halcyon House, 1929).

18. W. E. B. Du Bois, *Black Reconstruction in America: An Essay Toward a History of the Part Which Black Folk Played in the Attempt to Reconstruct Democracy in America, 1860–1880* (New York: S. A. Russell, 1935).

19. Foner, *Reconstruction*, xix.

20. See Alrutheus A. Taylor, *The Negro in South Carolina during the Reconstruction* (Washington, DC: Association for the Study of Negro Life and History, 1924), and Carter G. Woodson, *The Negro in Our History* (1922; repr., Washington, DC: Associated Publishers, 1962).

21. Among others, see John Hope Franklin, *Reconstruction: After the Civil War* (Chicago: University of Chicago Press, 1961); William Gillette, *Retreat from Reconstruction, 1869–1879* (Baton Rouge: Louisiana State University Press, 1979); Leon F. Litwack, *Been in the Storm So Long* (New York: Knopf, 1981); and Kenneth M. Stampp, *The Era of Reconstruction, 1865–1877* (New York: Vintage, 1965).

22. Foner, *Reconstruction*, xix–xxvii.

23. See, for example, Vann R. Newkirk II, "The Faux-Enlightened *Free State of Jones*," *Atlantic*, June 28, 2016, https://www.theatlantic.com/entertainment/archive/2016/06/the-faux-woke-state-of-jones/489071/.

5

From Griffith to Parker

The Representation of African Americans and the US South in *The Birth of a Nation* 1915–2016

Caroline Schroeter

This chapter explores the divergent portrayals of the American South presented in D. W. Griffith's 1915 epic *The Birth of a Nation* and Nate Parker's 2016 cinematic slave narrative by the same title.[1] Griffith and Parker both focus on the violation and destruction of the South by the Other. For Griffith, the white South is threatened by a political, economic, and, most disturbingly, racial landscape undergoing dramatic redefinition. Parker, however, tells the story of a long-oppressed black South struggling to claim its basic humanity against the cruel hegemony of a corrupt social order. Each director defines a version of the historical South, rejecting the Other in lieu of an appeal to the racial Same. Moreover, both films play with the idea of identity crisis, as both a national condition and a personal struggle. I argue that the black and white body are metaphors for the South in these two films and in their foundational literary canon. The violation of the body represents the abjection of the South's white and black cultural identity, in the form of brutal acts—or the mere threat—of physical, emotional, and sexual violence.

The thematic content of each film raises important questions about the America in which it is set, specifically the ante- and postbellum South. I regard each film as an artifact of its time, each reflecting the values, norms, and attitudes influential to the times in which they were made. My analysis, then, provides insights about the shifting representations of racial identity and southern culture as they appear on screen by examining the differing interpretations of race, slavery, and nineteenth-century southern society in the selected films. The roles these films play within their own historical circumstances are also of critical importance. Though causality has never been definitively demonstrated, it is no historical secret that the second iteration of the Ku Klux Klan almost immediately followed the release of Griffith's film.[2] Likewise, the critical acclaim Parker's film has received prompts the question as to its potential social and historical consequence, especially at a time when the Klan appears to be regaining traction in some southern states.

I view the term "identity" through the phenomenological framework of the Self and the Same and as a distinct social category in relation to the Other. This reductive distinction has had its place in philosophical thought and social practice for centuries, and, as Edward Said has argued, supported the us-versus-them social dichotomy that served as a justification for imperialism, contributing to the Atlantic slave trade. In this way, identity can be framed within the historical construction of power relations between black African and African American, and white European and American people. Because white, land-owning men and women, as the dominant social group, were (and are still) often considered the standard against which all Others are compared and defined, they have been "left unexamined, whilst the identities of those seen as 'Other' were constantly interrogated, investigated and monitored."[3] In the past, white people "seized the right to define and determine the status of the Other," while black people were "metaphorically dissected by white males constantly seeking reaffirmation of their superiority."[4] The construction of identity—whether in a personal or communal sense—especially for black Americans, has often been framed by a discourse about superiority versus inferiority and is defined by issues of oppression, particularly in consideration of race, class, gender, the body and sexuality. The concept of identity as defined by the subordination of the Other by the dominant Same is critical to the understanding of southern identity, especially in the context of the dynamics by which the Othered identities have been represented on screen over the past hundred years.

I define the dichotomy between the Other and the Same in order to widen the narrow impression of the term "Self," which enables a richer analysis of the relationship Parker's audience has with his film. Each of the films in question, as well as their filmmakers, makes explicit use of the body—both black and white—to appeal to identification with the idea of a Same. The body's consequent violation by the Other is used as a metaphor for the existential challenges that southern identity and representation have undergone in the hundred-year span between the two films.

From 1915 to 2016: Dixon, Griffith, and the Evolution of Mediatized Othering

Written in 1905, *The Clansman* is the second part of Thomas Dixon's trilogy about the Lost Cause of the Confederacy and sentimental notions of white cultural idealism, subtitled "A Historical Romance about the Ku Klux Klan." In character with white southern attitudes about the Lost Cause, Dixon's trilogy is set during the Reconstruction era and downplays the central role of slavery in the conflict of the Civil War. *The Clansman* offers a "vibrant testimony to the gallant, courageous, and transformative spirit of the South and its people," a correction to what Dixon "perceived as gross misrepresentations of the South in literary works."[5] Dixon suggests that with all members of southern society uniting, the "great beast of Reconstruction," as Kirkpatrick calls it, could be slain. Framed in a classic melodrama plot, two love stories emerge in between the Stonemans and the Camerons, two white families from opposing sides of the conflict, set against the changing social, political, and economic landscape of the South. These families come together, bringing with them the hope of reconciliation, healing, and order between the victorious North and the destroyed South.[6]

The Clansman sold more than a million copies in a short period of time and became the basis for the play that was an immediate success in theaters everywhere. Concerns arose, however, that the popularization of this story's Anglocentric message against a backdrop of anti-black sentiment would provoke conflict. All over the United States, tensions began to rise shortly after opening night, contributing to the riots that engulfed Atlanta and spread across the country in the early twentieth century.[7]

Despite the tense social atmosphere, Griffith and Frank E. Woods began working to transform Dixon's novel and selections from his play into a script that would eventually become the basis for the film. The work that resulted is often described as a "landmark and notorious film, which is praised for its many cinematic innovations while condemned for its overt racist agenda."[8] Regarded as an "aesthetic masterpiece," it is generally thought of as the first American blockbuster. The film was the first twelve- (as opposed to three-) reel production and redefined the meaning of feature length—three hours in comparison to the conventional half-hour shows. The film was considered to have played a "crucial pioneering role" that brought about a "revolution in American moviegoing," but it was also "one of the most controversial motion pictures of all time."[9]

Griffith attempted to portray his version of the true history of the South, to tell the story of its destruction during the Civil War and Reconstruction. The film argues that allowing former slaves the rights and political opportunities enjoyed by white people was an egregious mistake, tantamount to blasphemy and bringing about the ultimate degradation of the values and principles of southern society. Because Dixon's radical belief that "blacks must be denied political equality because [it] leads to social equality and miscegenation and thus to the destruction of both family and civilized society" is a theme running through *The Clansman,* it is no surprise that the 1915 *The Birth of a Nation* echoes the glorification of white supremacy and the ideal of racial purity.[10]

In the film, as in many other works of the southern canon, white women represent the core of the family and are the "repositories of all human idealism."[11] The purity of white womanhood demonstrates the need—the duty, even—of the southern white man to provide protection from the unjust political machinations of Emancipation and Reconstruction. The Klan, romanticized as an "institution of Chivalry, Humanity, Mercy and Patriotism," took on this protective role, defending women and children, upholding the Constitution, and bringing safety and order back to the disenfranchised and endangered South.[12] Southern white women not only shouldered the burden of symbolizing purity and family but also came to represent the fertile land of the South itself: beautiful, yet helpless, besieged and destroyed by the armies of the North and suffering from the postwar degradation of economic and political power at the hands of wealthy northern politicians, vagrant former slaves, and all those who did not belong to the South: the Other. This representation of southern white women as a "bastion of purity and goodness" contrasts with the counter-narrative of the antagonistic African American, who was already the target of much public hostility and often associated with treachery or incompetence.[13]

Griffith, drawing verbatim from Dixon's works, suggests a common misguided belief that contemporary Republican politics favored newly freed slaves—for example, encouraging black men to vote, become politically active, and pursue white women for marriage. The scene in which Flora Cameron (Mae Marsh), a southern belle and sister to the protagonist, Colonel Ben Cameron (Henry B. Walthall), plays in the woods, illustrates the harmony between her and the beauty of southern nature. Griffith contrasts her youthful innocence with the forceful pursuit of Gus, a lecherous black man (performed by Walter Long, a white actor in blackface). The scene shows a helpless

Flora—the heart of southern virtue—fleeing Gus's advances and in dire need of protection. The South, thus, is "frozen at its exoticized apex and nadir, relegated by tacit national consensus to a heaven-and-hell diptych of social types" and at the end of the scene is standing both literally and figuratively on the precipice of death and disaster.[14]

Griffith depicts black people, in contrast to Flora, as morally weak and brutish, an overriding theme that becomes especially clear in two scenes, the first of which is Flora's suicide. Flora is pursued and chased by Gus and is, at the end of the scene, on the precipice of death and disaster. She chooses to jump, tumble down a cliff, and die, protecting her purity, rather than to be involved with a black man. Second, newly elected African American legislators are portrayed as shoeless, their feet propped on desks, "eating chicken and leering at white women, apparently unable or unwilling to pay attention to the workings of democracy." Griffith conspicuously suggests that newly freed former slaves are unable to think "beyond primitive impulses" and are clearly unfit for political positions and inferior to their white counterparts, a common belief used for decades to "legitimize the South's efforts to deny African Americans the right to vote."[15]

Ben Cameron (Henry B. Walthall), a war hero also known by the moniker "The Little Colonel," is the eldest son of the southern Cameron family and the film's hero, who mobilizes the knights of the Klan to offer a way to fight back, to rescue the South and punish misbehaving former slaves. Griffith even portrays the Klansmen as gallant heroes "working to ensure a reunited white nation."[16] From the time of the film's first release until the present, these claims, along with the portrayal of the Griffith's white-power "truth," have been challenged and discussed vehemently by critics for their deeply controversial content and racism. The mythologizing and "glorification of the Old South, that world of tea, Spanish moss, buggy whips and summer dances" represents a "populist paean to recapture certain vestiges of an America undergoing dramatic change, similar to Donald Trump vowing to 'make America great again.'"[17]

As in *The Clansman,* Griffith's depictions of African Americans are as grotesque and offensive as they are clichéd. He applies Dixon's representation of black characters to the film and develops the story into an epic tale of good versus evil, pitting the incumbency of white society against its newest, black members. In his film, African Americans are reduced to a "series of physical characteristics, described in bestial terms, or to flawed personality traits"[18] that were common at the time. Their representation was also often dominated by caricatures and exaggerated depictions of the black body. Donald Bogle argues that black characters can be divided into distinct racial stereotypes or roles.[19] Black men were often stereotyped as "apelike savages," "buffoons" or criminals: the brutal, lecherous Buck, the docile Tom, the happy Sam(bo), the dancing Jim Crow, the harmless but good-for-nothing Coon. Black women were hypersexualized as the promiscuous Jezebel, desexualized as the bossy Mammy, portrayed as the sassy Sapphire or the tragic mulatto. Mulattos frequently served as reminders to the audience of the "dangers" of interracial mingling. All these stereotypes were portrayed often as fierce, cantankerous, and condescending to black men.[20] Many black characters from the first *The Birth of a Nation* comport with these personae.

The Tom, represented by a Cameron house servant (actor uncredited), is an obedient, good-natured slave or former slave who is loyal to his/her master and presents no threat to their authority and superiority. The Mammy, also represented by a servant of the Cameron household, is played by a white actress (Jennie Lee) in blackface. She is portrayed as a large, sassy, independent woman who is asexual and, therefore, of no temptation to her masters. She is responsible for raising the white children of the household and is fiercely loyal to her white family. The Mulatto/a, a character of mixed racial decent, is often portrayed as having been raised white, later discovering the tragic revelation of his/her black heritage. In the earlier *The Birth of a Nation*, the Mulatto stereotype is represented by two white actors in blackface: the lecherous and cruel Silas Lynch (George Siegmann) and the power-hungry, scheming, and sexual Lydia Brown (Mary Alden), who both work for the Hon. Austin Stoneman (Ralph Lewis), congressman and the Leader of the House.

Griffith also introduces the audience to the black Buck, aggressive and prone to hypersexuality. The black Union soldier Gus is a walking hyperbole: impudent, aggressive, and, problematic for Griffith's audience, obsessed with white women like Flora. Bogle suggests that while the Buck was already a stereotype, until Griffith's film, it was not part of the conventional range of cinematic stereotypical roles usually ascribed to black characters.[21] For the past century of film production, and to the incredulity and humiliation of black audiences, however, the Buck as a caricature in popular media has persisted as part of the repertoire of black characters in film.

Griffith's film creates and reinforces negative depictions of black people by Othering them through racial stereotyping and appealing to the South's struggle to find its identity amid the pain of racism, slavery, and civil unrest. The mediatized denigration of African Americans in a film that even President Wilson called an excellent work and *true* is profoundly troubling for the identity, self-identification, and Other-identification of black people and of the South in general, the more so since the Other have had little agency to challenge these mediatized stereotypes.

Nate Parker and *The Birth of a Nation*

Nate Parker's *The Birth of a Nation* was initially celebrated as "instant rapture," setting a sales record at the 2016 Sundance Film Festival.[22] A belated corrective to #OscarsSoWhite, the film was conceived, written, and performed by a black director and leading actor and portrays the reimagining of Nat Turner's 1831 slave rebellion against white slave owners and their families in Virginia. Parker presents his audience with a new perspective on African American slaves, who, through violent uprising, declared their autonomy and fought against the injustice of their enslaved circumstances rather than helplessly bearing the inhumanity and indignation of their victimization. His interpretation of this historical event, based on Nat Turner as a historical figure, thrusts the power of black masculinity into the spotlight.

What Parker brings to the table is the idea of profoundly revising master narratives, a history largely written from a white perspective, both in literature and in film. His film connects the deep undercurrent of racism in America's past to the pervasive effects of institutionalized racism in society today. The scene in which a young Nat Turner's father is confronted by a group of murderous slave hunters, for example, is a readily accessible and visual approximation of contemporary police shootings of black men.[23] In this context, Parker argues that Nat Turner's story is about "one person who stood against a system that was oppressing people. And if we can relate to that in 2016, we must ask ourselves, what are we willing to sacrifice for what we want our children, and our children's children, to enjoy?"[24] The contemporary *The Birth of a Nation* is one salient answer to the call for provocative cinema, offering highly topical subject matter. It also sparked considerable public dialogue about race and appeared to dovetail with the Black Lives Matter movement, in protest against, among other hot-button issues, police brutality and the decades-long rise of for-profit prisons, a judicial system that appears stacked against black communities, and the beginnings of the Klan's rebirth in some southern states.[25]

Parker received high praise for his reimagining of the Nat Turner story, both as a contradiction to the extant, white, account and for his portrayal of

Turner himself as a more multidimensional figure with considerable significance in African American culture. During the civil rights movement, for example, Nat Turner was considered a hero, one of the "revolutionaries and militants who waged a physical fight to free black people," shaping the decisions of black leaders like Malcom X and Martin Luther King Jr.[26]

Of particular interest, apart from the film's revolutionary content and the snowballing controversy around its maker, are its numerous intertextual references to literature and film from the last hundred years. The most conspicuous allusion is Parker's explicit use of Griffith's title: *The Birth of a Nation;* while his film was publicized as a challenge to the original, it is only the latest in a long line of work seeking to reclaim the meaning of Griffith's title.[27] Parker is not only working within the larger context of African American creative expression but also drawing from a variety of literary sources. These include the Bible, Thomas Gray's 1831 *Confessions of Nat Turner* and William Styron's Pulitzer prize–winning novel *The Confessions of Nat Turner* (1967). In Gray's work, the lawyer-turned-writer publishes his interview with Nat Turner before his execution, which became the only contemporary account of Turner's story. Styron's account focuses on teasing out Turner's fictional obsession with a teenaged white girl, Margaret Whitehead, portraying him as a hypersexualized, fanatical preacher. Parker intends to reclaim the story written by Gray and excoriated Styron's neo-slave narrative as a misguided work that removes any sense of Turner's autonomy, courage, and self-determination as a leader and, eventually, a martyr.[28] It is difficult, even today, to define the "boundary between fact and fiction, between Turner and Gray," which gave Parker the opportunity to develop his own vision and use creative license to redefine Nat Turner's story, the rebellion and the consequent large-scale punishment that was meted out. Indeed, Parker aims to bridge the gap between the "true" and the fictional account of the past, between what the audience knows and what we wish we knew, in this case, about Nat Turner and one of the largest slave rebellions in US history.[29]

Aiming to disabuse his audience of the negative stereotypes of African Americans prevalent in popular media, Parker not only offers a critique of the depiction of African Americans in popular culture over the last century but also makes a timely contribution to current debates on the state of race relations in the United States in the early twenty-first century. In a 2016 interview with Soheil Rezayazdi, he described the power cinema can exert and expressed his hope that his "black" *The Birth of a Nation* might be used as "a tool to challenge racism and white supremacy in America, to inspire a riotous disposition toward any and all injustice in this country (and abroad), and to promote the kind of honest confrontation that will galvanize our society toward healing and sustained systemic change."[30] Parker's *The Birth of a Nation* represents a changing narrative about the South, from a place where slavery existed among whitewashed estates and high culture to one where slavery dominated the existence of southern society, corrupting its values and traditions. Parker encourages his audience to think about slaves not as slaves but as enslaved *human beings.*

Representation of Racial Identity, History, and the South

Frantz Fanon articulated the double standard that Othered people—in this case, black Americans—face in the formation of social identity: "Only for the white man the Other is perceived on the level of the body image, absolutely as the not-self—that is, the unidentifiable, the unassimilable. For the black man . . . the historical and the economic realities come into picture."[31] White people in North America, Fanon argued, do not bear the burden of self-identification along the consequential lines of social or historical metrics; they just *are,* as opposed to black people, whose identity is interrogated through various lines of understanding and reasoning as a matter of the condition of their existence.

In both Griffith's and Parker's films, the body, and the body of the Other, serve as an important metaphor, but to opposed ends. Griffith uses the white body as a tool for self-definition and to glorify the purity of whiteness from the stain and the terror of blackness in the South. Parker uses the body for the purpose of self-identification, albeit in his work the roles of black and white bodies are reversed. He reimagines black self-identification against a white Other. Parker challenges the idea that the only effective way to portray black people on screen is by showing the "visual, bounded body of the Other," in this case, the black body.[32] He suggests that stereotypes about black people can and should attribute gladiatorial qualities like strength and ferocity to black characters. Parker, like Quentin Tarantino in *Django Unchained* (2012), aims to solidify the idea of a different African American character on screen: the black hero.[33] Parker's Nat Turner, hence, reinforces a modern pantheon of strong black characters that rise above the docility and victimization of many slave films of the past. Where Parker succeeds is in turning Griffith's Other into a self-identifiable Same for his audience, raising questions about how films address different kinds of audiences and how the film's message changes over time and within differing social contexts. By concentrating on black masculinity and empowerment, Parker provides his audience with a counterbalance to the message of white supremacy of Griffith's film.

Griffith focuses his attention on crimes supposedly committed against white people, as opposed to the more complex tensions arising from the wholesale wreckage brought about by the Civil War. Using white actors in blackface to portray black people as antagonists against the backdrop of a peaceful white coming-together story, Griffith plays with two-dimensional, mainstream, white conceptions of black villainy, constructing "Blackness as synonymous with being 'naturally uncivilized'" and unable to see African Americans as "possible partners in American civilization."[34] Parker, in contrast, seeks to develop holistic, well-rounded, complex characters with strong identities, motivations, and individual narratives. His film may be linear and couched in the simple language of revenge, yet he works to convince his audience that Nat Turner's rebellion was not just a "mindless massacre of innocents but a legitimate and righteous retaliation against a cavalcade of inhuman and vile acts."[35]

Audiences are commonly prompted to either identify with or reject the characters of a film, often resulting in an explicit acceptance of the Same or dissociation from the Other. How favorably an audience receives or how strongly an audience repudiates a character influences the power of the film and the work's subsequent reception. Often, a film's narrative addresses and appeals to the audience's ability to relate to a certain character; if, however, the narrative disrupts such identification, it also disrupts the way the audience perceives the film. In Parker's case, the black and white audience binary, as an explanatory reflection of the characters represented in the film, is confronted with two levels of identification. On the one hand, Parker depicts benevolent, likeable white people, like Elizabeth Turner (Penelope Ann Miller), who try to help slaves; white audience members can, for example, identify with her as the Same. On the other hand, Parker also presents the audience with the strong, caring, and intelligent Nat Turner (Nate Parker) and invites both black and white audiences to identify with him as the black Same. While the black audience has a variety of characters that represent the black Same to identify with, the white audience becomes caught in a dilemma, torn between associating with their likeable Same, caught in an unjust system, as well as the powerful Other, motivated by a just cause. Perhaps this is what led Parker to obscure the murder of Elizabeth Turner and other white women and children, to keep notions of Sameness bound in white audience members' minds.

Another possible explanation for the break from historical record is that Parker chooses not to include such scenes because opting to show Turner and his men killing innocent white people would have undermined his attempt to make the audience empathize with Turner, the likable Other. For the same reason, Parker also ignores another critical historical point, that Turner's rebellion led to the murder of several hundred enslaved African Americans, the passage of stronger anti-black legislation, and the implementation of more draconian punishments against black slaves.

It could be argued that "whiteness" and/or "blackness" are, in this regard, more of an indicator of shared experience. An audience's existing bias toward people that look like them make connections with a character easier (or more immediate). Films like Griffith's, which do not develop characters into complex multidimensional individuals, rest their whole argument on these biases. Parker, however, tries to create a more complex Other, whose development approaches a level of Sameness not granted at first. The film's white characters are generally not created to be relatable as the Same but rather as the Other—the unsympathetic, the unidentifiable, the unassimilable. Parker flips the concept of Fanon's Other for his black audience, redefining the role of the conventional Other as the Same; he now interrogates, investigates, and monitors the identities of those seen as Other as well as the Same.[36]

One of the major challenges is the moving away from the sexualized, unidimensional depictions of black characters—and, by association, of black people—toward a modern, independent, and fully rounded range of characters representing men and women who are complicated, imperfect, and "real." Black femininity and masculinity are crucial to the discussion of personal and cultural identity and to the evolving representation of stereotypes on screen. While decades of filmmakers gave preference to white skin over black, the role of the cinematic slave narrative is to counter this representation and its long-standing history.

When African slaves were brought to the New World, slave traders and owners designated them according to two defining features: skin color and the nakedness of their bodies. As far back as the 1600s, white Europeans documented their features, concluding from them a proclivity toward uncontrolled, animal-like hypersexuality. Based on this notion, interracial sexual activity was considered abhorrent and unimaginable, and it became a common belief that no virtuous southern woman would voluntarily be involved (sexually or otherwise) with a black man. Black men were often regarded as potential murderers and rapists, maligned as deviant Others in the broader white society—white was the norm, the Same; black was the deviation, the Other.[37] Consequently, for centuries, self-identification for black men and women was nearly impossible; developing their own identity was prohibited by law and strongly discouraged by society.[38] White men did not want to be black, but, to be recognized as human, black people tried to perform whiteness and adopt white culture.[39] Despite the long history of false representation in popular culture, these limiting representations have been challenged now by cinematic slave narratives and other black films by contemporary filmmakers like Nate Parker, such as Steve McQueen, with *12 Years a Slave* (2013), and Quentin Tarantino, with *Django Unchained* (2012) (also, Clement Virgo, with *The Book of Negroes* [2015]; Barry Jenkins, with *Moonlight* [2016]; Justin Simien, with *Dear White People* [2018–]; Salim Akil and Mara Brock Akil, with the TV show *Black Lightning* [2018–]; Ryan Coogler, with *Black Panther* [2018]).[40] As represented by Parker, black men are strong and powerful and fight back, standing in stark contrast to those without self-recognition or self-awareness in *The Birth of a Nation* (1915) and films that followed its path.[41]

Parker finds a counterbalance to white hegemony in his portrayal of black characters who embody wisdom and agency in the face of brutal injustice. This becomes clear during the verbal duel between Turner and the white Reverend Walthall (Mark Boone Junior). Filmed through a medium shot, a group of white men, including Sam Turner (Armie Hammer), Walthall, and another man, Jethro (Justin M. Smith), surround Nat. Using biblical verse to insist on the righteousness of Turner's enslavement, Walthall receives a powerful rebuke from Turner, who retorts with quotations from scripture, answering each of the reverend's passages with one of his own. Walthall's action triggers Turner's reaction, which, in turn, prompts Sam Turner to strike him down and later to administer punishment that will lead to Turner's alienation from Sam and further convince him to initiate a rebellion. As cracks in the veneer of white authority begin to appear, Sam Turner can only turn to violence to end the encounter. Turner's decision to stand his ground demonstrates not only his ability to use words as weapons, revealing the courage and the rage building within him, but it also indicates the importance of religion and faith during slavery times. The impact of external factors, such as religion, the church, and the abolitionist movement, influenced the style and message of the original slave narrative manuscripts, which often borrowed and subversively redeployed elements from sermons and other Christian literature. Kimberly Rae Connor suggests that "appropriating biblical language and appealing to religious sentiments was a profound way to overturn Southern apologies for slavery."[42]

Nat Turner's biblical clash with white men. *The Birth of a Nation* (2016).

Religious symbolism likewise plays a guiding role in a cinematic slave narrative like Parker's film. Building the story on Turner's faith, Parker uses religion to empower Nat, arm him with his words, a sword and a Bible, and exalt him as a leader and a hero. However, Parker fails to fully address the complexity of Turner's religious fanaticism and the intensity of his prophetic visions. While Parker weaves in spiritual themes from the outset, mixing Christian beliefs with African traditions, Nat's final decision committing him to the rebellion seems to hinge on the rape of his wife, turning a narrative about a religious leader into a "secular fable."[43]

Christianity was intricately interwoven into the cultural fabric of the "Old South," and Griffith leverages this strong adherence to faith and custom in his depiction of the KKK as Christian saviors of southern (as well as female) virtue. Griffith developed the Klan's burning cross, for example, as a tool of intimidation and fear "meant to sear the message of alleged white Christian superiority into people's minds."[44] His President Lincoln is a Christ-like figure, administering judgment and forgiveness to the captured sons of desperate and pleading mothers. Griffith also uses the metaphoric reunion of the North and South, represented by the marriage of Elsie Stoneman (Lillian

Turner's body tied to a makeshift cross in a Christ-like pose. *The Birth of a Nation* (2016).

Gish) and Ben Cameron under the watchful gaze of Jesus and a group of angels, their images superimposed over the scene, delivering his approval. Parker uses a similar approach near the end of his film: awaiting his impending execution, Turner is filmed standing, Christ-like, against a heavenly beam of light filtering in through his solitary prison window.

Two different filmmakers use similar source material to achieve very different ends. Griffith, on the one hand, paints a picture of a God-fearing southern population, guided by the Bible, which offers the hope of salvation and a justification for slavery. Parker, on the other hand, uses religion to motivate the slaves to keep faith despite the unending brutality of their existence and to transcend the limitations of a society built to prevent them from developing their own sense of humanity. In *The Birth of a Nation* (2016), religion is also the guiding element of the narrative that connects the dots and justifies the rebellion. Parker portrays Nat Turner as the chosen one who will lead his people to freedom. While the violation of his wife, Cherry (Asia Naomi King), is the catalyst for Turner's rebellion, his faith generates the momentum building up to his fateful decision. It is important to note that the rape of Cherry as the impetus for Turner's revolt is a break from the historical record and facilitates Parker's insistence on Turner as the black savior.

Each film presents its version of the Old South, depicting its population,

(*Top*) Turner in a prison cell before his execution, assuming a Christ pose, illuminated by divine light. *The Birth of a Nation* (2016).
(*Bottom*) Elsie Stoneman and Ben Cameron's wedding takes place under Jesus's watchful gaze. *The Birth of a Nation* (1915).

traditions, and conspirators in the light that seems most authentic and fitting to their makers. The portrayals of the Other and the Same, and of who fits the categories in these films, ultimately depend on the perspective of the director. Yet in both films the South is a dichotomy of good and evil, a battlefield of black versus white, a story of the Same versus the Other. Each director uses social predispositions to generate dichotomies between his constructions of the Same and the Other, often depicting these binaries in terms of the human body—and the violation of the body—intricately weaving into his respective narrative a story that tries to paint an accurate picture of the true South of the nineteenth and early twentieth centuries. For Griffith, black characters fulfill the role of the repugnant, intruding Other, endangering the beauty and prosperity of the white South, the white Same. His predominantly white audience could readily identify with this white Same, allowing the Klan to stand in as heroes, keeping the encroaching Other at bay while mending the chaos and restoring order. In contrast, Parker casts white people as the Other, allowing black characters to represent the Same, or at least giving Othered audiences a protagonist who crosses the border from Other to Same.

The American South and the Violation of the Body

In each film, the body and the violation of the body is used as a vehicle to communicate fear of change in the social order, reflecting the sentiments and attitudes of the times. In Griffith's film, African Americans are portrayed as violating the purity and innocence of the white South by insulting, offending, raping its women—violating their bodies—and profaning the enduring symbol of white southern identity. The bodies of the black South, however, are stereotyped as hypersexualized; Griffith paints a colorful portrait of "subservient, villainous, dangerous, dim-witted, and buffoonish" black characters.[45] He uses whiteness to convey the idea of the white South succumbing to the "black plague."

In the second film, the black body is violated by Parker's white Other. The beauty of the "black" South, which has suffered a long-time underrepresentation on screen, is disfigured by the crack of the whip, utterly devastated by the greed of the white population, as seen through the eyes of the black characters. However, Parker, unlike Griffith, does not make any assumptions about the fragility and purity of nature as some grand reflection of humankind, black or white. Instead, he uses the landscape's natural beauty to frame the dissonance inherent to slavery existing in such a pictorial setting as the South.

The most powerful, viscerally and symbolically, body-related themes in both films is, as I argued above, the rape or assault of women. Cherry, for example, is gang-raped and nearly beaten to death by a group of antagonistic slave patrollers. Here, Parker plays with the "visual power of the injured black body"; Cherry's face is almost unrecognizable from the beating she has received, calling to mind the 1955 lynching of fourteen-year-old Emmett Till, drawing the subject of abuse of black people in slave times to crimes against black people in more modern times.[46] Cherry's rape also represents the suffering and violation of the female black body in the Old South, standing in direct juxtaposition to the violation of the white female body in Griffith's film. While Flora in the 1915 film chooses to die rather than submit to the advances of a black man, Cherry has no such choice; rather, she must endure the pain, humiliation, and dehumanization. Cherry's role, then, is mainly to illuminate and support Turner's character: because she is abused, he is drawn to her, showing how tender he can be; because she is raped, he takes action, showing how outraged he feels and how his revolutionary consciousness is awakened; because he sees her battered body, his tears flow and the camera focuses, in a close-up, on his face, not her body. As Salamishah Tillet argues, women are "silenced by the violations against their bodies and then again when their victimization is cast as secondary to Turner's heroism, their voices sidelined to the plot of Turner's realization of his own manhood in the horror of slavery."[47] Side by side, these two scenes suggest similar images of two very different and degraded Souths, but the contrast between the events scrapes off the thin veneer of Griffith's fear-mongering, giving a glimpse into the lived experiences of enslaved women.

Like Harriet Beecher Stowe does in *Uncle Tom's Cabin* (1852), Parker creates the opportunity for his audience to identify with the black female Same by appealing to emotions and exposing audience members to her suffering.[48] Numerous critics have argued, however, that Parker's portrayal of women is one of this film's major flaws. These women lack agency on screen, and as a consequence of their violation, men are incited to exact revenge on other men. It would appear that Parker believes black men suffered more from the rape of "their" women than the women themselves did. Neglecting the female perspective and role of women as the violated Other in these scenes arguably hurts Parker's case, especially because he confronts the audience with explicit scenes of brutal violence against men but not against women, disregarding the role and importance of the violation of the female body and psyche. Cherry's and Esther's (Gabriel Union) silence, then, "mutes their [black women's] ability to act, rendering their rebellion virtually nonexistent in a film about revolt and freedom."[49]

Despite historical documents that indicate otherwise, Turner's mother, Nancy, played by Aunjanue Ellis; his grandmother Bridget (Esther Scott); Cherry; and her daughter Joanna are depicted as "helpless victims who suffer unspeakable horrors until Turner rides in on his horse and vows to seek vengeance on their behalf." Turner here is the black savior, the black leader, the black liberator of femininity and female purity. Parker neglects that "enslaved women fought for their dignity and freedom, and they exercised agency over their lives, in spite of unimaginable horrors."[50] Parker also disregards the fact that an enslaved woman was caught, tried, and executed for her involvement in the Turner rebellion for holding down her mistress during the onslaught.[51]

The two rape scenes offer the audience a soundless void, exemplifying this voicelessness through a silenced representation of the pain and the violation of the black South, the black body, the black Same. While the audience never witnesses the actual rapes, the scenes, rather than the women themselves, attempt to give voice to Parker's intentions: to shift the usual emphasis and focus on white people to the unspeakable suffering of black people. However, it is difficult to argue that black women symbolize the South, as white women do for Griffith, because it is the black male characters who represent Parker's South. Neglecting the female perspective and role of women in these scenes arguably hurts Parker's case, especially because his focus appears to be on the men who must confront the rapes of their partners, rather than on the violation of the female body. He confronts the audience with explicit scenes of brutal violence against men but not against women, disregarding the role and importance of the violation of the female body and psyche.

White men are never exposed to anything commensurate with the violence perpetrated against black women, men, and children, enslaved or not. Because the white man is Griffith's quintessential Same, any act of violence a white man commits against a(n Other) person is seen as right. Assaults on the institution of whiteness are merely incidental incursions against the dominant order, which Griffith restores with the heroic entry of the Klan and, at the film's close, overt allusions to heaven's blessing of the holy union of white families. Parker ignores the resulting backlash against southern black people after the failure of Nat Turner's rebellion and the restitution of the racial status quo. However, it comes as a surprise—in a historic diversion from conventional cinematic slave narratives and other films about slavery—that in

Parker's film white men are killed. With the working definitions of the Same and the Other in mind, the slaying of white men—especially at the hands of empowered black people—is outside the natural order. Enslaved black men and women are expected to sustain savage beatings, rape, and other forms of dehumanization; however, the audience is presented with a scene portraying the opposite, challenging the reality of violence against the white body.

When white men are killed, though—and he does indeed show the murder of a few key white people—Parker elides the violence of the rampage that killed between fifty and sixty white people, including many children and women. Instead, Parker focuses on the portrayal of the black hero, Nat Turner, to allow the audience to concentrate on a character created in accordance with the ideals of the Same. It seems that for the purpose of a making a Hollywood film, Parker censors elements of the story that would conflict with the narrative that Turner is a "good" Other to white people. In both films, the focus is not solely on the state of the South and on the harm inflicted by the Other on the Same. Both emphasize the consequences of such violations and on the subsequent reactions of violated people—consequences that center on the conflict between men and on male violence provoked by violations to "their" women's bodies.

Drastic measures are taken to revenge the deeds of the Other, the destroyer of the South. In Griffith's film, black men violate the bodies of white women, leading to the formation of a biblical savior, the Klan, and the victorious destruction of the "black plague." In Parker's film, white people violate black men, women and children, leading to the rebellion during which white people find themselves on the receiving end of physical violation at the righteous hands of a group of black people. Consequently, Turner's rebellion leads to the murder of several hundred slaves and stronger anti-black legislation requiring, for example, harsher punishments for misbehavior, a critical point Parker ignores. Instead, Parker both makes the case that Turner's actions make him a martyr and draws a straight line from Turner to black soldiers taking part in the North's Civil War victory.[52] Ultimately, both directors make emotional appeals to their audience based on popular sentiments of their times. The representations of the violation of the white and the black body, the Other and the Same, is functionally different in the two works, although in both films the development of the Same-Other dichotomy and the intent to build portrayals of godlike men seems more important than delivering an accurate picture of white and black bodies.

Conclusion

Since 1915, onscreen representations of African Americans and the South have undoubtedly reflected the nation's shifting definitions of and attitudes toward American whiteness, blackness and Otherness. In this chapter, I have discussed the divergent portrayals of African Americans, race, and the South in Griffith's and Parker's antithetical films titled *The Birth of a Nation.* More specifically, I have explored the roles of the Other and the Same in the context of the two films and their depictions of the violation of the southern body, considering the use of the Other as a complex tool for self-identification.

In Griffith's *The Birth of a Nation,* the newly freed former slaves are the Other, endangering and destroying the prosperity and beauty of the predominantly culturally white South. Griffith mediates his own truth and ideas about contemporary events, using negative stereotypes already widely used in popular media. Alluding to biblical verse, Griffith pits black people—the morally weak, aggressive, and uncivilized—against the white-robed knights of the Ku Klux Klan. This portrayal represented and codified the negative stereotypes, legitimizing racist conceptions of the South's apparent collapse during Reconstruction at the hands of African Americans, and the subsequent imagery of the Klan as the white South's savior.

In Parker's *The Birth of a Nation,* white people fulfill the role of the Other, threatening to destroy the beauty of life itself, while black people are the Same: the group the audience is asked to identify with, which needs to be rescued from the white Other. Griffith's Other becomes the Same, though the lines that separate acceptance from rejection of Parker's Same and Other become blurred. Parker's film appears to reflect its audience's changing demographic base, becoming what Baker and Nelson define as a phenomenon of the New South: the film reconfigures "our familiar notions of Good (or desperately bad) Old Southern White Men telling stories on the porch, protecting white women, and being friends to the Negro."[53] Moreover, the film casts black male characters into a more positive, or at least heroic light, challenging a century-old misrepresentation of African Americans in popular culture and trying to correct racialized exaggerations of nineteenth-century southern society. Like Griffith, who introduces the Buck as a character type not seen before in film, Parker aims to solidify the idea of a different African American character on screen: the black hero—if not the black Redeemer—a direct challenge to Griffith's KKK.

While Parker directs a historical piece, he uses allusions to events from the course of the past two centuries to strongly connect the struggle of African Americans in the South in the past and the present. Intimations of the Emmett Till lynching and of racialized police shootings, for example, show the audience that slavery's impact has not been relegated to history books. Parker furthermore wants to present his audience with a black perspective—a powerful tool for audience members who might otherwise not immediately identify with the Sameness inherent to the story of slavery—and to make a film that can be used as a tool to challenge the underpinnings of present-day racism. A general African American cinematic trend is heading away from caricatures toward more authenticity and historical accuracy.[54] Characters of the Old South—beautiful belles, "cheerful darkies," and the noble white gentlemen are giving way to more nuanced characters who resemble actual people more closely than racist cartoons.

The Civil War and the Reconstruction era destroyed the "civilization of the Cavalier" and the southern belle that Griffith held tightly.[55] Griffith appealed to an audience still trying to come to terms with the repercussions of that chapter in American history and the struggle, disbelief, and confusion that came with it. Since then, the representation of African Americans and the South have changed; however, southern iconography such as sweeping cotton fields, Spanish moss in gigantic oak trees, moonlit countryside, and dinners and dances in white-columned mansions remains.

While these two works portray the South and its people very differently, they do have several aspects in common: in both films, and for both filmmakers, the South is a place of unparalleled beauty and the home of America's most egregious violations against humanity. Both films are portraits of "society unfolding in time," a reflection of the time period's identity crisis.[56] The dominance of the Old (white) South's identity was breaking down during and after the Civil War, giving way to a new sense of identity for black and white members of society, whose interactions became fundamentally different after Emancipation. Different actions and reactions to new developments are reflected in both films. The narrative of the South's struggle to define itself around and outside of racial lines before and immediately after the Civil War are paralleled by the struggles faced by a present-day society internalizing the long-lasting impact of the institutionalized and systemic racism that is in part a result of Dixon and Griffith's work.

Though Parker aims to counter negative racial stereotyping, he, like Griffith, sacrifices the agency of women to prop up the apparent necessity of masculinity and male violence as the solitary remedy to antagonistic and invasive

Otherness. The white women of Griffith's Old South are the last bastion of purity and goodness, threatened by black people and in need of rescue by the KKK. Black women are obliging servants or lustful mistresses, unrecognized as human and most certainly unworthy of saving. Parker's women are hardly better off. White women like Elizabeth Turner are powerless if well-intentioned, and black women are objectified, subservient, and fragile, targeted for sexual violence at the hands of white men and needing the comfort and protection of their black partners. They are portrayed as silent in their oppression and unable to voice the same convictions that enslaved men readily possess and act on in Parker's film.

Religion plays an additionally powerful role in both films. On the one hand, it demonstrates the white justification for superiority as the dominant Same, yet, on the other hand, it simultaneously gives grounds for consequential and violent action in both films, leading the victims in each film to challenge the hostile Other. Of course, Griffith's use of Christianity is relatively one-sided, as the gentle, God-fearing white characters are threatened by a godless black menace and in the end are saved by the mounted knights of God. Parker shows the dissonance inherent in Christian justification for slavery and the arguably more Christ-like biblical interpretation that advocates brotherhood among men. His portrayal of Nat Turner at various times assuming a crucifixion pose (see figures on page 106 and at the top of page 107) pushes the religious envelope further, challenging the notion of a white-only Christian God, ultimately thrusting Turner's execution into the spotlight, a martyrdom that sets the stage for righteous victory in his prophesied war.

Ultimately, each filmmaker portrays his own version of the "Old South"—his idea of the Other and the Same and the violation of the black and white body. Questions about who or what is actually born in *The Birth of a Nation* films, however, remain unanswered. The discussion in this chapter shows that the only way to deal with the ramifications of America's dark past is to confront them. Indeed, a historical understanding of how slavery has influenced every social, legal, and economic institution in America is essential to combat modern injustices. It is important to remember, however, that the South in any given time period is not one place with a singular identity; rather, it is a collective of conflicting identities that have been and still are struggling for cultural dominance, if not for the fundamental rights to voice and equality expressed in America's founding principles.

Notes

Excerpts of this chapter have been published in Caroline V. Schroeter, "Nate Parker's *The Birth of a Nation*: Classical Hollywood Cinema or Independent Rebellion?" *Alphaville: Journal of Film and Screen Media 13* (Summer 2017): 135–55.

1. I define a cinematic slave narrative as one written, directed, and filmed for audiences of cinema or television. These narratives can contain elements of both original and neo-slave narratives, they can be works of total historical fiction, and they may exhibit features owed to the artistic license of the director and writers of the project (e.g., *Django Unchained* [2012], *12 Years a Slave* [2013], *The Book of Negroes* [2015], *The Birth of a Nation* [2016]). This modern form of the slave narrative is audiovisual and usually feature-film length, with the exception of television series. Cinematic slave narratives generally portray North American slavery, but the genre may be extended to cinematic narratives of slavery and slavery-like institutions in other cultures, countries and contexts (e.g., *Beasts of No Nation,* directed by Cary Joji Fukunaga [Los Gatos, CA: Netflix; 2015] or *13th,* directed by Ava DuVernay [Los Gatos, CA: Netflix, 2016]). In comparison to historical and neo-slave narratives, cinematic slave narratives offer an audiovisual component not present—or possible—in the other variations of the genre. Therefore, they can show iconic images to mass audiences and can be particularly powerful in reimagining history, giving the audience an opportunity literally to "see" the story through the eyes of the enslaved.

2. See Riché Richardson, *Black Masculinity and the U.S. South: From Uncle Tom to Gangsta* (Athens: University of Georgia Press, 2007), 43.

3. Lola Young, *Fear of the Dark: "Race," Gender, and Sexuality in the Cinema* (New York: Routledge, 1996), 31.

4. For example, scholars like Richard Dyer have tried to open up the debate about "white" and whiteness. See Richard Dyer, *White: Essays on Race and Culture* (New York: Routledge, 1997).Young, *Fear of the Dark,* 53.

5. DocSouth Staff, "Controversial History: Thomas Dixon and the Klan Trilogy," *Documenting the South,* last updated March 11, 2018, http://docsouth.unc.edu/highlights/dixon.html.

6. Mary Alice Kirkpatrick, "Thomas Dixon, 1864–1946 and Arthur I. Keller (Arthur Ignatius), 1866–1924, Illustrated by The Clansman: An Historical Romance of the Ku Klux Klan," *Documenting the South,* accessed September 23, 2016, http://docsouth.unc.edu/southlit/dixonclan/summary.html.

7. See also Melvyn Stokes, *D. W. Griffith's* The Birth of a Nation: *A History of "the Most Controversial Motion Picture of All Time"* (New York: Oxford University Press, 2007), 47, 54.

8. DocSouth Staff, "Controversial History."

9. Stokes, *D. W. Griffith's* The Birth of a Nation, 108, 5, 3.

10. James Kinney, "Thomas Dixon, 1864–1946," in *Encyclopedia of Southern Culture,*

ed. Charles Reagan Wilson and William Ferris (Chapel Hill: University of North Carolina Press, 1989), available online at *Documenting the American South*, http://docsouth.unc.edu/southlit/dixonclan/bio.html.

11. Ibid.

12. Thomas Dixon, *The Reconstruction Trilogy*: *The Leopard's Spots; the Clansman; the Traitor* (Newport Beach, CA: Noontide Press, 1994).

13. Kirkpatrick, "Thomas Dixon, 1864–1946 and Arthur I. Keller (Arthur Ignatius), 1866–1924."

14. Allison Graham, "The South in Popular Culture," *The Cambridge Companion to the African American Novel*, ed. Maryemma Graham (Cambridge: Cambridge University Press, 2004), 335.

15. Daniel Bernardi, *The Birth of Whiteness*: *Race and the Emergence of U.S. Cinema* (New Brunswick, N.J.: Rutgers University Press, 1996), 87–88.

16. Daniel Bernardi, "The Birth of a Nation: Integrating Race into the Narrator System," in *Film Analysis*: *A Norton Reader*, ed. Jeffrey Geiger and R. L. Rutsky (New York: Norton, 2013), 58–73.

17. Jeffrey Fleishman, "A New 'Birth of a Nation' Dredges up the Complicated, Ugly Legacy of the Groundbreaking 1915 Film," *LA Times*, September 20, 2016, http://www.latimes.com/projects/la-ca-mn-birth-nation/.

18. Kirkpatrick, "Thomas Dixon, 1864–1946 and Arthur I. Keller (Arthur Ignatius), 1866–1924."

19. For more details on the categorization and stereotyping of African Americans see Donald Bogle's discussion on black stereotypes in *Toms, Coons, Mulattoes, Mammies, and Bucks*: *An Interpretive History of Blacks in American Films*, 5th ed. (New York: Bloomsbury Academic, 2016), 1–14.

20. Laura Green, "Stereotypes: Negative Stereotypes and Their Effect on Attitude towards African-Americans," *Journal of Perspectives on Multiculturalism and Cultural Diversity*, 11, no. 1 (1998–99), available online at the Jim Crow Museum of Racist Memorabilia Web site, https://ferris.edu/HTMLS/news/jimcrow/links/essays/vcu.htm.; Gary D. Engle, ed., *This Grotesque Essence*: *Plays from the American Minstrel Stage* (Baton Rouge: Louisiana State University Press, 1978).

21. Bogle, *Toms, Coons, Mulattoes, Mammies, and Bucks*, 7.

22. Brooks Barnes, "Sundance Roars for a Black Film, and Fox Searchlight Bids $17 Million," *New York Times*, January 26, 2016, http://www.nytimes.com/2016/01/27/business/media/fox-searchlight-bids-17-million-for-the-birth-of-a-nation.html?_r=0.

23. Brooks Barnes and Cara Buckley, "'The Birth of a Nation,' Nate Parker's Heralded Film, Is Now Cloaked in Controversy," *New York Times*, August 17, 2016, http://www.nytimes.com/2016/08/18/movies/the-birth-of-a-nation-nate-parkers-heralded-film-is-now-cloaked-in-controversy.html.

24. Tasha Robinson, "Nate Parker Answers the Question 'How Does Birth of a Nation Relate to Black Lives Matter?'" *Verge*, September 11, 2016, http://www.theverge.com/2016/9/11/12878604/nate-parker-birth-of-a-nation-black-lives-matter-racism.

25. Brooks Barnes, "Tricky Goal for 'Birth of a Nation': Inspire but Don't Incite,"

New York Times, October 2, 2016, http://www.nytimes.com/2016/10/03/business/media/tricky-goal-for-birth-of-a-nation-inspire-but-dont-incite.html; John Archibald, "Klan Will 'Hold Trump's Promises Close'; Drops Fliers in Alabama," *Birmingham News,* November 9, 2016, http://www.al.com/opinion/index.ssf/2016/11/klan_will_hold_trumps_promises.html.

26. Terry Bisson and John Davenport, *Nat Turner: Slave Revolt Leader* (Philadelphia: Chelsea House, 2005), 84.

27. Earlier examples by African American artists include John Noble's *The Birth of a Race* (1918); Oscar Micheaux's *Within Our Gates* (1920); D. J. Spooky's remix, *Rebirth of a Nation* (2007); and Spike Lee's short film *The Answer* (1980). Many black filmmakers, too, have used the Nat Turner story as the basis for historical recreations, most notably Charles Burnett's *Nat Turner: A Troublesome Property* (2003), a multi-perspective documentary.

28. John H. Clarke, ed., *William Styron's Nat Turner: 10 Black Writers Respond* (Boston: Beacon, 1972), 7.

29. Headnote to excerpt from *The Confessions of Nat Turner* Nat Turner (1800–1831), in *The Oxford Book of the American South: Testimony, Memory, and Fiction,* ed. Edward L. Ayers (New York: Oxford Univ. Press, 1998), 23.

30. Soheil Rezayazdi, "Five Questions with *The Birth of a Nation* Director Nate Parker," *Filmmaker Magazine,* January 26, 2016, http://filmmakermagazine.com/97103-five-questions-with-the-birth-of-a-nation-director-nate-parker/.

31. Frantz Fanon, *Black Skin, White Masks* (New York: Grove Press, 1967), 161.

32. Houston A. Baker and Dana D. Nelson, "Preface: Violence, the Body and 'The South,'" *American Literature* 73 (June 2001): 232.

33. *Django Unchained,* directed by Quentin Tarantino (Culver City: Sony Pictures Releasing, 2012), DVD.

34. Stokes, *D. W. Griffith's* The Birth of a Nation, 12; Roger Ebert, "The Birth of a Nation," *Rogerebert.com,* March 30, 2003, http://www.rogerebert.com/reviews/great-movie-the-birth-of-a-nation-1915.

35. James Berardinelli, "Birth of a Nation, The," *Reelviews Movie Reviews,* October 6, 2016, http://www.reelviews.net/reelviews/birth-of-a-nation-the.

36. Young, *Fear of the Dark,* 31.

37. That white slave masters raped their female slaves was often completely disregarded. To remain within the scope of this chapter, however, the objectification and sexualization of enslaved women cannot be discussed.

38. Young, *Fear of the Dark,* 35.

39. Pramod K. Nayar, *Frantz Fanon* (London: Routledge, 2013).

40. *12 Years a Slave,* directed by Steve McQueen (Century City, CA: Fox Searchlight Pictures, 2013), DVD.

41. *The Book of Negroes,* miniseries directed by Clement Virgo and Lawrence Hill, aired January 7–February 11, 2015 on CBC, BET, miniseries; *Moonlight,* directed by Barry Jenkins (Beverly Hills: Plan B Entertainment, 2016); *Dear White People,* directed by Justin Simien (Los Gatos, CA: Netflix, 2017–), television series; *Black Lightning,* television

series developed by Salim Akil, airing January 16, 2018–, on The CW; *Black Panther*, directed by Ryan Coogler (Burbank, CA: Walt Disney Studios Motion Pictures, 2018).

42. Kimberly Rae Connor, *Imagining Grace: Liberating Theologies in the Slave Narrative Tradition* (Urbana: University of Illinois Press, 2000).

43. Jackson McHenry, "The Birth of a Nation Downplays Nat Turner's Fanaticism but Can't Figure Out What to Say about His Religion," *Vulture*, October 7, 2016, http://www.vulture.com/2016/10/birth-of-a-nation-nat-turner-visions.html.

44. Mark Karlin, "'The Birth of a Nation' 100 Years Later: Why Woodrow Wilson's Embrace of the KKK Still Matters," *Buzzflash*, accessed December 9, 2016, http://www.truth-out.org/buzzflash/commentary/white-supremacists-have-always-baptized-their-perverted-cause-in-christianity.

45. Mark Karlin, "'The Birth of a Nation' 100 Years Later: Why Woodrow Wilson's Embrace of the KKK Still Matters," *Buzzflash*, accessed December 9, 2016, http://www.truth-out.org/buzzflash/commentary/white-supremacists-have-always-baptized-their-perverted-cause-in-christianity.

46. Jessica Carew and Jennifer Thompson, "From Blackface to Blaxploitation: Representations of African Americans in Film-Duke Library Exhibits," Duke University Libraries Web site, accessed December 5, 2016, http://exhibits.library.duke.edu/exhibits/show/africanamericansinfilm.

46. Baker and Nelson, "Preface," 232.

47. Salamishah Tillet, "How 'The Birth of a Nation' Silences Black Women," *New York Times*, October 12, 2016, https://www.nytimes.com/2016/10/16/movies/how-the-birth-of-a-nation-silences-black-women.html.

48. Harriet Beecher Stowe, *Uncle Tom's Cabin* (1852; repr., West Berlin, N.J.: Townsend Press, 2006).

49. Tillet, "How 'The Birth of a Nation' Silences Black Women."

50. Leslie Alexander, "'The Birth of a Nation' Is an Epic Fail," *Nation*, October 6, 2016, https://www.thenation.com/article/the-birth-of-a-nation-is-an-epic-fail/.

51. *The Confessions of Nat Turner and Related Documents*, ed. Kenneth S. Greenberg (Boston: Bedford / St. Martin's, 1996).

52. See Schroeter, "Nate Parker's *The Birth of a Nation*.

53. Baker and Nelson, "Preface," 232.

54. Tom Brook, "Slavery on Film: What Is Hollywood's Problem?" BBC, October 21, 2014, http://www.bbc.com/culture/story/20131015-hollywood-scared-of-slavery.

55. Edward L. Ayers, preface to Ayers, *Oxford Book of the American South*, ix.

56. Ibid.

6

Roots Reimagined

Todd Simpson

When *Roots* the miniseries originally aired, it became the preeminent cultural touchstone for Hollywood's depiction of the historic South, permanently antiquating *Gone with the Wind*'s romanticized fantasy by recontextualizing it. In his introduction to the thirtieth anniversary edition of Alex Haley's book *Roots: The Saga of an American Family,* Michael Eric Dyson writes, "Each generation must make up its own mind about how it will navigate the treacherous waters of our nation's racial sin. And each generation must overcome our social ills through greater knowledge and decisive action. *Roots* is a stirring reminder that we can achieve these goals only if we look history squarely in the face."[1] In his review of the original production, Sander Vanocur writes that while this was not the first miniseries to portray the evolution of a family over time, it was the first to do so within the context of slavery and "that distinction is of major importance, since the introduction of slavery into this country is the continuing central issue of our national existence."[2] Forty years after David L. Wolper produced the original, his son Mark Wolper attempted to show it to his children, and when he saw through their eyes how dated the production had become, he realized that the material deserved a reboot. LeVar Burton, star of the original, was initially skeptical, "Mark Wolper . . . called me to say he was doing a new version. My first question was: Why? He said he had tried to show the original to his children and there was resistance—pushback even. They likened it to their father's music: They got why it was important to him, but what relevance did it have to them? That hit me right between the eyes. We will never get to where we should be, once and for all, unless we examine how we got here and that means coming to terms with America's original sin."[3] While the media landscape has changed drastically since the original aired, the current cultural moment, from social justice movements like Black Lives Matter to racist political campaigns that demonize the other, demonstrate that themes inherent to an African American family romance have only become increasingly relevant and fertile for artists to explore. It is in this context that the film industry in Hollywood finds itself stumbling over issues of diversity, in stark contrast to the worlds of Broadway and television, and is being called out by grassroots social media campaigns like #OscarsSoWhite and entertainment executives alike. Universal's Jeff Shell asserts that "the film business is about 10 years behind the TV business" in embracing diversity, and this could arguably be due to the foundation created by the unparalleled success of the original television production of *Roots.*[4]

In September 2016 the Media, Diversity, and Social Change (MDSC) Initiative, a think tank based out of USC's Annenberg School for Communication and Journalism released a study, titled "Inequality in 800 Popular Films," that purports to be "the most comprehensive and rigorous intersectional analysis of independent speaking and named characters in popular motion picture content to date."[5] The MDSC has been releasing a yearly report since 2007 (excluding 2011) and has now been expanded to include assessment of women composers in film and characters with disabilities. While the merits of the study and issues of correlation and causality may be discussed, the question of disproportionate representation both in front of and behind the camera is indisputable, as further evidenced by the US Equal Employment Opportunity Commission opening a "wide-ranging and well-resourced investigation into the industry's hiring practices," following an ACLU request to specifically address the striking disparity in hiring of women directors.[6]

The MDSC report found that in front of the camera out of the "4,370 speaking or named characters evaluated, 68.9% were male and 31.4% were female across the 100 top grossing films of 2015." Furthermore, in these same films "73.7% of characters were White, 12.2% Black . . . together, a total of 26.3% of all speaking characters were from an underrepresented racial/ethnic group," and, in fact, 17 percent of these films featured zero black speaking or referenced characters, and that percentage increases significantly for Latino and Asian characters. A credible argument can be made that this is because that the situation behind the camera is even less diverse than that in front of it. Of the 1,365 directors, writers, and producers of these same films, 81 percent were men and 19 percent were women, and of the 107 directors alone, 92.5 percent were male and 7.5 percent were female, a total of 4 were black or African American and 6 were Asian or Asian American. To find directors who are women of color, one has to refract out to the 800 films and 886 directors tracked cumulatively since the inception of the MSDC; out of this total we find only 3 black and 1 Asian female directors.

Across the metrics compiled since 2007, there is no meaningful change discernable anywhere, and the fact that the numbers remain so consistent and disproportionate from the population at large is revelatory of why television has increasingly drawn actors, directors, and writers known for their work in film. With deference to the groundbreaking opportunities that the original production of *Roots* provided black artists, Stephane Dunn argues that the producers of the new version deftly used the opportunity to address Hollywood's diversity problem:

> The actor LeVar Burton, who played Kunta Kinte in the original *Roots,* is among the producers, as are several women; Will Packer is an executive producer alongside Wolper and Marc Toberoff. Black historians and experts served to varying degrees as researchers or consultants. The prolific costume designer Ruth Carter—who was nominated for an Academy Award for her work on Spike Lee's *Malcolm X*—led a team through the vast task of creating a striking canvas of colors and looks throughout the series' changing locales. *Roots* has two black male directors (Mario Van Peebles and Thomas Carter), and a black woman (Alison McDonald) has a writing credit on one episode.[7]

And yet, he laments women of color missing from the directorial team, naming Julie Dash, Ava DuVernay, Kasi Lemmons, and Dee Rees as examples of successful directors who should have been considered.

In 2015, when Viola Davis, previously nominated for the Academy Award for Best Supporting Actress (*Doubt,* 2008) and then for Best Actress (*The Help,* 2011), became the first black woman of any nationality to win an Emmy for Outstanding Lead Actress in a Drama Series (*How to Get Away with Murder*) her acceptance speech—wherein she quoted Harriet Tubman and stated that "the only thing that separates women of color from anyone else is opportunity. You cannot win an Emmy for roles that are simply not there"—went viral.[8] The following year, Courtney B. Vance took home the Emmy for Outstanding Lead Actor in a Limited Series or Movie for his portrayal of Johnnie Cochran and afterward he stated to reporters, "Actors and directors follow the writing . . . the writers in TV are writing for different hues of color. Hopefully the movies start to see that if you want to get the people you better do the writing."[9] Vance's placement of writing as the cornerstone of broadly relevant entertainment demands close consideration of how themes and characters were altered between the two versions. This chapter examines—through a close comparison of the original with the reboot—what strategies the new production employed, thus articulating the greater knowledge the next generation had and the decisive action it consciously took. In doing so, it identifies how issues of race and gender have affected the world of corporate television entertainment in the time since the first production changed the paradigm by placing the African American narrative at the center of depictions of the historic South.

The original begins with the narrator describing *Roots* as an epic saga, "the television event of the year, from primitive Africa to the Old South," showing scenes of rural village life, an African pastoral, over the sounds of a woman giving birth. The new version opens with Kunta Kinte (Malachi Kirby) in the belly of the slave ship resisting his chains but quickly takes the audience back to the Muslim city of Juffure, in Gambia, West Africa, circa 1750. This Juffure is depicted in stark contrast to the flat, idyllic village that consisted of a sparse collection of identical huts in the original. The scoring of the original, split between Quincy Jones and Gerald Fried, generally remains traditional in its approach by reflecting the context depicted. Its highlight is the dances and music performed in the village when Kunta successfully returns from manhood training. Questlove takes on the reboot beginning with drums creating a sound both ancient and current, connecting past and present. This Juffure is a "rich and sophisticated city," depicted as urban, cosmopolitan, a grid of streets with variety in its architecture. There is certainly nothing 'primitive' about it. The narrator tells us: "Like the Greeks, Romans, and Hebrews, Mandinka kept slaves as servants. Some slaves married into these families, others paid ransoms to be free. Then Europeans arrived in great sailing ships. Some Mandinka were corrupted by European guns and gold, creating a violent market for slaves, but the many Africans who fought European plundering suffered brutal reprisals. Kunta Kinte's family were warriors loyal to the king. On the day that Kunta was born, the Kinte family had a violent clash with their rivals, the Koros, who were loyal only to their greed." In complete contrast from the original, social distinction is emphasized, and Juffure is not a uniform Garden of Eden.

We see Kunta's father, Omoro (Babs Olusanmokun), leading an armed contingent of warriors on horseback tracking African slavers transporting their prey. At first, the characters are speaking in Mandinka and subtitled, but this soon transitions to English spoken in an unidentifiable accent. Like

Questlove's music, there is an attempt at authenticity here, though an unspecified one. Omoro holds his rival, Djeliba Koro (Prince Sonni Ochuba), at gunpoint, as an argument ensues over whether the king has granted permission for the transport of slaves through this territory. Juffure has a complex social order and is a place of tribal conflict and political intrigue with stark differences between neighbors, which range from how they dress to their moral code. Omoro accuses Koro of taking slaves from upriver and trading them to the English for guns. Slavery has a history, and is the constant among many cultures and periods, which participate in it with varying levels of severity. Omoro unleashes the "cargo," enraging Koro just as drums in the distance announce that a baby is arriving. Drums are not just musical instruments but a sophisticated method to convey codes of information. In both versions, Omoro is barred from the house until the birth has taken place. In the original, he finds relief when the baby cries, and the update introduces a device here that will be used to unify the series. Omoro knows that his wife, Binta, and the baby are fine when he hears her singing a lullaby to comfort and quiet her newborn child. This melody, which Questlove created, reappears at different times in each episode throughout the series and provides one of the few threads of connection and inheritance unifying the Kinta family tree.

In both versions, Omoro takes his offspring out into the night to perform a naming ceremony under the stars, and this ceremony, like the lullaby, is repeated with each successive generation. There is something mystical about it in both versions, but the reboot savors the moment, expands on it. Omoro rides on horseback, telling the child who he is, listing his parents and grandparents, instructing him to always honor his ancestors as they are the ones who love and watch over him. One's name is given extreme significance: "Your name is your spirit, your name is your shield." He presents the sky to his child and says, "Behold, Kunta Kinte, the only thing that is greater than you." We immediately transition to the fully grown Kunta fishing in the Kamby Bolongo, gossiping and flirting amid his community. While the African costuming in the original was almost uniform in its simplicity, costume designer Ruth E. Carter uses a much wider palette, infusing rich patterns and colors with varieties of jewelry, and some range from clothes worn for play and work to more formal occasions, including masks, hats, and turbans.

Before they are circumcised, the boys learn that the first responsibility of a Mandinka warrior is to have a family, raise children, and pass on their way of life. Returning to Juffure as a warrior, Kunta finds his mother, Binta (Nokuthula Ledwabak), setting up his new home. In stark contrast to her admonishment before he left, she now bows out of respect for the new warrior. She hands him a necklace of beads she has made for him. These beads are the only tangible item he will take with him when he is captured and then pass on to his descendants. They become a symbolic device reappearing in each episode, joining her lullaby, ceremony, and language—all forming an inheritance that allows the Kinte family to retain a shared African identity. The scene is infused with connection, in stark contrast to a similar scene in the original version where Kunta returns and scolds Binta (Cicely Tyson) that "a woman should not tell a man what to do," testing out his new status as an adult male. Yet the original quickly follows this up with a charming counterpoint: his grandmother Nyo Boto (Maya Angelou) chases him out of his new hut and demands respect.

As their guests dine in celebration, Omoro presents Kunta with a stallion, which he will need as a member of the king's cavalry. Kunta bucks his father's assumptions and states that he wants to study at the university in Timbuktu and test himself against other students—demonstrating ambition for and knowledge of life beyond Juffure, whereas Kunta in the original had no sense of context for Juffure or anything resembling this level of sophistication and independence of thought. In that version, Kunta does not even understand the concept of the ocean. In the reboot, Koro's men come upon Kunta in the forest and at first intend to capture and ransom him back to the Kinte family, but after Kunta gives chase, possibly killing Koro's son in the process, he is sold to the "English." Kunta is the target, subject to past grudges, greed, and revenge. In contrast, in the original, Kunta is just unlucky, in the wrong place at the wrong time.

Absent in the 2016 version are the conspicuously Christian Captain Davies (Ed Asner) and his tormented conscience, as well as Slater (Ralph Waite) his amoral steward. These characters were invented to give a white audience an identifiable entry point into the narrative, but in the reboot we see the "English" for the first time when Kunta is on a beach in chains being prepared for transport, and they are given no specific characterization. Likewise, throughout the Middle Passage the audience sees these men from their victims' perspective; they are not articulated beyond the abuse and torture they inflict. The effect is that of unifying Kunta's perspective with the audience in a horrific intimacy, as opposed to the original, which continually alternates perspective among Captain Davies, Slater, and Kunta. While in both versions Africans attempt a revolt during the voyage, in the reboot their means of communicating and planning is greatly expanded on, utilizing language and song, subtitled, which cannot be understood by their captors. And as a survival strategy, Kunta sings Binta's lullaby to himself, some small comfort in the brutal, gruesome hell of the slave ship.

The slave auction, where Kunta is named Toby and meets Fiddler (Louis Gossett Jr.), is completely excised from the reboot. Kunta continues to speak in Mandinka, the words for the most part subtitled, as he is taken to Annapolis to be sold and transported to the Waller plantation, where he becomes the responsibility of Fiddler (Forest Whitaker). Phillip Noyce uses flashback, where the original doesn't, when Kunta is working in the fields, as he daydreams about life in Juffure while humming Binta's melody. One night, Fiddler is admonishing Kunta and generally complaining about the day's events, while Kunta prays, holding the beads Binta made for him as he sings her song. When Fiddler's musician ears hear Binta's song, he is stopped him dead in his tracks. He wants to know what the tune is and swears that his grandmother sang him the same one before he was sold away. He says he has been chasing that tune in his head for a long time, and he is going to figure it out. Kunta responds, sternly, that the song belongs to him and that no one in this place can have it.

As the Waller plantation celebrates Christmas, we are given a contrast between how slaves sing and dance, reminiscent of celebrations in Juffure, and how the farm owners socialize, as in some formal court. Kunta uses this opportunity to make an escape attempt, and when Fiddler finds him having filed through his chains, he returns to the farmhouse and distracts everyone by playing Binta's melody on his violin. Noyce uses flashback again here, connecting Kunta with Binta, before he rides away. He is captured, and what ensues is the pivotal scene where the overseer whips him, demanding that he answer to the name of Toby. In both versions, this same overseer states that you don't buy a slave, you make a slave, as if he understands the same idea Omoro imparted to Kunta about the essential nature of identity. The overseer wants to strip Kunta of his spirit and his shield, to be sure he self-identifies as Toby the slave. This scene remains almost entirely unchanged, except that Noyce shows Omoro and Binta looking for their son and concluding that he will not return, as if to suggest Kunta accepts that he will never see either of them again as he finally relents and utters the name assigned to him. Fiddler steps in to care for Kunta's wounds and reminds him that he is the son of Omoro Kinte, returning his shield to him and reminding him of his duty to live.

In the next episode, directed by Mario Van Peebles, Kunta gets further in his second escape, establishing the historical context of the Revolutionary

War. His abilities as a warrior are made more clear, as he murders the overseer chasing him, before he joins both Native Americans and other escaped slaves aiding the British in exchange for the promise of freedom. However, it is clear that the British value neither as anything more than fodder into the breach. Kunta assesses and reacts quickly, abandoning the British and fighting for his own escape. In an extended action sequence, Kunta is forced to reassess and react multiple times. As he canoes past slaves working by the river, they begin to sing, just as slaves did during his crossing: song as communication, instruction, direction, and encouragement. The reboot opts to use Kunta's escape attempts to place him in the context of historical events, as opposed to the original, in which Kunta's first escape references no historical context and the second is to find Fanta (Renn Woods), the girl he loved back in Gambia, whom he had learned was living on a nearby farm. The reboot edits out these elements of historical romance and replaces them with history, contributing to the overall sense that Kunta is vulnerable to social forces from every direction but also stripping his motives of sentimentality and rendering them down to the will for autonomy.

After another failed escape attempt by Kunta, we are introduced to Belle Reynolds (Emayatzy Corinealdi), an accomplished apothecary tending to him after he is recaptured and maimed. Belle and Fiddler have no patience with their patient once they see his major ailment transitions from the loss of his foot to an ensuing depression. As Kunta learns to cope with his injury, his relationship with Belle develops, and soon they are committed to each other. The naming ceremony of Kizzy, the daughter born to Belle and Kunta, is perilous in both versions, but completely dissimilar. In the original, prior to her birth, Kunta has driven Dr. Waller to a neighboring plantation for a celebration and he recognizes drums playing nearby. There, he discovers another African slave, and they have a conversation that ends in the instructions that when he hears the drums again he must run and join in an escape attempt. The original Belle (Madge Sinclair) knows that Kunta wants to run at the drum signal, and when they start to play while he has taken Kizzy for the naming ceremony, she is terrified that she has lost both of them. In the reboot, none of this occurs, and Fiddler joins Kunta in the trek out under the stars, playing Binta's tune. However, they are interrupted by white men who demand they hand over the baby. Fiddler distracts them and is murdered, while in the original, Fiddler dies of old age. In both versions, this is the point at which Kunta commits to staying with Belle and protecting Kizzy, bringing an end to any future escape plans.

In the new version, we are shown Kizzy's childhood, while it's just referenced in the original. Kizzy is played by three different actresses, who portray her at age six, as a teenager, and as an adult. When we first see the young Kizzy (Saniyya Sidney) helping Belle, she is being told to count in her head, not aloud, and she then goes on to show us that she is bilingual, alternating freely between Mandinka and English. In the original, Kizzy (Leslie Uggams) knows the names of places, Juffure, the Kamby Bolongo, and that her father was a Mandinka warrior, but that seems the limit of her knowledge. In the reboot, the girl Kizzy (Saniyya Sidney) is the favorite companion of Missy Waller (Kiera Strauss), Dr. Waller's niece, and during their play they come across a group of abolitionists preaching and baptizing adherents in the river. Kizzy demonstrates an inquisitive intelligence when she asks her parents whether slave owners will suffer hellfire damnation, as she heard the preacher claim. Belle quickly reprimands her for saying this aloud, and Kunta tells her in Mandinka that preachers are stupid, establishing his close relationship with Kizzy and also his influence, in affording her the space to be skeptical of Christianity. We are shown Missy absconding with Kizzy and teaching her to read, although they both are aware that this is prohibited. When they are teenagers, Missy (G. Hannelius) directly states that she knows Kizzy (Emyri Crutchfield) doesn't believe in God as they continue to read together, and, before she begins to expertly read aloud from a book on human anatomy, we learn that the extent of Kizzy's education includes all of Shakespeare.

It is notable that Missy refers to her as Kizzy Waller while Kunta uses Kinte as Belle's, his, and Kizzy's last name—in each case, her name anchors her in one of her dual identities. When Dr. Waller states that soon it will be time to "breed" Kizzy, Kunta reacts quickly, forcing his daughter to train as if she were to be a Mandinka warrior so that she is prepared at all times. It is a mental preparation as well as physical; Kunta states: "Do not allow yourself to be defeated; they can put the chains on your body, never let them put the chains on your mind. You are the daughter of Belle Kinte and Kunta Kinte; anything is possible." Knowing he cannot protect her, Kunta creates rites of passage that are truly perilous as well as physically challenging. She learns how to mount a horse, ride without a saddle, use anything within reach as a weapon, tell which direction is North, and recite the names of her ancestors in order. He warns her explicitly that this country will always be dangerous for her. Their relationship is one of not just filial love and affection but mutual respect. He speaks to her very directly: "Many masters, masters' sons, overseers rape slave women and pay no price. Now if you ever feel you must kill a toubob, then do it without hesitation, only if you are prepared to die yourself. That is your choice to make. Do you understand?" Kizzy then goes on a mission off of the plantation, exploring the river by canoe, navigating uncharted territory at great risk. When she returns unscathed and triumphant, Kunta presents her with the beads Binta gave him, passing on the only physical object that connects Kizzy to Africa and her free ancestors. Here, Peebles uses a flashback to underscore the parallels; we are shown Binta giving Kunta the beads, then Kunta presenting them to Kizzy.

The level of Kizzy's literacy is much higher than in the original, where we witness her reading from the Bible and writing her own name in soot on the fireplace. In the reboot, she teaches a fellow slave how to read and discusses with him the writings of Frederick Douglass and his use of argument and logic to assert that no man should deny another liberty. While Kunta had the physical agility of a warrior and had known what it was like to be literally free, Kizzy has the strength born of intellect and literacy enabling her to navigate an internal world of thought and ideas that affords her an abstract form of freedom. When Kunta angrily confronts her about another slave knowing of her literacy and how vulnerable that makes her, she responds, "Reading is my way of being a warrior, of being free inside, and it's worth jail to me or whatever comes." When Dr. Waller (Matthew Goode) discovers that Kizzy can read and write, to the level of being capable of forging documents, she is sold, and Kunta's worst fears are realized; the trauma of irrevocable separation is repeated. The modernized Kizzy demonstrates skill and strength as she tries, unsuccessfully, to escape and fight off Tom Lea (Jonathan Rhys Meyers), the man to whom she is sold. The 2016 version presents a definite feminist revision, or, rather, expansion of her character, and while there is a palpable intimacy between Kunta and Kizzy in both versions, the reboot articulates their shared space in a way that illustrates how identity is both individually forged and given.

In the original, familiar, friendly faces from American television, like Robert Reed, Lorne Greene, and Sandy Duncan were cast against type. In the reboot, these roles were cast with British actors, such as Matthew Goode and James Purefoy, both of whom have résumés spanning genres and reflecting a range of types, including significant villains. Aside from plot points, these roles have nothing in common, not even names, as they appear in the different versions. It is almost as if the white characters are the parts from the original series that have aged the worst, the dated tatty edges in most need of mending. But Jonathan Rhys Meyers's performance as the odious Tom Lea achieves an eerily consistent amplification of Chuck Connors as Tom Moore; both seem unhinged and make the viewer recoil with a visceral combination of fear and disgust. Patricia Lea (Shannon Lucio), is relentlessly pitiable, beaten down and ineffectual, but sane and aware, whereas Mrs. Moore (Carolyn Jones) ranges from batty to hysterical. It is merely implied that she knows her husband rapes Kizzy, whereas Patricia explicitly witnesses the horror of sexual violence as she stands in the rain outside of the barn listening to Kizzy's screams for someone to kill her.

Kizzy is impregnated by her rapist and is at her greatest crisis point after she gives birth and attempts to drown herself and the child in a river, when, in another flashback, her ancestors are shown, as if they are watching over her as Omoro had once told Kunta they would. This moment parallels the one in which her father was whipped and forced to say his name was Toby. When she calls on them for help, she recalls their names and their stories and that that the first duty of a Mandinka warrior is to raise a family. These memories do serve as a shield, because she will not let their stories end here, at her lowest moment; she will not let her oppressors put chains on her mind. She is arguably the strongest branch in the Kinte family tree; she had never known freedom like her father had or her son will; she will be denied a significant partner, as they are not, and she will never leave the Lea farm. While she is not allowed to choose a name for her son, George, instead of ending their lives, she emerges from the river, holds him up to the sky, and repeats the words of the naming ceremony. She is impelled to live so that she can tell her child where and who he comes from, because it is the only way he will know who he is and be able to form an identity independent of his circumstances. This is significant, as it establishes a motif, whereas the original jumps from Kizzy recovering from being raped by Tom Moore to berating her grown son for mocking stories about her father. At the beginning of the third part, before Kizzy, now played by Anika Noni Rose, leaves her cabin she grabs the beads Binta made and speaks in Mandinka to her father, "Papa, your strength is my strength. I will be strong, like you taught me. I won't fail you," again demonstrating a level of literacy and an independence of thought. Kizzy's spiritual incantation is familial rather than religious.

In a more stratified picture of white southern society, Tom Lea, an Irishman, is looked down on by his neighbors. For the most part, in the original version the white characters are a monolithic group; the picture of southern society is literally split between blacks and whites. In the reboot, however, southern society is depicted with nuance. One can identify and differentiate manners, class, and wealth among the white characters. Tensions of status are on display among the white landowners as, for example, Tom and Patricia try to find a place to sit in church. Outside, not far from the church, where the slaves gather to hold their own services, we meet Kizzy's grown son (Regé-Jean Page), who is trying to impress the preacher's daughter Matilda (Erica Tazel), quoting from Song of Solomon. Page is reminiscent of Ben Vereen as he imbues Chicken George with the same vibrant charisma, adding perhaps some sexual ambition. Marcellus (Michael James Shaw), shares only a rogue's sense of style with his counterpart from the original series, Sam Bennett (Richard Roundtree), each of whom becomes Kizzy's love interest. In the original, Sam is the slave of Stephen Bennett, who visits the farm of Tom Moore. In the reboot, Chicken George competes against Marcellus at a chicken fight and learns that the latter is a free man. Marcellus informs George that it is becoming increasingly possible to buy one's way to freedom and that Tom Lea should be giving him a cut of the prize money. This broadens the picture of what the slave experience was in the South, again in contrast to the original's binary black-and-white definition of southern society.

After Tom Lea refuses to sell Chicken George to Mr. Jewett (Mark Rolston), a wealthy neighbor, Jewett invites Tom to join him and friends at an Easter dinner, an irresistible offer to the social climber Lea. William Byrd (Brett Rice), another wealthy neighbor, is appalled to see the Leas included. Byrd turns the conversation to the election of Andrew Jackson, arguing that he is "too boorish to be President, he's a warmonger. Only ignorant men without land or education would back him." Lea cannot resist taking the bait: "Old Hickory will be a damn good president." Byrd asserts that Lea has proven his point and that lowborn men should not be given the vote. Mrs. Byrd chimes in, relating that they are soon to visit her cousin in New York, and they have been warned that the streets are "foul" with horse droppings and "Irish," giving Lea the side-eye. He loudly disrupts the dinner and a violent conflict ensues, ending when Byrd challenges him to a duel. Kizzy is distraught that George has been designated Tom Lea's second and afraid that Byrd will murder him as well. Marcellus informs her that it is actually Mr. Jewett that she should be afraid of and that whole conflict had been orchestrated so Jewett could get his hands on George.

Just as in its depiction of Juffure, in this version's South there are complex layers of motivations and levels of discrimination that encompass skin color, country of origin, and socioeconomic status, the consequences of which must be known and navigated by those on the margins if they want to survive. The fates of Kizzy and George are subject to prejudices and discrimination of all varieties, for in addition to suffering racial discrimination, they must also contend with the fact that Tom Lea is barred from the southern gentry and easily preyed on by those with more social capital. The cohesion of their family unit is subject not just to the volatile whims of Tom Lea but also to those who reject him.

And yet, their family grows, as Matilda agrees to marry George. At George and Matilda's wedding, Marcellus drops his hat at Kizzy's feet, which Kizzy recognizes as an African tradition by which a man declares his intentions. We soon see Marcellus and Kizzy in bed, and she's singing Binta's tune. Their parting scene differs greatly from the parting of Kizzy and Sam Bennett in the original. In the reboot, Kizzy wants to stay and protect the people she would be leaving behind, even though she and Marcellus share a genuine connection. As Marcellus leaves, Kizzy tells him her daddy would have liked him. In the original, when Kizzy witnesses Sam Bennett's reaction to his owner berating him, she declares that he does not know who he is; he does not have the connection to a proud origin that she does, and it is precisely because her father would not have liked Sam that she turns him down.

Before Tom Lea and George leave for an extended journey to Charleston, George reassures Kizzy that he has no worries, since she will be watching over his family. Kizzy responds by presenting George with the beads Kunta gave her and says, "And my daddy going to watch over you." At the Charleston Jamboree, there is cockfighting on a grand scale, with participants from abroad ready to make larger wagers than anything Tom and George have experienced in their hometown among their neighbors, and Tom is expecting to make more money than he ever has before. Tom Lea's class consciousness is his defining characteristic, and after winning and promising George his freedom, he is easily goaded into a bet beyond his means when Sir Russell suggests, "Even an Irishman understands fair play." Again, the society is presented as hierarchical, Sir Russell far above Tom Lea and consequently even farther above George. When Sir Russell wins the wager, and George is given to him to cover the bet, the reboot takes the audience with George to England, where he spends the next twenty years working off the debt. In the original, when George leaves he exits the story and abruptly reappears later in the narrative. Maintaining a focus on George illustrates how slavery was integrated into the global economy rather than existing as a peculiarity of the American South. The effect is to reinforce how his experience is bound with Kunta Kinte's; on George's return, we see him crossing the Atlantic in the belly of a ship, holding the African beads Kizzy hoped would protect him, only this time, instead of being taken from the family he doesn't want to forget, he is returning to the family he hopes has not forgotten him.

He returns to Tom Lea's farm now in shambles one year before the Civil War, to find Kizzy's grave and his family sold off to the Murray family plantation. George's confrontation of the declining Tom Lea, which does not appear in the original, provides a necessary catharsis, along with clarification that his character has transformed:

> TOM LEA: You and me have the same blood boy. I'm your daddy.
>
> CHICKEN GEORGE: No, the blood in me from Kizzy, not you—blood that kept me strong all these years away. What few good things I done, that the blood of my granddaddy. And every damn bit of foolishness in me, everything weak, everything selfish—that's you, Tom Lea, 'cause that's who you is. You ain't smart enough to change yourself. And the truth is, your whole damn life, you was a slave, too. You just never knew it. God damn you.

After the confrontation, Chicken George leaves Tom Lea to his degradation and heads out to locate the Murray plantation, where he hopes to find Matilda and his children. There, we are introduced to George's son, the adult Tom (Sedale Threatt Jr.), a blacksmith who defines himself in defiant contrast to his flamboyant father. Tom keeps his head down and provides invaluable hard labor; he can be depended on, and this is his strategy for not being sold away. The Murray plantation in the reboot is the stereotypical plantation of the Antebellum South; it is Tara, from the Greek-Revival architecture to the costumes. Frederick Murray (Lane Garrison), is the Confederate soldier counterpart to the earlier series' Even Brent (Lloyd Bridges), and while both use humiliation and seethe with potential violence, Brent is a working man, whereas Murray is the son of privilege and gentility. He forces George to wait by the roadside until Matilda finishes her workday, Questlove using the gospel classic "Trouble of the World" to underscore the sweet pain of delay before their reunion. In the original, George's return is a joyful but privately domestic scene, literally a homecoming—he seems to appear out of thin air. In contrast, the new version openly displays the intimate connection between George and Matilda as they embrace in the dusk, somewhere between a lurking Frederick and their enslaved children returning from the fields. That George and Matilda get to reunite at all feels like the first time this family has triumphed over fate in generations.

The two versions completely diverge in their depictions of the impending Civil War. In the original, Even Brent announces secession to the townsfolk amid whoops and hollers, and soon he, his brother, and other men are uniformed and departing. The war is external to the narrative; it is taking place elsewhere as Tom's story goes forward on the farm. It is only when the Brent brothers periodically return from the war that we are given updates as to its progress. In the modern version, the Civil War is taking place everywhere simultaneously. Matilda is serving the Murray family as Frederick's fiancée, Nancy Holt (Anna Paquin), reads the family his published letter calling for secession. Frederick's father, Benjamin Murray (Wayne Pére), depends on Tom's skills in designing and developing domestic munitions production in preparation for war. Conflict arises between George and Tom, as George attempts to disabuse his son of the notion that he can work his way into the good graces of Benjamin Murray or any white master. There are hints in Tom's reaction that he sees Mr. Murray as something of a father figure.

When the Murrays host a ball, the musicians begin playing a waltz that is instantly recognizable as Binta's lullaby.

> Chicken George: That's my mama's song.
>
> Matilda: Every band in the county plays it now. It's changed some but always the same. I can hear mama Kizzy humming it. These folks don't know where it come from.
>
> Chicken George: Well, we do, Mornin' Dove. Dance with me.

This connects George and Matilda thematically with every generation preceding them, going back to Juffure, where Binta and Omoro were free, and provides a textbook illustration of cultural appropriation, reminding us of when Kunta told Fiddler that the song was his and "these people" could not have it. In both versions, George's status as a free man is dependent on him leaving the state, and hence he is forced to flee. In the modern version, as Matilda and George say their goodbyes, George hands her Kizzy's beads, once again an object of protection and connection, amplifying what is at stake.

In the original, when George leaves, the narrative stays centered on Tom at the farm. The modern version splits the narrative, showing the Civil War from both sides of the conflict. On his flight North, Chicken George befriends Cyrus (T.I. [Clifford Joseph Harris Jr.]), and they both end up fighting for the Union. Cyrus provides some comedic relief, and this part of the narrative begins to feel like a buddy picture. Meanwhile, Nancy Holt reveals herself to Tom as a spy for the Union and attempts to recruit him to help her pass intelligence on Mr. Murray's plans for arming the Confederacy. Both Cyrus and Nancy are refreshing innovations, one a humorist who serves as a sidekick in arms and charms to Chicken George, the other an abolitionist challenging Tom to risk his life and abandon his sense of security by undermining Mr. Murray, and consequently the Confederacy. Cyrus engages, while Nancy compels. After Confederate soldiers rape his wife, Tom throws himself wholeheartedly into Nancy's plans. Before he sets out on his mission, he tells his wife: "Chicken George used to say his mama used to talk to Kunta Kinte all the time. Said the African used to come to her when she was scared. Don't know if it's for true, but maybe ain't no difference. It's the askin' him to help us makes the difference." Like Kizzy, this is Tom's form of prayer and indicates he has embraced his heritage, aligning himself with the father he disdained and no longer dismissing any mention of "the African" as just stories.

The reboot depicts Chicken George and Cyrus narrowly escaping the Fort Pillow Massacre, an elaborate battle scene ending in the intentional murder of captured Union troops. In contrast to the original, historic events are portrayed rather than referenced, lending the story both scale and plausibility. The original goes far past the end of the Civil War to include references to Reconstruction and the origins of the Ku Klux Klan before the denouement, when Chicken George declares to his ancestor that the family is now finally free, as they embark on an unspecified exodus. The reboot quickly finishes the story after the conclusion of the Civil War. While his siblings struggle with the reality of sharecropping, Tom sets out to find Chicken George, whom they learn has been fighting bushwhackers, and the series turns to the fantastic or supernatural as Kunta Kinte appears in Mandinka attire guiding Tom to Chicken George. George and Matilda are given a final reunion, and the family sets out with the stated mission of settling in Henning, Tennessee, the birthplace of Alex Haley.

Traditionally, Hollywood had populated stories set in the Old South with various stock character versions of the happy slave, and just as those subjected to the institution of slavery were once considered property, so these characters were relegated to supporting roles and functioned as little more than props with limited human dimension. The original series permanently antiquated any Hollywood depiction of the historic South that disregarded the perspective of the enslaved. The reimagined version builds on this by articulating nuances of that point of view and placing it in a far more complex context. The theme of how identity serves to inspire, connect, and protect is developed with the repetition of motifs represented as song, ceremony, language, and beads. These threads of inheritance are woven together to represent a painfully beautiful family romance that is both African and American. While forty years ago it was an innovation to merely place the African American experience at the center of the narrative when depicting the historic South, this new version of *Roots* carefully enriches the African setting, emphasizing how the Third Passage was a violent interruption of a rich narrative already in place.

Three factors have come into play in the interim between when the original miniseries surprised corporate television culture with its profound success and when it became clear that an updated version would be felicitous. First, advocacy groups have been formed whose mission is to convince the entertainment industry that there is "a moral mandate to tell stories that cover the entire human family."[10] Organizations such as the Multi-Ethnic Media Coalition have established relationships within the television industry for more than a decade, whereas they are just beginning to focus their energy on the film industry. With television, the coalition has demonstrated that what began as an adversarial relationship, operating as a "watchdog," has developed into a successfully collaborative one. It said to the industry, "We are watching you" in both senses; the industry is being monitored and "we are increasingly your audience." This has led to better business practices; corporate television is paying closer attention to the changing dynamics of their audience. The *Los Angeles Times* notes, "By most accounts, the small screen has become a more culturally inclusive place over the last decade, and for several reasons. The TV audience itself is diverse—one estimate is that black viewers spend 37% more time watching TV than other racial groups—which has forced network executives to find programming that reflects the people watching at home."[11]

It was tactical genius for advocacy groups to begin with television, as there are far more productions to supply content to platforms that are expanding exponentially, while at the same time the film industry is contracting. Growing diversity among the few gatekeepers who make decisions about television programming is the third element. Channing Dungey made history when she became the president of ABC Entertainment, "the first black executive to run one of the Big Four networks' entertainment divisions."[12] Before *Roots* first aired, television executives considered it risky material unlikely to find an audience, hence their decision to air the episodes on consecutive nights. It was a lucky accident. Before the rebooted version of *Roots* aired, corporate television's sense of risk aversion determined that the production would comprise a diverse cast and crew and that it would be supplied with ample resources invested in ensuring authenticity. While the culture of corporate television remains undoubtedly risk averse, concerted efforts to understand and incorporate the complexity of diversity is now a part of that definition. Dungey states, "In television, we are fortunate because we get to try a lot of things; we get to take a lot of shots . . . it gives us a great opportunity to tell many different stories from diverse points of view."[13]

Notes

1. Michael Eric Dyson, introduction to Alex Haley, *Roots: The Saga of an American Family,* Thirtieth Anniversary ed. (New York: Vanguard, 2007), 30.

2. Sander Vanocur, "Dramatic 'Roots' of America," *Washington Post,* January 23, 1977; "Everyone Was Talking about 'Roots' in 1977—Including Ronald Reagan," *Washington Post,* May 30, 2016.

3. "Historical Presence: LeVar Burton on Why He's Co-Producing a Remake of the Groundbreaking, Emmy-Gobbling Miniseries Roots," *Town & Country,* June–July 2016, 6.

4. Dominic Paten, "Les Moonves Calls Not Embracing Diversity 'Stupid,' Universal's Jeff Shell Tells Confab Movie Biz 10 Years behind TV," *Deadline,* May 4, 2016, http://deadline.com/2016/05/less-moonves-jeff-shell-milken-conference-cbs-universal-dreamworks-animation-1201749243/.

5. Stacy L. Smith et al., "Inequality in 800 Popular Films: Examining Portrayals of Gender, Race/Ethnicity, LGBT, and Disability from 2007–2015" (University of Southern California Annenberg School for Communication and Journalism, 2016).

6. "ACLU Statement on Federal Probe of Gender Discrimination in Hollywood." American Civil Liberties Union Web site, May 11, 2016, https://www.aclu.org/news/aclu-statement-federal-probe-gender-discrimination-hollywood.

7. Stephane Dunn, "Why the 'Roots' Remake Is So Important," *Atlantic,* May 29, 2016, http://www.theatlantic.com/entertainment/archive/2016/05/why-the-roots-remake-is-so-important/484661/.

8. Rachel Syme, "Viola Davis Speaks about Her Emmy, Diversity, and Women on TV," *New York Times,* September 24, 2015, https://www.nytimes.com/2015/09/24/arts/television/viola-davis-emmys-interview.html.

9. John Koblin, "Marcia Clark Has Moment to Savor at Emmys," *New York Times,* September 20, 2016, C1.

10. Steve Green, "Multi-Ethnic Media Coalition Tells Hollywood: You're Next," *IndieWire,* February 4, 2016, http://www.indiewire.com/2016/02/multi-ethnic-media-coalition-tells-hollywood-youre-next-26259/.

11. Scott Collins, "How TV Beats Film in Giving Women and Minorities Greater Opportunities on Screen," *Los Angeles Times,* February 24, 2016, http://beta.latimes.com/entertainment/tv/la-et-st-tv-film-diversity-20160224-story.html.

12. Nellie Andreeva and Lisa de Moraes, "ABC Shakeup: Paul Lee Exits as President, Channing Dungey Named to Succeed Him," *Deadline,* February 17, 2016, http://deadline.com/2016/02/paul-lee-out-abc-president-channing-dungey-1201704333/

13. Collins, "How TV Beats Film."

7

The South as a Space/Place of Reclamation of Black Fe/Male Inheritance

Kwakiutl Dreher

I dedicate The South as a Space/Place of Reclamation of Black Fe/Male Inheritance to Georgia Anne Bellamy Robinson, my Aunt Georgia or, Aunt G, depending on the swing in our conversations. Aunt Georgia, along with her brothers, Paul and Owen, ushered into the family the Great Migration of the United States. Bear with me as I tell you her story. Born in 1919 in Green Sea, a rural town in Horry County, South Carolina, Aunt Georgia migrated to Brooklyn, New York, as soon as she graduated from high school. She may not have known it then, but she joined millions of black southerners who left the South in the 1930s and 1940s to escape the practice of white supremacy, poverty, oppression, and discrimination, and to search for better socioeconomic opportunities in the North. Her son, Martin, sheds more light on Aunt Georgia's reason for leaving: "She knew after high school, the only opportunities for her would be work in the fields, get married, and have children. She left."[1]

Aunt Georgia married Elliott "Uncle E" Robinson, who also migrated from Blackville, South Carolina, to "up the road" as is spoken in the southern vernacular. The Wilmots, a Jewish family, hired Aunt Georgia as their domestic; thereafter, Aunt Georgia and Uncle Elliott began a family. The Wilmots facilitated the family's move into a two-bedroom apartment in their complex on St. Mark's Avenue in the Bedford-Stuyvesant neighborhood; the Robinsons were the second black family in the area. On September 6, 1967, at the age of forty-eight, Aunt Georgia had the forethought to certify her domestic caretaking skills. She enrolled in the State of New York Medical Aid Training Schools and earned a certificate of completion, No. 1113B, in the "instruction of New-Born and Child Care, Geriatrics and Convalescent Care for Homes and Hospitals."

Then, in 1976, Aunt Georgia retired, packed up her family, and made the trek from up the road down South to Columbia, South Carolina, where she and my mother nurtured their close sisterhood. I wondered through starry eyes, though, *why not just stay in the big city of New York?* Martin revealed, "For my mother to be able to purchase a home and to have a yard meant something. . . . Brooklyn never was home for her—the south was. Plus, paying rent on an apartment . . . something she never would own. . . . No. a house and land . . . mother wanted those things."

On her own, Aunt Georgia purchased a three-bedroom brick home and secured the deed in *her* name.[2] It has a porch and generous front and back yards. She lived comfortably, and on many a visit I would find her sitting on the porch talking with Uncle E. In her twilight years, she changed gracefully into grand- and great-grandmother; when she died in 2012, she was ninety-three years old.

My Aunt Georgia's story is that of a black female teenager who bravely "stepped out on faith," as the church folk would say, to reach for the northern promised land. The North gave her wide berth from an expected, if not an *exclusive,* lived experience in the South: marriage, children, fieldwork—the latter, literary critic Thadious Davis defines as a "constructed, tilled, planted, and cultivated . . . work-specific site . . . of production."[3] This lived experience, she knew, would extend to her children. "Sharecropping and picking cotton were degrading to my mother," Martin informed me. "When we would visit Grandmother down the country [in Horry]," he remembered, "Mother would not let us pick cotton with our cousins, so we played in Grandmother's yard. Mother would sit on grandmother's porch and shell peas . . . look out on the fields." The return to the South for Aunt Georgia, more importantly, meant the opportunity to own land and, as matriarch, to pass it down to the next generation. Martin resides in her house to this day. In addition, that my cousin Martin could tell me her story interjects the black woman's voice in the Great Migration to the North and the return to the South's histories.

I desired to find out, however, Martin's reasons for following his mother to Columbia. After all, he came into young manhood in Brooklyn, and even now, I hear the cadence of the city in his voice. He replied, "Well, cousin, I was not doing so well [during the 1970s], and while I had my hesitations, the move down south was needed . . . it was *necessary* for me to be there and get myself and my life together." Southern decorum forbade me from further inquiry. My Aunt Georgia, I hazard, intuited his need, and, therefore, acted on her faith that the South would rescue him from his travails in the big city. He did not disappoint her.

In his screenplay *Down in the Delta,* screenwriter Myron E. Goble tells a similar story of reverse migration in. In 1993, Goble won the Don and Gee Nicholl Fellowship in Screenwriting to develop the script, and *Down in the Delta* made its nationwide film debut in December 1998, with Maya Angelou as director.[4] Goble revealed to me his experience with the story: "I read an amazing book called *The Promised Land* [: *The Great Black Migration and How It Changed America*]. In that book are stories about people who migrated from the Mississippi Delta to Chicago. Yet, at the end of the book is a little throwaway: people maintained family ties. I didn't really think much about it, but somehow out of that came my story—a story about women facing challenges in Chicago who find opportunities for redemption by moving the nuclear family back to the South."[5]

This chapter pays close attention to one black woman in the film, Rosa Lynn Sinclair (Mary Alice), who "fac[ed] challenges in Chicago," and initiated a forced reverse migration in three stages: Chicago to the Mississippi Delta, the Mississippi Delta back to Chicago, and Chicago back to the Mississippi Delta. Each journey is undertaken to deliver to the next generation its ancestral inheritance. Rosa Lynn, the in-law of interest here, maintains southern family ties in a distinctive way. As the sister-in-law to Earl Sinclair (Al Freeman), the family's patriarch, she disrupts the family's patrilineal legacy to bestow upon her firstborn, Loretta Sinclair (Alfre Woodard), the right of passage to full black female adult/motherhood. Even though she reminds Earl, who resides down in the Delta, "Nathan gets passed down from oldest child to oldest child, so he stays right up here [in Chicago] until Thomas comes of age," Rosa Lynn determines that Loretta will earn the right to pass down Nathan and all of its symbolism to Loretta's son, Thomas (Mpho Koaho).[6] On first screening of the film, it appears Goble has entrusted Loretta to save Thomas, the next Sinclair patriarch. A deeper analysis reveals, however, Goble accords to *Rosa Lynn,* the sister-in-law, the authority to open a space for the black *female* firstborn to articulate a matrilineal narrative of (reverse) migration.

Only the South can deliver the particular yearnings for redemption *and* salvation curried by Rosa Lynn, the mother, and Loretta, the daughter. Rosa Lynn and Thomas assume the roles of secondary caretakers of his sister, Tracey (Kulani Hassen), who is autistic. In his mother's absence, Thomas sometimes misses school to take care of Tracey. Loretta, who is unemployed in Chicago, strives to exist. After the father abandons the household, she and her children move back into her mother's apartment. She medicates her feelings of worthlessness with alcohol and drugs, but her desires are compelling: to find gainful employment and to provide for her family as a single parent. When she binges after another failed job search, Rosa Lynn arranges for her and her children to spend the summer down in the Mississippi Delta with Earl. Goble contends, "When it came time for salvation for her daughter, Rosa Lynn knew the South was only one place to send her, and it was the right choice."[7] There in the Delta, Rosa Lynn believes, Loretta will pull herself out of her pain and, more important, come into her own as a woman and responsible single mother.

In the analysis of the black female's voice interpolated in *Down in the Delta*, I take my cue from nineteenth-century author and speaker Anna Julia Cooper. She writes, "In the clash and clatter of our American Conflict, it has been said that the South remains Silent. . . . One muffled strain in the Silent South, a jarring chord and a vague and uncomprehended cadenza has been and still is the Negro. *And of that muffled chord, the one mute and voiceless note has been the sadly expectant Black Woman.*"[8]

Goble liberates the voice of one black woman in his story. Once it is free, just as my Aunt Georgia passed down her story and southern land to her family, the black woman with ancestral roots in the South can learn of her family's history and confer the same to the next generation. For Rosa Lynn, the South *and* Chicago are those spaces.

Goble's insertion of the Black female's voice in the retelling of Mississippi Delta ancestry is important, because outside of Fannie Lou Hamer, Mississippi conjures a nimiety of visions: the lynching of fourteen-year-old Emmett Till (Money, 1955); the assassination of civil rights activist Medgar Evers on his front lawn (Jackson, 1963); and, the murders of civil rights workers Andrew Goodman and Michael Schwerner, white students from New York, and James Chaney, a black native of Meridian, Mississippi (Philadelphia, 1964). More haunting, not only does the Mississippi Delta carry a reputation for extreme poverty, the state also bears a violent history of white supremacy: the state ratified the Thirteenth Amendment to the United States Constitution on *March 16, 1995.* That amendment abolished slavery *in 1865.* In the documentary *The Untold Story: Slavery in the Twentieth Century,* Mae Louise (Wall) Miller (d. 2015), the daughter of the late Cain Wall Sr. and Lela Wall, recounts to genealogist and historian Antoinette Harrell her family's horrific experience of involuntary servitude, a.k.a. peonage, in Gillsburg, Mississippi. Alfred Aubry, the narrator, informs the viewer, "peonage occurred primarily in three areas of Mississippi: the deltas, the Mississippi Bluff, and the Black Belt." The unnamed plantation owners enslaved Cain and Lela along with their seven children in a barn; the family escaped in 1963. Miller recalls, "The plantation owners had the capability of killing you . . . burying you alive or whatever they felt like they wanted to do. . . . We had been beat so much and had been threatened so many times you really didn't know who to tell."[9]

Ms. Mae Louise was four years into her freedom when Marian Wright Edelman, founder of the Children's Defense Fund, invited Senator Robert Kennedy and other senators to tour the Mississippi Delta in 1967 to investigate the Economic Opportunity Act of 1964 and the Head Start Program of 1965—the latter to which the state of Mississippi refused to subscribe. Edelman remembers Senator Kennedy "saw a very malnourished baby with a bloated stomach sitting on a dirt floor while his mother . . . was washing out of a tin cup. He came out after trying to get a response [from the baby], which he did not get from this child . . . and he was visibly angry and moved and said he'd never seen anything like this in the United States, not even West Virginia."[10] Kennedy's own remarks about poverty in the Mississippi Delta are poignant: "I have seen children in Mississippi—here in the United States—with a gross national product of $800 billion—I have seen children in the Delta area of Mississippi with distended stomachs, whose faces are covered with sores from starvation. . . . I don't think that's acceptable in the United States of America and I think we need a change."[11]

Not one vestige of these traumas circulates within the film; instead, Goble sidesteps Mississippi Delta's present past and concentrates on *a* distant history of enslaved Africans in North America and the nation's Civil War. In his script, through Rosa Lynn and her brother-in-law, Earl, Goble generates nineteenth-century black history, and William Wages, the film's cinematographer, carries it forward via the visual art of the flashback. Angelou's film direction, too, brings to life the spirit of Goble's vision. In the screenplay's dedication, Goble writes, "Maya Angelou: What could bring more pleasure than finally seeing the film that I wrote? Seeing the film that I *meant* to write."[12] Historian Terrence Tucker agrees, "[Angelou] reject[s] the myth . . . [of] the rural South as a site from which blacks must always escape. African Americans carve . . . out a life for themselves by *directly engaging in stories of their ancestors' survival* as a means to garner strength."[13] The Mississippi Delta in the film, Davis would argue, "functions as a crucible of a landscape of racial memory," a "part of the material culture grounding physical relations and psychological dramas of human beings."[14] The oral histories of "psychological dramas" heard within *Down in the Delta,* stabilize the foundations on which the Sinclair family stands. The Mississippi Delta also extends corporeal freedom the concrete jungle of Chicago cannot. As she prepares Loretta, Thomas, and Tracy for the trip to the Delta, Rosa Lynn remarks, "Down in the delta there are great big fields to run and play and nobody's chasing after you but your own shadow. . . . If you don't want to play in the fields you can learn to swim."

Down in the Delta, more general, is a story of the white Sinclairs and the enslaved blacks on their plantation and the enduring symbolism of a silver candelabra named Nathan. When Jesse Sinclair was six, he witnessed, along with his mother and other enslaved people, the auction of his father; the Sinclairs paid for him with the candelabra. Later, he joined the Union army, and, at the end of the Civil War, he made his way to the Sinclair plantation and retrieved the silver candelabra. He believed that "as long as it was in the Sinclair family the family was going to stay together." On his deathbed, Jesse passes down to his young son the candelabra and the story behind it. Nathan stayed down in the Mississippi Delta until Clayton Sinclair (never seen onscreen, Earl's brother, married Rosa Lynn).

The couple migrated to Chicago during the great migration; they brought Nathan with them to the city, since Clayton was next in line to inherit it. Loretta is Clayton and Rosa Lynn's only child. Upon Clayton's death, Rosa Lynn—the in-law—breaks protocol: she refuses to repatriate Clayton to the Mississippi Delta; instead, she buries him in Chicago soil. What is more, Rosa Lynn has the audacity to secrete the candelabra in a local church in Chicago (where she feeds the homeless) rather than return it to her brother-in-law. For those travesties, Earl has yet to forgive Rosa Lynn. He protests, "[Nathan] belongs right here in this house and you know it Rosa Lynn! He never should have been kidnapped to Chicago in the first place."

Thadious Davis maintains, "Place is a powerful signifier of identity that cannot be overestimated, particularly in terms of the South with its specific history and sociology. No section of the United States has taken on so contested but persistent an identity or role in the creation of an image as the South."[15] For instance, in an interview by literary critic Henry Louis Gates Jr., celebrated actor Morgan Freeman underscores the reason he moved back to Mississippi. Freeman replied, "We built the South, *and we know it*. . . . What *I own* is my place here, because my mother, my father, my grandmother, my grandfather . . . all the way back to my great-great-great-grandmother, who happened to be Virginian—that's where they had the farms. . . . Traveling around the country and living in different places. I could never see that any place was any better racially than Mississippi. . . . This is where my parents are buried. This is where I've always felt safest."[16]

Freeman's revelation brings to relief his southern inheritance, a territory "marked" and "bought" for him by the labor of his ancestors. That they traveled "around the country" and "liv[ed] in different places" indicate the *descansos,* or the markers by the side of the road as memorials to those who died thereon. Freeman's presence in Mississippi at the burial site of his parents serves as a living descanso to the sweat and toil of his ancestors on southern land. African American labor conveys the deed to the southern land, and Freeman claims his southern heritage and his identity as well.

Jazz and song stylist Cassandra Wilson is another celebrity artist who migrated "up the road" and returned to her southern roots. Born in Jackson, Mississippi, she moved to New York in the 1980s to carve out her identity and hone her vocal skills. In 2000, "needing time off to 'get [her] bearings" and to care for her ailing mother, Mary Fowlkes, Wilson set her mind to return to Jackson.[17] She notes, "Returning to Mississippi helps create a certain tempo, a pace. I couldn't have gotten the same tempo in New York. . . . Our ancestors spilled blood here. . . . We have to stay here. . . . There's a color, cadence, timbre and tone in Mississippi that contains all our memories, dreams, fears and hopes. . . . My mother sang to me, communicated to me in every color imaginable. That's what the Africans brought to this land. It's all they had."[18] Wilson speaks of the South in the language of music, and Mississippi infuses her own work with a more nuanced sound. As does Freeman, Wilson discerns the descansos left behind by her ancestors. Wilson's (re)assessment of Mississippi's significance makes possible for her to produce from a mental space of home or community.

Angelou, the late poet and activist as well as director of the film, believed this pull of the South and ultimate respect for its history by many who return can "make their places in the land of their fore parents. They find and make friends under the shade trees their ancestors left decades earlier. Many find themselves happy, without being able to explain the emotion. I think it is simply that they feel generally important." Angelou understood this interior feeling; after all, she left her hometown of Stamps, Arkansas, and emerged a "big-city, internationally wise, sophisticated" woman who later joined the faculty at Wake Forest University in Winston-Salem, North Carolina, where she taught for thirty-two years.[19]

Freeman, Wilson, and Angelou sustain Davis's idea of the South as a "powerful signifier of identity" that the North only partially allows.[20] In fact, *Ebony* magazine's review of the film acknowledges, "the North was considered a promised land, a place where Blacks could journey for hope of better days. Today, some folks are heading back home to the South for the same reasons."[21] In his analysis of the film, Tucker states, "Maya Angelou's *Down in the Delta* sees the South as an important regenerative space for African Americans, a place where blacks can reestablish connections to their roots and encounter a supportive community that pushes back against the crushing isolation and nihilism of Northern, urban spaces."[22] For these entertainers, the film director, and the screenwriter, the South nourishes a sense of belonging; even more specific, the Mississippi Delta accords an ancestry and an ancestral home to which they have a right to return. These artists make their way back South; some, also, nurture the places that contributed to their artistic growth. Wilson and Angelou traveled back and forth from Mississippi and North Carolina, respectively, to their homes in Harlem, New York. In the same trajectory, Rosa Lynn retains Chicago as her home; it is where she came of age as wife, mother, and grandmother. She acknowledges, however, the South as sanctuary for Loretta.

The film reviews and scholarly critique concur: Goble's "wise and eloquent script" offers up belief in the curative dynamic of the South.[23] "The Healing Power of a Delta Family's Roots," the title of film critic Stephen Holden's review, denotes the film's theme. Florence Anthony writes that *Down in the Delta* is about "a troubled woman changing her life around by moving to her uncle's home in Mississippi."[24] Jim Farber, *Entertainment Weekly* film critic, says, "The surest cure for what ails the troubled modern, industrialized African American is good Southern country living and the love of a family proud of its heritage."[25] Tucker writes, "As she and her children adjust to the life in the South, Loretta moves from a woman objectified by the urban environment of poverty and drugs to a (re)constructed self—built around a fuller understanding of her heritage and the development of a reciprocal relationship between herself and her community."[26]

These reviews and critiques appraise the South as therapeutic for Loretta. Rosa Lynn, the in-law, and her overall function in the story draws little if any attention. In the film, we meet Rosa Lynn, a retired domestic, as caretaker of African violets, a houseplant adaptable to any environment but with a high demand on the gardener. Mrs. Charles S. Hawley, a gardener, lists "ten factors that unite to produce a beautiful African violet." These include "Proper Soil,

Water and watering methods, Fertilizer, Light, Temperature, Air circulation and spacing, Humidity, Potting and Spraying."[27] Rosa Lynn's African Violets are in full bloom, and each of the plants lined up neatly on the shelves in her apartment testifies to her care and attention. Indoor gardening, among other artistries black women undertake, observes novelist Alice Walker, sheds light on "a vibrant, creative spirit that the black woman has inherited, and that pops out in wild and unlikely places. . . . [It signals] her ability to hold on, even in very simple ways."[28] In essence, Rosa Lynn's gardening orders her everyday ordinary after Clayton's death. She assumes the role of the primary financial and emotional caretaker for Loretta and her children, her "African Violets."

Rosa Lynn as widow, in-law, mother, and grandmother yields a recognition of the ways these categories operate for her. According to Helena Znaniecki Lopata, "the absence of the husband dramatically or gradually changes the routine, what is thought about, and what is felt in response to events."[29] As the "main inheritor" of her husband's estate, Rosa Lynn "put . . . the *marriage bond ahead* of the lineal succession bond."[30] The break with protocol or the changes in routine after Clayton's death upholds the black patriarchal "protection," or what I would term "marital surrogacy." She mentions to Loretta, "Nathan needed to stay up here to look after us after your father died." In other words, Clayton resides with Rosa Lynn, still, through Nathan.

Clayton's death no doubt resulted in the loss of some income in the family; Rosa Lynn therefore, enacts "gradual . . . changes in the routine[s]" of the household.[31] In her retirement, she assumes the role of primary breadwinner for her extended family. In one instance, Loretta arrives home disheveled the morning after a night of partying and drinking; she wobbles through the apartment with hands raised in a "don't bother me; I don't want to hear it" gesture. She is unanchored. Rosa Lynn's concern, though, is only for Loretta's unemployed status and the interruption of time. She yells, "How you gonna find a job when you're out playing all night huh? You tell me that! . . . We've wasted enough time this morning!" Eventually, Rosa Lynn comes to the bitter realization: a job alone cannot solve Loretta's distresses. Her daughter's emotional and spiritual life is in need of restoration.

As mentioned, in-law Rosa Lynn redirects Nathan's journey. Her decisions are a "compensatory mechanism" used to "expan[d] [her] definition of primary kinship membership."[32] The initiation of reverse migration comprises Rosa Lynn's expansion for Loretta to begin her journey to self-actualization and healing from the ravages of alcoholism and drug addiction that hold her hostage. She consults Earl, who declines his sister-in-law's request to host his niece and her children for the summer. In turn, Rosa Lynn invokes her right of lineal kin and Nathan's "legacy to use in bargaining for services from children and other relatives."[33] She threatens, "She's your niece, Earl! If it comes down to it, I'll sell Nathan if I have to. . . . If it comes down to saving Nathan and saving my family, you know what I'll choose." Earl relents.

Matriarch Rosa Lynn's successful arrangement for a summer's reprieve for her daughter and grandchildren, however, calls for her to strategize how to acquire the funds for bus fare. She decides to pawn Nathan. That she hocks Nathan reveals not only the dire necessity of Loretta's journey; it also shows the journey's compulsory expediency. Peaches Pawnbrokers, the pawn shop, suits Rosa Lynn's scheme because "just about anyone can borrow on a pawn loan. No bank account, job, or credit check is required—just the collateral and a valid photo ID."[34] Peaches (Sandi Ross), the pawnbroker, advertises on her storefront "Instant Cash Paid," "EZ Credit Loans," and "Buy Now Pay Later."

To Loretta's chagrin, when the family enters the shop, Peaches calls her out on previous visits to the pawn shop for small loans. "Hey Loretta!" she hollers. "You got something for me today?" As Rosa Lynn displays Nathan in the pawn shop in the presence of her family members, Loretta recoils, holds her stomach, and exclaims, "No! No! You can't do it! Nathan is too important. . . . He been in our family forever, Momma!" Rosa Lynn rightly intuits Loretta's appreciation for Nathan's value, and bargains with Peaches for the requisite funds for Loretta and her family to take the trip. Peaches, however, assesses Nathan's capital value. She curries no interest in its historical currency, even though Rosa Lynn informs her of the same:

> "Silver plate—maybe $100," she offers Rosa Lynn as she unveils Nathan.
>
> "Solid Sterling nothing less than $500," counters Rosa Lynn.
>
> "Can't be any older than 1950s . . . maybe I go as high as $200—maybe . . ."
>
> "Antique silver, I'll have you know; 1852. Look close here on the bottom: silversmith, signed, engraved and dated . . . easily $450"
>
> "American $300."
>
> "British $400."
>
> "Alright $350—final offer or else you can go someplace else."
>
> "$375 and it's done."
>
> "Done."

Peaches counts on Loretta's forfeiture of the loan, however, following the closure of the deal. "This will melt down real nice," she says in anticipation of the resale of the collateral. Even though this statement makes plain generational apathy for black history, that Peaches would "melt down" or "inflict harm" on Nathan creates audience investment in Loretta's success. Just as the heirloom remained hostage on the mantel in the white Sinclairs' home, it will remain captive in the pawn shop under the care(less disregard) of Peaches, the pawnbroker until the family can earn it back. *Nathan has to be rescued from Peaches. Loretta has to win.*

Loretta rejects the pawn ticket but immediately rushes to recover it from the trash can once Rosa Lynn tosses it there. Rosa Lynn's highly prized "collateralized pledge" is a dangerous gamble but one with the lowest probability of default. Her pawn of the hyper-sentimental heirloom is a "commitment mechanism to give [Loretta] a greater incentive to act optimally" during her tenure down South.[35] Rosa Lynn waged a similar gamble with Earl by threatening to sell Nathan.

Down in the Delta

As did my Aunt Georgia's community and family celebrate her return, Loretta's kin and the black community welcome her home. These members include her Uncle Earl, cousin Will Sinclair (Wesley Snipes), and Zenial (Loretta Devine), caretaker of Aunt Annie (Esther Rolle), Uncle Earl's wife, who has Alzheimer's. A close reading of this part of *Down in the Delta* points out those culturally influenced features of the South that begin to contradict the life Loretta lived in Chicago. These features build on black entrepreneurship and social activism.

The first order of business pivots on Loretta's employment via black entrepreneurship. This brings to light a rich history of black men and women who ventured into the risk of self-employment, for example, Peaches, the pawnbroker; Earl, the restauranteur; and, later, Loretta the waitress/assistant manager. The Reverend Vernon Johns (1892–1965), Martin Luther King Jr.'s predecessor as pastor of the Dexter Avenue Baptist Church in Montgomery, Alabama, is an early example of black entrepreneurship. According to civil rights historian Taylor Branch, Johns, farmer and Oberlin College graduate, "peddled hams and onions, potatoes and watermelons, cabbages and sausage" from the back of his pick-up truck and "cultivated a garden behind the parsonage on Jackson Street."[36] Negroes should be self-sufficient to lessen their patronage of white businesses and funnel profits into their own neighborhoods Johns reasoned. Malcolm X, too, advocated for black entrepreneurship: "The black man himself has to be made aware of importance of going into business; once you and I go into business we own and operate—at least the businesses in our community—what we will be doing is developing a situation wherein we will actually be able to create employment for the people in the community."[37]

Earl engages the history of black entrepreneurship in Just Chicken, a restaurant he opened after retiring from the poultry plant in the Delta; the community's plant is one of the primary economic engines. The restaurant is successful, and Earl employs two waitresses Gina (Quancetia Hamilton) and Isabelle (Kim Roberts). Earl is the primary cook. Loretta's apprenticeship under Uncle Earl nullifies the indignity she experienced during an interview with a grocery store manager (Phil Akin) in Chicago. He explains to Loretta the logistics of the job as he eyes her with contempt: "The job pays minimum wage, and if you're lucky enough to get in 30 hours, you'll take home about $110 a week. And the first time you don't show up you're outta here, ok? Oh, and uhm, one more thing . . . basic math test—just to make sure you know your dollars and cents: what is five dollars minus three dollars and eighty-seven cents?"

Loretta fails the test but demonstrates her will to work. She asks in desperation, "Is there something else I could do? I could put stuff on the shelf; I'll mop . . . anything . . ." The manager turns his back as he throws her application into the trash. Humiliated, Loretta runs out. Rather than go home, she proceeds to a drug den and smokes marijuana, received in exchange for her son's Walkman. When Rosa Lynn finds her there intoxicated and dazed, she sets in motion her plan to send her daughter and grandchildren to the Mississippi Delta.

Once Loretta arrives, her Uncle Earl educates her in black business ownership, and we see her develop a strong work ethic and joy in her work. Free from the menace of the streets and drug culture, Thomas teaches his mother how to make change. Under Uncle Earl's tutelage, she perfects the art of turning ground chicken into sausages. When she eventually graduates to waitressing, Uncle Earl accepts her customer-service tips: "Why don't you go walk around and visit with the customers? Ask them is everything ok . . . try it." The men and women in the community, in addition, treat her as a capable person—not contemptable and weak, as had many in Chicago. More powerful, Loretta finds her voice in Just Chicken when she and her cousin, Will, rouse the community to activism after receiving notice of the chicken plant's closure. Will calls her up to the front after his introduction. Loretta, though hesitant, responds: "I wasn't born here, but I kind of got reborn here, and I learned to appreciate Just Chicken. And I also found out here that you . . . nobody do stuff for you, you got to do it yourself. Everybody sitting around wanting somebody else to do stuff for them. So I'm asking you can we do this for ourselves and for our children. . . . Can you do it? Uncle Earl? Can we do it?"

Uncle Earl and the attendees heartily agree to Loretta's call to action. The time spent in the Mississippi Delta, then, makes it possible for Loretta to recast herself as an industrious businesswoman. The expression of community harmony baptizes Loretta into black entrepreneurship as, at Uncle Earl's request, she agrees to manage the restaurant—symbolizing her further growth into a responsible mother and caretaker. Her self-esteem and self-respect are apparent.

I have demonstrated the success of Rosa Lynn's enterprise of reverse migration. Now, I chart how Goble allows for the black woman to speak during black masculine intrafamilial storytelling as it relates to Nathan's history. More central, Goble lays the groundwork for the black woman's voice to be heard in the story of Jesse, the black Sinclair patriarch. From a patriarchal perspective in the Delta, Uncle Earl relays the first half Nathan's story to Thomas and Loretta. Rosa Lynn passes down the second half of Nathan's story in Chicago, a black woman's frame of reference, with Nathan on her dinner table, to Loretta, after she has earned the money to bring Nathan home from the pawn shop.

The Story of Nathan in the Delta

In the family's cemetery outside of the ancestral church, Thomas and Loretta witness Uncle Earl's story at different times. Thomas listens to his great uncle tell the history of the Sinclair family, which has lived down in the Delta for five generations. Gesturing toward the tombstone of Thomas's great-great-great-grandfather, Jesse, Uncle Earl says, "So maybe you and *my son, Will*, will tell your children about our family history." The tombstones and stories of the Sinclair *women*—Anne Claire, and Clara, Jesse's wife, whose name is engraved under her husband's—are not mentioned; nor does Thomas ask about the women. It is obvious, then, that Uncle Earl endorses a patrilineal vision of the family's history, and he passes this vision down to his grandnephew. On another occasion, he retells the same story to Loretta—also in the family's cemetery. His narrative centers on the Union soldier, Civil War, postwar decline of the South, and Jesse as patriarch of his family. Cinematographer Wages brings into view the Sinclair women but Jesse's story strikes at the heart of Uncle Earl's narrative. He remembers in flashback: "There is over one hundred and fifty years of family history right here. . . . During the Civil War . . . southern soldiers and freed slaves all running around trying to get their hands on anything they could find. Jesse took Nathan off that mantelpiece right in that house we're in now. . . . Jesse would take Nathan out and talk to him. . . . Ever since Annie got sick, I've been thinking how I can get Nathan and Will back down here in the Delta so we can talk to Nathan."

Loretta offers, "There's gotta be something you can do, Uncle Earl," and Earl replies, "Looks like I've gone about as far as I was meant to go." That Rosa Lynn is Nathan's custodian confirms Uncle Earl's limitations here.

The Story of Nathan in Chicago

By contrast, Rosa Lynn, with rag and silver polish, cleans Nathan after its retrieval from the pawn shop as she shares with Loretta the second part of its story. At the dinner table, Rosa Lynn establishes the genesis of Jesse's motivation to retrieve Nathan: "Jesse was just a little boy when the white Sinclairs first came over from Alabama, and they didn't come over with much—just their animals and their slaves, and to get the land and things they needed they had to sell off a few of their slaves. Jesse was only six years old when he lost his father that way . . . sold away . . . right before his very eyes. His mother never got over it; and Jesse? Jesse never ever forgot it."

Wages interposes the faces of Jesse's community—in particular his mother and another enslaved woman who comforts her as potential buyers bargain for Nathan—then he closes in on six-year-old Jesse. Rosa Lynn adds the mother's grief Uncle Earl neglects to recount. The music of the all-female a capella group Sweet Honey in the Rock stands in for the wails of the enslaved women as the white auctioneer conducts Nathan's sale.

The whole of Nathan's story is important here, and only in the Mississippi Delta could Loretta earn the right to hear it in its entirety. The stories of families and slavery and its horrors, suggests Goble, cannot be passed down all willy-nilly; no, they have to be given up to those who are ready to receive them. Without an appreciation for slavery and all of its sociocultural and economic implications, black histories run the risk of being shunted to the side, as Peaches did in the pawnshop. When Loretta asks her mother why she withheld the "whole story of Nathan," Rosa Lynn replies, "When your father died, you were too young to really understand; later on I wasn't sure the time was ever right for you to appreciate it. I thought it best to keep him safely put away until things got better." This "safety" includes guardianship of the story and the object to which it is tied. There is, however, one other significant aspect of Rosa Lynn's story about Jesse and Nathan and the women who grieved Nathan's sale. At the end, Loretta wraps her fingers around Nathan's base, looks into her mother's eyes, and says, "I can appreciate that, momma." For all of its symbolism, however, neither Rosa Lynn nor Uncle Earl discloses the source of Nathan's name. In Chicago, Loretta pieces together parts of the story. She asks, "Was Jesse's father named Nathan?!!" Rosa Lynn answers, "Yes. And he was traded off . . . traded away for this silver candelabra." Now, Nathan can be taken from Chicago and returned to the Mississippi Delta.

Rosa Lynn Repatriates Nathan to the Mississippi Delta

Down in the Delta, Loretta finds her ancestral heritage and, more important, her own interior core. There, she and Thomas hear pieces of the story. In Chicago, Rosa Lynn completes the narrative. When Loretta returns to the Delta, Rosa Lynn accompanies her, with Nathan in tow. There, Uncle Earl bestows on Loretta the honor of guardianship of Nathan. He hands her the heirloom and says, "Well, I guess Nathan rightfully belongs to you, Loretta." Loretta places Nathan on the mantelpiece. Thomas asks, "Why do you call it Nathan anyway?" The mother begins to relate the story to her son, "Let me tell you a story about a family staying together. Remember when your Uncle Earl told you about your great-great-great granddaddy Jesse? Well, when Jesse was a boy—just a few years younger than you, his father . . ."

Rosa Lynn lands on a continuum of black women who have changed the course of history and saved their families from the "class and clatter of . . . American Conflict."[38] From generation to generation, the story of the black Sinclairs has been voiced from man to man; no doubt the "one mute and voiceless note" was the black female Sinclair. Rosa Lynn intervenes and performs an act of resistance: she supplements Nathan's story with a mother's grief and anguish over the auction of the patriarch and makes certain the Sinclair lineage does not pass over the females. My cousin, Martin, listened to my Aunt Georgia's recollections and watched her manage the majority of family matters. More meaningful, he described how the South restored him and gave him a sense of purpose; he told me Aunt Georgia's story. Rosa Lynn's dare ceded to her firstborn daughter her due right and privilege *only* after her baptism down in the Delta.

Notes

1. Martin Robinson, in conversation with the author, February 2017. (His name has been changed to protect privacy.)

2. Aunt Georgia managed all of the family's business because Uncle Elliott could not read.

3. Thadious Davis, *Southscapes: Geographies of Race, Region and Literature* (Chapel Hill: University of North Carolina Press, 2011), 80.

4. *Down in the Delta* premiered August 5, 1998, at the Urbanworld Film Festival in New York. It stars Al Freeman, Alfre Woodard, and Esther Rolle. The film would be Rolle's last appearance in film; she died on November 17, 1998. Unless otherwise noted, the film, not the screenplay, is the subject of this chapter.

5. Myron E. Goble, in conversation with the author, July 2017.

6. *Down in the Delta,* directed by Maya Angelou (1998; Amazon Prime Video, 2016).

7. Goble conversation.

8. Anna Julia Cooper, "Our Raison D'Être," in *The Voice of Anna Julia Cooper: Including a Voice from the South and Other Important Essays, Papers, and Letters,* ed. Charles Lemert and Esme Bhan (New York: Rowan & Littlefield, 1998), 51 (emphasis mine).

9. "The Untold Story: Slavery in the 20th Century," Vimeo video, 27:36, posted by Mephisto Productions, 27:36, Monday, February 8, 2010, accessed March 11, 2018, https://vimeo.com/9310529.

10. "JFK50: Robert Kennedy Continued JFK's Pledge to Serve—Marian Wright Edelman," YouTube video, 2:41, posted by Harvard Kennedy School, April 4, 2011, accessed November 2, 2016, https://www.youtube.com/watch?v=rE3m3Bdpbc8.

11. Robert F. Kennedy, "Remarks at the University of Kansas, March 18, 1968," Available online at the John F. Kennedy Presidential Library and Museum Web site, accessed November 3, 2016, https://www.jfklibrary.org/Research/Research-Aids/Ready-Reference/RFK-Speeches/Remarks-of-Robert-F-Kennedy-at-the-University-of-Kansas-March-18-1968.aspx

12. Myron E. Goble, *Down in the Delta: A Screenplay* (New York: Hyperion 1998), n.p.

13. Terrence Tucker, "Healing the (Re)Constructed Self: The South, Ancestors, and Maya Angelou's *Down in the Delta,*" *College Language Association* 58 (2014): 91 (emphasis mine).

14. Davis, *Southscapes,* 113, 115.

15. Ibid., 6.

16. Henry Louis Gates Jr., *America Behind the Color Line: Dialogues with African Americans,* (New York: Warner, 2004).

17. Ted Panken, "Cassandra Wilson: Country Strong: The Beloved Vocalist Steps Out of Her Comfort Zone," *Jazz Times,* October 8, 2012, http://jazztimes.com/articles/54766-cassandra-wilson-country-strong.

18. John Leland, "Going Home with Cassandra Wilson; Jazz Diva Follows Sound of Her Roots," *New York Times,* March 7, 2002, http://www.nytimes.com/2002/03/07/garden/going-home-with-cassandra-wilson-jazz-diva-follows-sound-of-her-roots.html.

19. Maya Angelou, "Why Blacks are Returning to Their Southern Roots," *Ebony,* April 1990, 48, 44.

20. Davis, *Southscapes,* 6.

21. "Down in the Delta: In Her Feature-Length Movie Debut as a Director, Maya Angelou Brings the Story of Human Truths to Life," *Ebony,* February 1999, 96.

22. Tucker, "Healing the (Re)Constructed Self," 91.

23. Stephen Holden, "The Healing Power of a Delta Family's Roots," *New York Times,* December 25, 1998, http://www.nytimes.com/1998/12/25/movies/film-review-the-healing-power-of-a-delta-family-s-roots.html.

24. Florence Anthony, "'Down in the Delta' Makes Impressive Debut; Iron Mike Explodes," *New York Amsterdam News,* December 17, 1998,16.

25. Jim Farber, "Down in the Delta," *Entertainment Weekly,* January 1, 1999, http://ew.com/article/1999/01/08/down-delta-4.

26. Tucker, "Healing the (Re)Constructed Self," 91.

27. Mrs. Charles S. Hawley, "Back to the Basics," *African Violets,* June 1981, available online at the African Violets Society of America Webs site, http://avsa.org/learn-violets101.

28. Alice Walker, *In Search of our Mother's Garden: Womanist Prose* (New York: Harcourt Brace, 1983), 239, 242.

29. Helena Znaniecki Lopata, "Self-Identity in Marriage and Widowhood," *Sociological Quarterly* 14, no. 4 (1973): 411.

30. Helena Znaniecki Lopata, *Current Widowhood: Myths and Realities* (Thousand Oaks, CA: SAGE, 1995), 134.

31. Lopata, "Self-Identity," 411.

32. Ann Goetting, "Patterns of Support among In-Laws in the United States," *Journal of Family Issues* 11 (March 1990): 80.

33. Lopata, *Current Widowhood,* 134.

34. Susan Payne Carter and Paige Marta Skiba, "Pawnshops, Behavioral Economics, and Self-Regulation," *Review of Banking and Financial Law* 32 (2012–13): 194.

35. Ibid., 194, 195.

36. Taylor Branch, *Parting the Waters: America in the King Years 1954–63* (New York: Simon & Schuster, 1988), 17–18.

37. "Malcolm X on Black Business," YouTube video, 0:54, posted by NuFroot, June 15, 2008, accessed November 16, 2016, https://www.youtube.com/watch?v=WrHub0ASEQs.

38. Cooper, "Our Raison D'Être," 51.

8

Hollywood's Southern Strategy

Portraying White Christianity in Late Twentieth-Century Civil Rights Melodramas

Megan Hunt

As consecutive Republican presidential candidates failed to secure more than 14 percent of the African American vote in the 1980s and early 1990s, concerns grew about a deepening racial divide and America's failure to live up to the promises of the 1960s. The perceived southernization of America through the culture wars of the late twentieth century encouraged many Americans to reconsider the legacy of the civil rights movement, an era that was being concurrently reshaped by Hollywood film. "The civil rights movement contained all the elements to inspire creative writers," Sharon Monteith writes: "courage in the face of violence, conflict in the face of social change, a moment in history when an old order fell." It also offered the obvious heroes and villains so crucial to Hollywood's often simplified narratives, as bitter white southerners, embarrassing a nation under Cold War scrutiny, brutalized peaceful black activists.[1]

Television and cinema audiences in the 1990s saw more depictions of the civil rights movement of the 1950s and 1960s than viewers in the 1960s, 1970s, and 1980s combined. "Constantly used as a reference point for judging the state of contemporary race relations and for defining what constituted racial progress," Jennifer Fuller writes, "civil rights drama became an arena to explore these issues and to articulate competing political ideologies."[2]

Focusing on the religious language and iconography evident in the civil rights genre, this chapter will analyze the films *A Time to Kill* (1996), *Ghosts of Mississippi* (1996), and the earlier but hugely controversial *Mississippi Burning* (1988), to demonstrate how, in the midst of the culture wars, late twentieth-century Hollywood fashioned a simplistic binary of good and evil by consistently conflating southern white religiosity with reactionary, even racist politics.[3] I shall argue that the perceived religious backwardness of many segregationists supports Hollywood's presentation of the South as an irrational region, where a zealous religiosity and rabid racism clouds all judgment.

In general terms, Hollywood flattens the diversity of white involvement in civil rights discourse. More specifically, it denies the complex and disparate nature of white evangelical responses to the African American struggle for equal rights, from those who were inspired to join the movement to those who expressed their commitment to segregation in a much more refined manner than through the Ku Klux Klan. By limiting its portrayal of white religious expression in this period to the margins of segregationist society, Hollywood not only denies white religious activism in the pursuit of civil rights but it also overlooks what historian Carolyn Dupont recognizes as "the racial hierarchy's powerful but often subtle articulation by more polished religious leaders and prominent laymen."[4]

The future of the South was a nationwide debate in the mid-twentieth century; transcending regional or religious divisions, it was discussed by Americans of all faiths, as well as secular citizens. Religious activism in the form of civil rights protest or massive resistance was neither limited nor marginal. However, as Kevin Schultz and Paul Harvey note, as a result of the sporadic inclusion of religion in American historiography, "religion has yet to become central to the way in which most historians of modern America (since 1865) tell their story—except in areas that are either racialized (the civil rights movement) or considered to be politically marginal (the New Right). . . . Religion, it seems, is acceptable for outsiders, not for 'us.'"[5]

This has ensured the memorialization of vindicated civil rights leaders as "prophets," leading America to a better tomorrow through the biblical concept of equality before God. However, many key figures of the religious right have been understood as demagogues, conflating politics with a self-serving understanding of biblical teachings in order to lead America in a very different direction from that which civil rights leaders and other cultural liberals proposed in the 1960s. Accepting historian Matthew J. Hall's understanding of evangelicalism as "a broad and unwieldy" canopy, this chapter provides evidence that white southern Protestant responses to the civil rights movement were often incongruent—a complexity that rarely figures in Hollywood's constructions of the era and its legacy.[6]

That the southern civil rights struggle should be a key focus for Hollywood's assault on reactionary America in the late twentieth century reflects the distinctly southern accent of much of the then contemporary revived right. At the dawn of the millennium, the United States' most populous region, the South, was home to three in every ten Americans. Sweeping gains there proved essential to the Republican Party's huge electoral success in the 1994 midterms, headed by Georgia congressman Newt Gingrich. As a result, all but one of the new congressional leaders appointed during the "Republican Revolution" of 1994 were Southern Baptists, including Strom Thurmond (South Carolina), Trent Lott (Mississippi), and Gingrich himself. By 1997, political scientist Oran P. Smith argued that "the Republican party and the Southern Baptist Convention (SBC) are not only in firm alliance, they are sometimes indistinguishable from each other."[7]

That Democratic president Bill Clinton was a Southern Baptist only seemed to rile his conservative opponents more. Religious historian Gary Scott Smith writes, "Southern Baptists designated the first forty days of 1994 as a special period to pray "diligently and consistently" for Clinton, guided by a booklet titled *Pray for the President,*" while delegates at the 1998 annual denominational convention urged Congress to overturn the president's executive order banning homophobic discrimination in the federal work force. An amendment calling on Clinton's home church in Little Rock, Arkansas, to discipline the president for his support of gay rights—one of eight fielded during his presidency—was only narrowly defeated.[8]

By 1979, fundamentalists effectively controlled the SBC, the nation's largest Protestant denomination, replacing a more liberal leadership that had shaped Clinton's views. The transition was solidified in 1988, when Richard Land overtook the liberal Foy Valentine as the leader of the SBC's influential policy arm, the Ethics and Religious Liberty Commission (ERLC). Land, who would later argue that Valentine's "liberal antinomianism" was at least "partially responsible for producing people with the tragically flawed moral compass of a Bill Clinton," closely aligned the denomination with conservative Republican policy. Polls conducted in 1986 showed that 55 percent of SBC leaders who self-identified as "fundamentalist" disagreed or were unsure that the civil rights movement had led the nation in the right direction, as opposed to just 10 percent of moderates. And yet, Southern Baptist opinion on these matters was not dramatically different from that of other southern white Protestants. As Mark Newman notes, "the majority of southern white Disciples of Christ, Episcopalians, Presbyterians, Southern Baptists and United Methodists believed that the federal government had no obligation to improve black living standards, and they also believed homeowners had the right to sell to whomever they chose, including the right to refuse African-American buyers."[9]

Such attitudes reflected a growing trend in the decades following the civil rights victories of the 1960s, as the defendants of what media scholar Kelly J. Madison calls "white identity, domination, and privilege" began to articulate their fears through "policy disagreements, concerns about 'reverse discrimination,' and assertions that racism is a thing of the past."[10] The conflation of many of these ideas with religious rhetoric is crucial to our popular understanding of the culture wars, and evangelicals such as the SBC figured conspicuously in the rise of the religious right in the 1980s, after prominent Baptist Jerry Falwell founded the Moral Majority in 1979.

Despite orchestrating the SBC's official apology for its role in slavery and Jim Crow in 1995, as well as other drives to establish more black churches within the denomination, Richard Land's leadership paradoxically endorsed what African American journalist Bill Maxwell called the Republicans' "cynical attack on affirmative action . . . the one federal program that modestly attempts to redress some of the wrongs of discrimination." Journalists and critics derided the denomination's incredibly delayed admission that slavery was wrong and that racial divides remained a barrier in religious worship and many other aspects of American life. "Forgive me for being underwhelmed by this astonishingly belated act of contrition," Jack E. White wrote in *Time* magazine, but "I would have been more impressed if the revelation had come a generation ago, when prominent Southern Baptists like George Wallace were standing in the schoolhouse door and never-miss-a-Sunday Ku Klux Klansmen were murdering fellow Christians who believed in civil rights."[11]

Those disappointed at the SBC's recommendation that the Supreme Court's 1954 *Brown v. Board of Education* desegregation decision was "in harmony with the constitutional guarantee of equal freedom to all citizens" wrote to their state SBC newspapers in their thousands, reflecting what Andrew Manis recognizes as a "significant schism between the views of the Southern Baptist laity and much of the ministerial leadership." By the early 1960s, several other mainline church groups had committed themselves to social action, including the National Council of Churches, the United Presbyterian Church, USA, and the United Church of Christ. And yet, as Ellen Rosenberg writes, the majority of white southern Christians "reacted to the whole trauma [of desegregation] by flights from city neighborhoods . . . establishing "Christian schools," deflecting to the Republican Party, and becoming deeply involved in a politico-religious amalgam called the New Right."[12]

For southern white Christians like activist Joan Browning, however, the journey from all-white to mixed congregations "seemed natural." For Browning, "the Freedom Movement was the all-inclusive true church, and the church was the logical center of the movement." Welcomed at Shiloh Baptist Church in Albany, Georgia, in December 1961 following her release from prison after participating in the Freedom Rides, Browning was brought up Methodist just one hundred miles away in rural Wheeler County. "Perfectly at home" at Shiloh, Browning was not alone; numerous whites were compelled to work for racial justice as a result of strong religious faith. In *Personal Politics,* historian Sara Evans argues that "virtually without exception white southern women who joined the civil rights movement came to it first through the church." Many were from strong religious backgrounds and extended their political and social consciousness on college campuses across the country.[13]

Reviewing white women's accounts of the civil rights movement, Wini Breines concluded in 2005 that "it is difficult to imagine that religion functioned in such a democratic political manner, encouraging so many young people, white and black, to become active in social change for racial justice."[14] Reflecting on the religious views of many activists through a twenty-first-century lens, Breines offers a restricted understanding of spirituality. She effectively argues that those religious white southerners who fought for racial justice are as much a product of their time as the racists they opposed—the supposedly timeless nature of their preoccupations frozen in a very specific historical moment, where the conflation of Christian dogma and social activism was apparently not as "odd" as it appears now. More contemporary white evangelicalism, Breines suggests, is associated with anything but tolerance and social activism. Despite electing its first African American president in 2012, the SBC remains 85 percent white.[15] The ERLC continues to focus almost exclusively on what Emma Green of the *Atlantic* calls "conservative social issues, rather than topics like poverty and mass incarceration, which have a significant impact on racial disparities in America." As a result of the changes of the 1960s and the subsequent culture wars, racial and cultural identity are such entrenched ideological battles that it often proves difficult for more contemporary critics and scholars to appreciate the religious preoccupations of those whites who in the 1950s and 1960s were compelled by their faith to join civil rights groups and demonstrations.[16]

Perhaps most significantly, it is hard to imagine Breines's comments about the implausibility of an intersecting social responsibility and religious faith being leveled at an account documenting the significance of Christianity to

African American activists. Certainly, black spirituality has proved to be a consistent and seemingly unproblematic trope within civil rights historiography and filmmaking.[17]

In *A Time to Kill,* passionate religiosity is reserved entirely for African Americans and white supremacists. Like his white hero counterparts in numerous other films, young Mississippi lawyer Jake Brigance (Matthew McConaughey) represents a progressive and national, rather than southern, white identity. Having "risen above" the deeply established confines of his southern homeland, Jake appears to have rejected his region's religiosity just as he has shunned its racism. Mainstream white Christianity only features in *A Time to Kill* when Jake's in-laws are in town: its singular appearance undoubtedly associated with older, more conservative generations. Jake's appearance in church therefore appears much more about maintaining pretense than spiritual involvement. Following the service, his in-laws express their concern that he has taken such a racially explosive case: defending Carl Lee Hailey (Samuel L. Jackson), an African American man who murdered the white men who raped his young daughter. The case is complicated, the specifics of the crime often secondary to the racial legacies at work in late twentieth-century Mississippi. Like most southern moderates, the film suggests, Jake's in-laws would prefer a quiet life.

Jake's wife Carla (Ashley Judd) is visibly shocked that her husband wants to talk to the press outside their church, telling him, "This isn't the time." Uttered in church and in the presence of her parents, Carla's comments provide an insight into her theological and political backgrounds, neither of which seem to compel social action. Like her parents, Carla appears concerned about how much they, a middle-class white family, have to lose from her husband's involvement in the trial. It is therefore symbolic that Carla retreats to her parents' home when Klan retaliation and subsequent marital strife further sour her interpretation of Jake's case.

Thus, it is somewhat ironic that Jake uses his presence at a mainstream southern white church to publically pledge himself to social justice and Carl Lee's case. The representative inertia of his congregation is made all the more apparent by the fact that the scene is bookended by two distinctly more zealous religious ceremonies. It is preceded by Freddie Lee Cobb's (Kiefer Sutherland) attempts to recruit his friends to the Klan so they might join "the war to protect our Christian homes and families" and "resurrect our country from the fires of racial degradation." Then, immediately following the scene in Jake's church, the film cuts to the service underway at Mount Zion CME and the rapturous response to the entrance of Hailey's family. Reflecting continuing de facto segregation of public worship in the 1990s, the juxtaposed scenes of Jake's and Carl Lee's churches also communicate a very different attitude toward the social purpose of religion. While Mount Zion is actively committed to supporting the community, the mainstream white church appears more as a place to "be seen," lest your neighbors (or in-laws) think less of you. Denied the protection of this white, middle-class Presbyterian existence, the poorer members of white society are, in Hollywood's logic, attracted to the more extreme white theology that manifests outside the mainstream church.[18]

Based on John Grisham's 1989 Mississippi courtroom thriller of the same name, *A Time to Kill* uses the religious rhetoric and iconography of the newly reformed Klan to tie the South's history of racial trauma to an easily recognized group, presenting a lineage of intolerance that is southern rather than American, poor rather than middle class, rural rather than urban, and—most importantly for this chapter—religious rather than secular. "The Klan's always been here," the Grand Wizard of Mississippi (Kurtwood Smith) advises Freddie Lee Cobb, "just waiting for the opportunity to deliver God's justice."

Just twelve days before the film's release on June 24, 1996, President Clinton spoke at the dedication of the newly rebuilt Mount Zion AME Church in Greeleyville, South Carolina, announcing a federal investigation into a spate of church arsons that brought back painful memories of the Jim Crow era.[19] By November 1996, two local Klan members admitted that they were responsible for the attack on Mount Zion—one of seventy-three African American churches torched across the South in just one year. Yet, when investigations confirmed that the majority were apparently random attacks, rather than the work of organized white supremacy groups, several journalists interpreted the lack of a coherent organizational conspiracy as evidence that the attacks were therefore not racially motivated. Several even argued that the mainstream media was overreacting to a series of information carefully drip-fed by leftist groups such as the Center for Democratic Renewal. The federal government remained committed to a more straightforward understanding. "The conspiracy," Vice President Al Gore concluded on June 19, "is racism itself."[20]

Several civil rights leaders argued that the fires were the product of the racial, religious, and political divisions of recent years, with C. T. Vivian acknowledging a specifically "crafted environment of bigotry and hatred," in which there was "a slippery slope between conservative religious persons and those who are really doing the burning." When Ralph Reed of the Christian

Coalition pledged to raise up to $1 million for the rebuilding of damaged churches, few civil rights leaders were convinced. Mary Frances Berry of the U.S. Commission on Civil Rights dismissed Reed's gesture: "You have the very people who created the context for the fires rushing over and saying 'Let us help put them out.'"[21]

Political rhetoric on both sides of the debate was testament to the fractured racial, religious, and political relationships of the culture wars at the time of *A Time to Kill*'s release. Conservative journalists began to use the words "deliberate hoax" and "sham" to describe a sense of panic that they argued had been carefully constructed by left-wing activists. Liberals like Democratic congressman John Conyers responded that key figures of the Religious Right had created an atmosphere of "blame and hate."[22]

In contrast to apparently arbitrary acts of contemporary racial terrorism, *A Time to Kill* provided a reassuring reminder of days when racial fanatics were readily identifiable by their white hoods and burning crosses. "It's no longer clear in white America who the good guys are," sociologist Bernard Beck argued in 1997, concluding that contemporary race relations made many white liberals "pessimistic [and] confused. They like to remember a time when things made sense, when we were the good guys."[23]

And yet, though *A Time to Kill*'s scenes of the Klan marching through the streets in broad daylight in their full regalia may seem somewhat anachronistic, they are true to Grisham's novel and more credible when one considers that the Klan did march in Greensboro, North Carolina, in 1987, garnering some national press coverage.[24] They had also opened fire on anti-Klan protesters in 1979, killing five in what became known as the Greensboro Massacre. Events in Greensboro reignited debates about the Klan's role in the South, discussions further stimulated by the subsequent spate of church burnings, and the numerous political escapades of David Duke, a former Grand Wizard who ran unsuccessfully for president in 1988, before securing a seat in the Louisiana State Senate.[25] There was also the highly publicized 1994 retrial of Byron De La Beckwith for the 1963 murder of the NAACP Mississippi field secretary, Medgar Evers.

In *Ghosts of Mississippi*, James Woods's Oscar-nominated portrayal of Beckwith proved "a reminder of the viciousness of a dark time in a dark place," according to the *New York Times*. A pantomime villain, were Beckwith a fictional character film critics could easily dismiss him as a frankly ridiculous archaism, spouting no limit of racial and religious hatred. And yet, Beckwith was real. He stood trial twice for Evers's murder but was never convicted, the result of two hung juries. Refusing to take the accusations against him seriously, Beckwith "appeared to enjoy himself immensely" during his original trials, resting his feet on chairs, offering cigars to the prosecutor and often wandering around the courtroom greeting friends, politicians, and sometimes even members of the jury.[26]

When the case reemerged in the late 1980s, the result of tireless efforts by Evers's widow, Myrlie, and the NAACP, National Public Radio reported that listening to the former Klansman "was like listening to someone who's been locked away in a time capsule for the last three decades. . . . You have to look long and hard to find Mississippians today who express agreement with Beckwith's racist rantings." Reflecting this and other coverage, Woods's performance in *Ghosts of Mississippi* is of an "unregenerate hater," who "won't talk to no Jew" and jokes about African American homes burning down. This was perhaps particularly provocative given the contemporary political debate over arson attacks.[27]

Beckwith's lawyers—apparently aware of their client's limited public appeal—kept Beckwith off the stands in 1994. Therefore, because he had no courtroom speech, *Ghosts of Mississippi* relies on reconstructions of interviews and statements Beckwith gave before and during the case to communicate his toxic racism and zealous Christianity to the audience. Woods perfected his performance watching videos of the white supremacist, including Beckwith's ninety-minute interview with Ed Bryson that aired on WLBT in Jackson in 1990.[28] Presented in the same style as the original television interview, these scenes require Woods to "smile the mocking smile of a man who has gotten away with murder," according to the script. They formed the basis of the teaser trailer that was shown in advance of the movie's release across the United States in late 1996. According to Mississippi writer Willie Morris, who served as a consultant on the film, the trailer caused a stir in many cinemas, as audiences shouted at the screen and in at least one recorded case pelted it with popcorn.[29]

Despite the film's actual focus on the man who eventually secures Beckwith's conviction, Assistant District Attorney Bobby DeLaughter (Alec Baldwin), this first trailer suggests that Beckwith is the movie's central character. The specific religious and racial nature of Beckwith's inflammatory rhetoric was clearly recognized as something that would incense but ultimately intrigue potential audiences, far more than DeLaughter's commitment to justice, or the courage of Medgar Evers and his bereaved family. Indeed, initial discussions between the film's producers show that they considered the Beckwith characterization crucial to the film's appeal and certainly its best chance at securing Oscar recognition. This was later vindicated, when the film received two Academy Award nominations: one for Woods as Best Supporting Actor and one for the makeup team that managed to transform him from an actor in his forties to the seventy-four-year-old Beckwith.[30]

Beckwith is never shown in private moments; the cinematic gaze directed toward him remains consistently public and judgmental. Continually implicating him as the horrible racist he undoubtedly was, Beckwith's outbursts also reflect a deep religious preoccupation. Yet, there is a clear assumption that audiences will recognize his religion as a rhetorical tool designed to obscure racial agendas, especially in the wake of inflamed racialized rhetoric. In this sense, the interviews repeat what media scholar Allison Graham recognizes as the "permissible (i.e., bankable) southern and racial imagery [that] has obsessed Madison Avenue" since the 1950s and 1960s. They reflect the centrality of media conventions to the civil rights melodrama, whereby authenticity is attempted through the adoption of rhetorical and visual reminders of the fact that for most Americans the movement unfolded as a media spectacle.[31]

Specifically noting Mississippi as "a poor depressing place," London-born Alan Parker was convinced that racial attitudes had yet to change in the Deep South and injected *Mississippi Burning* with several clips from "interviews" conducted with Jessup County residents, designed to give a broader sense of a fictional place that the *Washington Post* described as "an inbred bigoted community." Parker therefore attempted to justify his controversial fictionalization of the 1964 murder of civil rights workers James Chaney, Andrew Goodman, and Michael Schwerner near Philadelphia, Mississippi, by contending that the sheer scale of his movie's distribution would force people to think about racism in new ways. "There have been a lot of documentaries on the subject," Parker contended. "They run on PBS and nobody watches them. . . . I'm trying to reach an entire generation who knows nothing of that historical event, to cause them to react to it viscerally, emotionally, because of the racism that's around them now. And that's enough of a reason, a justification, for the fictionalizing."[32]

Parker had no doubts as to who the film's racial villains would be: "It was always the poor white who performed the violence," he claimed. "What I've tried to say in the film is that the roots of racism are economic." Though Parker makes no specific reference to religion, he could easily have replaced "violence" with "religion." The two are interwoven throughout his narrative, separating the good from the bad, at least among the white characters. Parker's thesis is explicit in the film when Agent Alan Ward (Willem Dafoe) asks his partner, Agent Rupert Anderson (Gene Hackman), "Where does it come from, all this hatred?" Anderson responds with a story about his father, who killed a mule belonging to a black neighbor out of jealousy. "The old man was so full of hate, he didn't know that being poor was what was killing him," Anderson concludes. Immediately after this exchange a brick flies through the window, alerting the agents to the burning cross outside their window and the legacy of the racial hatred and corrupted religion that marked the life of Anderson's father and continues to stifle southern progress.[33]

Like so many other popular accounts of the Klan, *Mississippi Burning* discredits what historian Kelly Baker recognizes as "the religious vision of the order," presenting it as little more than a "tiresome declaration of false religion." According to Baker, the "desire to set up boundaries between true and false religion does nothing to further the scholarly enterprise," marking the "religion of the hate movement as somehow not religion." Because this religion is considered unauthentic, it is not properly explored, thus its impact is lost. Most importantly, Baker argues that "presenting the religion of the Klan as false religion allows an assumption that religion is somehow not associated with movements and people who might be unsavory, disreputable, or dangerous. Religion is at best, ambiguous, which means that it can be associated with movements we label 'good' and 'bad.'"[34]

Baker's comments raise questions about the Klan's presentation in popular culture. If the religion of the group is depicted as illegitimate, as Baker suggests, what does it mean that this "false religion" is the dominant manifestation of white southern religion in Hollywood cinema? Does the continued association of white southern religion with the Klan, plus the subsequent delegitimizing of those religious concerns, have lasting impact on popular understandings of white religion in the region as false and self-serving? The films discussed here would suggest that it does, while the often juxtaposed positive portrayals of African American Christianity reflect a hierarchical understanding of religion within popular culture, whereby associated with one group religion becomes positive, and with another negative. As such, civil rights dramas relegate their villains to a subcultural status rather than attempting to communicate the religious practices and societal systems that fostered and supported their racial attitudes.

Beckwith's sense of Christianity as a vengeful faith committed to the protection of white supremacy forms *Ghosts of Mississippi*'s only presentation of religion, equating his archaic religiosity with the horrendous nature of his crime. His exceptional hatred and refusal to take his case seriously reflects the jarring presence within the "New South" that DeLaughter represents. "The growth I've had," the real DeLaughter once said, "is symbolic of the growth people of our age have had." According to Jerry Mitchell, screenwriter Lewis Colick and producer Fred Zollo were both committed to the idea "that DeLaughter was the story: a young prosecutor, son of Ole Miss, who overcame the objections of his own racist family to join forces with Medgar Evers's widow and win the longshot case to finally put Beckwith behind bars. "You're looking for things where you can get a movie star," Colick says. "This was a movie star role."[35]

Though director Rob Reiner acknowledged that the real DeLaughter was actually "a very principled, religious man," his film's constructed Beckwith/DeLaughter dichotomy would apparently have been compromised by an insight into the latter's religious and conservative preoccupations. A deacon at his Baptist church, DeLaughter later claimed that he found inspiration "from the depths of my conservatism" during the Beckwith case and firmly believed he was "under God's guidance." He later expressed regret that the movie depicted only Beckwith's religious motivations, and denied his own. Faced with the seriousness of his case, DeLaughter remembered that "there wasn't but one alternative but to say a lot of prayers. And probably if I had had the authority to say, 'I want one scene to convey one thing that did not make the final cut,' it would be a scene to illustrate that in some way."[36]

Frequently placed in the domain of the outcast, religion is never prominent in the lives of Hollywood's central white protagonists. White southerners who prove to be significant, progressive characters—like Bobby DeLaughter and Jake Brigance—often surpass the deeply established confines of regional identity, abandoning the white South's religiosity just as they have rejected its racism. In Hollywood's logic, enthusiastic religiosity shapes only African Americans and white supremacists.

A key scene in *Mississippi Burning* mirrors this understanding that only marginalized groups are preoccupied with religion, as an African American church service is juxtaposed against the increasing numbers of Klansmen gathering outside. As the congregation sings the hymn "When We All Get to Heaven," the tensions mount, and we see more men in white hoods forming their own counter-assembly. Soon, the animated chatter of the departing churchgoers descends into terrified screams on recognition of the waiting mob. Klan members begin to chase and beat congregation members. The same hymn can then be heard again, this time sung at a slower tempo by Lannie Spann McBride, who served as director Parker's gospel music consultant. Through McBride's reserved delivery, the song loses the triumphalism of its lyrics ("When we all get to heaven, what a day of rejoicing that will be! When we all see Jesus, we'll sing and shout the victory!"). The music has no inspirational or confrontational element; rather than encouraging resistance, the song acts as a salve, promoting dignity in the face of tragedy or potentially indicting religion's failure to deliver justice in the world. Nevertheless, the African American congregation's stoicism is cast in dramatic contrast with the zealous violence of its opponents. As one young black boy simply kneels in prayer, a Klansman kicks him in the face and threatens him with death.[37]

Pitting the film's only two presentations of religious involvement against each other, the scene illuminates Paul Harvey's contention that the southern civil rights movement reflected American Christianity "at its most tragic and its most triumphant." The scene undoubtedly reflects the very different ways these two groups of Mississippians have interpreted and enacted Christian teachings, but neither could be said to mirror dominant American culture. Mississippi was and remains a deeply religious state, and though historians' and activists' accounts have shown that mainstream denominations were often quietly complicit with segregation, they seldom supported Klan vigilantism. Instead of contrasting the Klan against a more liberal or even mainstream religious or political organization, *Mississippi Burning* pits it entirely against the secular, federal power of the FBI, ensuring that the film's heroes and villains are starkly projected, with little room for theological or political complexity. White churches and other institutions seem not to exist. Prominent businessmen and employees of the sheriff's office, the Klansmen of *Mississippi Burning* are hardly marginal figures. However, there appears no theological, social, or political alternative to the Klan in fictional Jessup County.[38]

Reverend Clay F. Lee, minister at First Methodist Church, Philadelphia, Mississippi, in 1964, recalled that religious worship was profoundly important to several of the FBI agents stationed in the town during the actual investigation into Chaney, Schwerner, and Goodman's disappearance. According to Lee, several of the agents attended local churches while stationed in Philadelphia and experienced varying degrees of hospitality. "One [agent] was from Cincinnati, he was a very faithful Presbyterian," Lee recalled. "He went to the Presbyterian prayer meeting, and he nearly gave them all a heart attack. It was really very funny. Another was a young Methodist man from Dallas. Another was a young single man from North Carolina, a member of the Church of Christ. The Presbyterian man went to the Presbyterian Church regularly on Sundays. The other two came to our church regularly on Sundays, and my wife and I befriended them just as human beings."[39]

It is almost impossible to imagine *Mississippi Burning* presenting this religious bond between agents and members of the local community. First, it would require recasting religion as an acceptable and commonplace aspect of national American life rather than a further indictment of southern exceptionalism. Second, few of Reverend Lee's congregation extended their pastor's welcome to the FBI agents. Florence Mars, an active member of Lee's church writes that no mainline church group expressed "even perfunctory sympathy for the missing young men or concern for their welfare." In her memoirs, Mars describes how her congregation had planned to raise money to rebuild the burned Mount Zion Methodist Church that Chaney, Goodman, and Schwerner had visited before their murder. However, fearful of Klan reprisals, First Methodist offered the money on the grounds that "the [new Mount Zion] building would never be used for anything other than church activities." Refusing to "relinquish control of the church in exchange for white support," the African American congregation of Mount Zion worked alone.[40]

Mars's account demonstrates the real level of Klan intimidation in the area and its determination to extinguish any hope of racial cooperation. And yet, when internal politics at First Methodist forced Mars to eventually resign from her teaching roles, she concluded that the reconciliatory wing of the congregation was more limited than she first suspected. She was, in the eyes of the congregation, "irrefutably connected with 'Communist civil rights agitation.'" "People were angered by the civil rights movement and afraid of being branded 'integrationists,'" Mars recalls. "There was a "prevailing attitude toward hoax and federal conspiracy" in the town, while groups such as Americans for the Preservation of the White Race circulated fliers urging citizens not to "cooperate in any way with any agents of the National Government."[41]

Yet, despite an obvious lack of support for integration in the local white community, *Mississippi Burning* fails to present these nonviolent strands of white resistance to civil rights activity, denying segregationist endeavors that fall short of the extreme violence of Klansmen. As R. Milton Winter has noted, few Mississippi church leaders advocated the rhetoric of the Ku Klux Klan or even Governor Ross Barnett. Yet, in his study of Mississippi Presbyterians, Winter writes that though the group tended to reject "violent and illegal opposition to civil rights," it also "condemned marches, protests, and other strident efforts to achieve integration."[42]

In a September 1964 *Christian Century* article, Baptist minister–turned–historian Richard Marius described Mississippi as both "embarrassing and enraging"; a simultaneously violent and devout place that forced him to "wonder how the church there can stand its own shame and cowardice." Carolyn Dupont writes that Marius's critique of the Magnolia State was somewhat "softened" by his conclusion that "the problems of the church in Mississippi are but warped and distorted reflections of the problems of the church in American society." Yet, it was unlikely that many of Marius's "left-leaning" readers welcomed this analysis, preferring, as Dupont recognizes, to "hone in on the apparently yawning chasm between conditions in Mississippi and those in the rest of the country, rather than to believe that America shared the South's racial dilemma."[43]

This commitment to southern racial exceptionalism endures throughout *Mississippi Burning*'s narrative, which sees the all-American righteousness of the FBI agents displace the Klan's southern bigotry, contributing to what David Jansson calls "a 'geography of racism.'" The film juxtaposes "the brutality of white Southerners with the morality of two FBI agents," Jansson writes, "reproduc[ing] an American national identity that stands for tolerance, justice and peace" and is very much at odds with the bureau's historical record under J. Edgar Hoover's leadership.[44]

Presenting the Klan as the natural manifestation of a pathologized town, *Mississippi Burning* does not attempt to explain the radicalization of these men. We do not see the initial development of a local Klan branch ("Klavern") or the recruitment of members. As such, the Klan of *Mississippi Burning* can simply be eradicated, the roots of the organization—religious, political, or otherwise—never truly explored.

Like other cinematic villains, Klan members take actions that "place them outside the pale of civilization," to use Christopher Ames's words, enabling "their pursuers" to stop them by any means necessary. In *A Time to Kill,* this logic justifies double murder, as Carl Lee guns down the men who abused his daughter. In *Mississippi Burning,* redemptive justice manifests through a black FBI agent, who threatens the local mayor with castration, despite that there were no black FBI agents in 1964. With this sudden and unrealistic shift in tactics, the FBI's actions become increasingly suspect: they are now "in the gutter" with the enemy, as the agents acknowledge. Yet, as Ames continues, crime films often grant heroes "the moral right to abandon the restrictions of law." Alan Parker admitted that the studio, Orion Pictures, wanted the film to be "a detective story that just *happened* to be set against the civil rights struggle." Thus, *Mississippi Burning* not only offers no judgment or punishment for the FBI's aggressive behavior but also actually engages in a Tarantino-esque redemptive fantasy.[45]

Rather than foreground black and white grassroots activists or the paid informants who really secured convictions in the case, *Mississippi Burning* "purposefully rewrites history" according to Monteith, centering its southern morality in Mrs. Pell (Frances McDormand), the deputy sheriff's wife. Downtrodden by the hypermasculine, segregationist mind-set that rules the town, Mrs. Pell recalls being taught the "segregation what's said in the Bible . . . Genesis 9, Verse 27." Eventually implicating her husband (Brad Dourif) in the murder of the missing activists, Mrs. Pell is unable to hate blacks as she has been taught to do. Her husband, a prominent Klansman, abuses her mentally and physically, treatment that provides yet another indictment of his already despicable character. Indeed, violent misogyny appears prominently in southern civil rights dramas, from *To Kill a Mockingbird*'s (1962) underlying insinuation that racist villain Bob Ewell (James Anderson) violently rapes and beats his daughter Mayella (Collin Wilcox), to the violence inflicted upon Tonya Hailey (Rae'Ven Larrymore Kelly) in *A Time to Kill*'s opening scenes, and law student Ellen Roark's (Sandra Bullock) later kidnapping and abuse at the hands of the newly reformed Klan. In all of these films, violence against women and girls—often specifically sexual violence—contributes to a wider characterization of mindless depravity that is deeply gendered.[46]

Though David O. Selznick may have removed all *Gone with the Wind*'s (1939) direct references to the Klan when adapting Margaret Mitchell's novel in what he called the "fascist-ridden 1930s," the organization has become an essential signifier of southern white intransigence in more recent film, regardless of whether the period reflected in the movie actually saw large-scale Klan activity. "Initiated into violence," Nancy Bishop Dessommes argues, more contemporary audiences have come to expect Klan extremism in presentations of a racially volatile South. Almost entirely "sinister" (as in *Mississippi Burning*), or "ludicrous" (as in *O Brother, Where Art Thou?* [2000] and Quentin Tarantino's *Django Unchained* [2012], despite the latter being set roughly a decade before the organization's first incarnation), Hollywood's presentation of the KKK traces what film scholar Melvyn Stokes calls "the growing disapproval of the Klan" through the twentieth and twenty-first centuries. Other than a couple of exceptions in the 1950s, "most films about the Klan were looking back on the Klan from a post-Klan era," imposing contemporary judgment that can often undermine the organization's historical threat and influence. "More concerned with evoking an acceptable audience response than with adhering to historical accuracy," Dessommes continues, most filmmakers opt for a timeless rendition of the Klan as little more than a band of ignorant bigots.[47]

Many scholars have argued that dismissing segregationists as toxic white trash enables filmmakers to offer a clear culprit for the South's—and therefore the nation's—legacy of racial intolerance and violence. Such displacement denies the structures that have continually enabled America's mistreatment of minorities, reinforcing misconceptions that segregation and racism are simply southern, largely lower-class, male phenomena. Yet, while numerous scholars and critics have dissected Hollywood's presentation of white heroes and subjugated, silent blacks, there have been considerably fewer examinations of its other reoccurring civil rights character: the segregationist villain. *Mississippi Burning, Ghosts of Mississippi,* and *A Time to Kill* do not, as most critics suggest, simply celebrate whiteness at the expense of black activism; rather they create divisions within whiteness along regional, class, and religious boundaries, projecting the idea that dominant, secular, consensus liberalism is stronger and more resilient than the values of an anomalous, racist region. Presenting only the Klan as the gatekeepers of segregation, many Hollywood films project white supremacy as a dubiously religious, yet simultaneously class- and gender-based identity. This denies not only widespread white concern about the implications of integration but also the considerable range of white Protestant involvement in the civil rights movement.[48]

On the whole, mainstream white churches rejected violence and illegal activity in defense of segregation, just as many opposed the protests that aimed to ensure integration. Yet, as white redemption narratives, few civil rights films contain any reference to white mainstream Christianity, as religious preoccupations would presumably complicate the hero's claims to secular righteousness. Intersecting extreme racial views with vengeful religious preoccupations, each of the films explored in this essay contributes to Hollywood's consistently negative portrayal of white southern religion.

In direct contrast to this trend, the recent release *Selma* (2014) offers an unparalleled presentation of white religious involvement in the civil rights movement, through its depiction of the 1965 voting rights campaign in Alabama. Perhaps the exception that proves the rule, *Selma*'s departure from the patterns of bias and misrepresentation so prominent in earlier films makes their shortcomings all the clearer. The film captures the tensions at the heart of the civil rights movement, humanizing many of its key players in a manner previously unseen in a Hollywood civil rights picture.[49]

While debates continue to rage about diversity in mainstream cinema, studios and distributors do appear to be finally awakening to the power and marketability of black stories. *Selma* would not have been made in the 1990s, despite the plethora of civil rights films released in that decade, and Ava DuVernay is testament to a new generation of African American filmmakers. However, hugely popular films with predominantly minority casts are still reported as "surprise hits," despite increasing evidence that African Americans and Hispanics buy more movie tickets than their white counterparts. They are also subject to gentrification, the idea of "the black film," despite dramatically different stories, characters, and timeframes.[50]

Selma may not always be entirely accurate in its presentation of chronological history, but it refuses to marginalize African American activists in order to foreground a white story. Most importantly for this chapter, *Selma* has encouraged critics, scholars, and religious groups to notice and discuss religion's place in the civil rights drama. "Never in the history of the United States has organized religion collaborated to such an extent on an issue of social justice," Warren Hinckle and David Welsh wrote of the Selma voting rights campaign in 1965.[51] In its presentation of these events, *Selma* provoked difficult conversations for white evangelicals, forcing them to acknowledge the conspicuous absence of their denominational forbearers in this most ecumenical of gatherings. Others discussed the film's use of spiritual music or its limited presentation of Jews.[52]

These conversations reflect the fact that *Selma* acknowledges the deep spirituality that moved figures such as King and his African American followers, without simply denying any white religious consciousness outside of the Ku Klux Klan. Thus, *Selma* manages two things that no other film discussed in this chapter can claim: it undoubtedly centralizes the role of blacks in the voting rights campaign—and rightly so—but also presents a broad coalition of races and religions coming together in pursuit of greater American freedom.

Notes

1. Consecutive exit surveys by CBS News and the *New York Times* are stored by the Roper Center Public Opinion Archives Web site at Cornell University, accessed February 23, 2016, http://ropercenter.cornell.edu/polls/us-elections/how-groups-voted/; Sharon

Monteith, "Civil Rights Movement Film," in *The Cambridge Companion to American Civil Rights Literature*, ed. Julie Buckner Armstrong (New York: Cambridge University Press, 2015), 123.

2. Jennifer Fuller, "Debating the Present through the Past: Representations of the Civil Rights Movement in the 1990s," in *The Civil Rights Movement in American Memory*, ed. Renee C. Romano and Leigh Raiford (Athens: University of Georgia Press, 2006), 167.

3. *A Time to Kill*, directed by Joel Schumacher (1996; Burbank, CA: Warner Home Video, 1998), DVD; *Ghosts of Mississippi*, directed by Rob Reiner (1996; Atlanta, GA: Turner Home Entertainment, 2010), DVD; *Mississippi Burning*, directed by Alan Parker (1989; Los Angeles, California: 20th Century Fox Home Entertainment, 2001), DVD.

4. Carolyn Renee Dupont, *Mississippi Praying: Southern White Evangelicals and the Civil Rights Movement, 1945–1975* (New York: New York University Press, 2013), 6.

5. Kevin M. Schultz and Paul Harvey, "Everywhere and Nowhere: Recent Trends in American Religious History and Historiography," *Journal of the American Academy of Religion* 78 (March 2010): 129, 135.

6. Matthew J. Hall, quoted in Justin Taylor, "Jim Crow, Civil Rights, and Southern White Evangelicals: A Historian's Forum," *Gospel Coalition*, February 5, 2015, http://www.thegospelcoalition.org/blogs/justintaylor/2015/02/05/jim-crow-civil-rights-and-southern-white-evangelicals-a-historians-forum-matthew-j-hall/.

7. Frank Hobbs and Nicole Stoops, "Demographic Trends in the 20th Century," *Census 2000 Special Reports*, November 2002, https://www.census.gov/prod/2002pubs/censr-4.pdf, 18–19; Oran P. Smith, *The Rise of Baptist Republicanism* (New York: New York University Press, 1997), 2. With the exception of Tom Daschle and Richard Armey, Smith continued, "our nation's leaders are entirely Southern Baptist. . . . This is particularly noteworthy considering few Southern Baptists have ever held any of these positions at any other point in our nation's history, much less simultaneously."

8. Gary Scott Smith, *Religion in the Oval Office: The Religious Lives of American Presidents* (New York: Oxford University Press, 2015), 340; Richard Vara, "Southern Baptists Set Sights on Clinton," *Sun-Sentinel* (South Florida), June 12, 1998, http://articles.sun-sentinel.com/1998-06-12/news/9806110511_1_southern-baptists-clinton-s-home-church-combat.

9. Richard Land, quoted in Tom Strode, "Newsweek Article: Baptist Moderates Laid Groundwork for Clinton morality," *Baptist Press*, October 30, 1998, http://www.bpnews.net/2780/newsweek-article-baptist-moderates-laid-groundwork-for-clinton-morality; Nancy Tatom Ammerman, *Baptist Battles: Social Change and Religious Conflict in the Southern Baptist Convention* (New Brunswick, NJ: Rutgers University Press, 1995), 103; Mark Newman, *Getting Right with God: Southern Baptists and Desegregation, 1945–1995* (Tuscaloosa: University of Alabama Press, 2001), 202.

10. Kelly J. Madison, "Legitimation Crisis and Containment: The 'Anti-Racist-White-Hero' Film," *Critical Studies in Mass Communication* 16, no. 4 (1999): 404. For detailed examinations of the coded political rhetoric that replaced overt white supremacy, see Michael Omi and Howard Winant, *Racial Formation in the United States: From the 1960s to the 1990s* (London: Routledge, 1996); George Lipsitz, *The Possessive Investment in White-*

ness: How White People Benefit from Identity Politics (Philadelphia: Temple University Press, 1998).

11. "Resolution on Racial Reconciliation on the 150th Anniversary of The Southern Baptist Convention, Atlanta, Georgia, 1995," Southern Baptist Convention Web site, accessed September 23, 2016, http://www.sbc.net/resolutions/899/resolution-on-racial-reconciliation-on-the-150th-anniversary-of-the-southern-baptist-convention; Bill Maxwell, "A Moral Duty to Correct Old Wrongs," *Florence (AL) Times Daily*, June 28, 1995, 7B; Jack E. White, "Forgive Us Our Sins," *Time*, July 3, 1995, 29.

12. *Annual of the Southern Baptist Convention, June 2–5 1954*, St Louis, Missouri, 56, available online at the Southern Baptist Historical Library and Archives, accessed October 3, 2016, http://media2.sbhla.org.s3.amazonaws.com/annuals/SBC_Annual_1954.pdf; Andrew M. Manis, *Southern Civil Religions in Conflict: Civil Rights and the Culture Wars* (Macon, GA: Mercer University Press, 2002), 108; James Findlay, *Church People in the Struggle: The National Council of Churches and the Black Freedom Movement, 1950–1970* (New York: Oxford University Press, 1997), 3; Ellen M. Rosenberg, "The Southern Baptist Response to the Newest South," in *Southern Baptists Observed: Multiple Perspectives on a Changing Denomination*, ed. Nancy Tatom Ammerman (Knoxville: University of Tennessee Press, 1993), 149.

13. Joan C. Browning, "Shiloh Witness," in *Deep in Our Hearts: Nine White Women in the Freedom Movement*, ed. Constance Curry, Dorothy Dawson Burlage, and Joan C. Browning (Athens: University of Georgia Press, 2002), 39–41; Sara Evans, *Personal Politics: The Roots of Women's Liberation in the Civil Rights Movement and the New Left* (New York: Knopf, 1979), 35.

14. Wini Breines, review of Debra L. Schultz, *Going South: Jewish Women in the Civil Rights Movement* (New York University Press, 2001) and Constance Curry, Dorothy Dawson Burlage, and Joan C. Browning, eds., *Deep in Our Hearts: Nine White Women in the Freedom Movement* (Athens: University of Georgia Press, 2002), in *Signs* 30 (Winter 2005): 1673.

15. Racial and Ethnic composition among Members of the Southern Baptist Convention, Demographic Information, Religious Landscape Study, Pew Research Center, 2014, accessed November 11, 2016, http://www.pewforum.org/religious-landscape-study/religious-denomination/southern-baptist-convention/#demographic-information.

16. Breines, review of Schultz, *Going South* and Curry, Burlage, and Browning, *Deep in Our Hearts*, 1673; Racial and Ethnic Composition among Members of the Southern Baptist Convention; Emma Green, "Southern Baptists and the Sin of Racism," *Atlantic*, April 7, 2015, http://www.theatlantic.com/politics/archive/2015/04/southern-baptists-wrestle-with-the-sin-of-racism/389808/. ERLC president Richard Land stepped down in 2013 after accusing President Obama and civil rights leaders such as Al Sharpton and Jesse Jackson of using the Trayvon Martin case to widen racial divides and "gin up the black vote" during the 2012 presidential election. See Lillian Kwon, "So. Baptist Leader Richard Land Reprimanded over Trayvon Martin Comments," *Christian Post*, June 1, 2012, http://www.christianpost.com/news/so-baptist-richard-land-reprimanded-over-trayvon-martin-comments-75927/#yrrXYPU100DoqPLT.99.

17. Of all the films discussed in this chapter, only *A Time to Kill* features a mainstream white church (briefly) in its narrative, while only *Ghosts of Mississippi* fails to portray a black church. *Mississippi Burning* is more representative of the civil rights genre in its depiction of solely African American church worship, a trope that has been repeated in other successful films, including *The Long Walk Home*, directed by Richard Pearce (1990; Santa Monica, CA: Lionsgate Home Entertainment, 2013), DVD and *The Help*, directed by Tate Taylor (2011; Burbank, CA: Walt Disney Studios Home Entertainment, 2011) DVD. As white redemption narratives, none of these films contain any reference to mainstream white Christianity, suggesting that religious preoccupations might complicate the protagonist's claims to liberal righteousness.

18. Though the film does not specify the denomination of Jake's church, Grisham's novel explains that Jake, originally a Methodist, and Carla, who was brought up Baptist, elected to join their town's Presbyterian congregation once they were married. While "the Baptists had more members and more money," Grisham writes, "the Presbyterians and Methodists adjourned earlier on a Sunday and outraced the Baptists to the restaurants for Sunday dinner." Thus, Jake and Carla's spiritual realignment does not appear to have been too taxing and probably reflects their now-elevated social status in the community. On Sundays, Grisham describes, Jake and Carla "sat in their usual pew, with [their daughter] Hanna asleep between them, and ignored the sermon." Jake focuses instead on his legal cases, while Carla is "mentally redecorating the dining room." John Grisham, *A Time to Kill* (1989; repr., London: Cornerstone Digital, 2010), 11

19. Both houses of congress passed the Church Arson Prevention Act of 1996 on July 3, 1996. The law increased the maximum penalty for arson and provided funds for rebuilding targeted churches. Mount Zion would burn again in June 2015, almost twenty years to the day. Though initial reports indicated that the fire had been caused by an electrical storm, tensions were already high, following the racially motivated murder of the Reverend Clementa Pinckney and eight parishioners at Mother Emanuel A.M.E. church in Charleston just days before.

20. Eric Harrison, "A Clan and the Klan in S. Carolina," *Los Angeles Times,* November 30, 1996: http://articles.latimes.com/print/1996-11-30/news/mn-4270_1_klan-members; Fred Bayles, "Burning Churches," *Free-Lance Star* (Fredericksburg, VA), July 5, 1996, A4; Jim Campbell, "America's Long History of Black Churches Burning," *Los Angeles Times,* June 16, 1996: http://articles.latimes.com/1996-06-16/opinion/op-15599_1_separate-black-churches; Michael Fumento, "Politics and Church Burnings," *Commentary,* October 1, 1996, 57–59; Vice President Al Gore, Press Briefing, White House, Washington, DC, June 19, 1996, available at Clinton Presidential Materials Project, National Archives, https://clinton6.nara.gov/1996/06/1996-06-19-vp-gore-and-others-briefing-on-governors-meeting.html.

21. Reverend C. T. Vivian, and Mary Frances Berry, quoted in Fumento, "Politics and Church Burnings," 58.

22. Ibid.; quoted in Bob Herbert, "In America; A Church Destroyed by Hate," *New York Times,* May 24, 1996, http://www.nytimes.com/1996/05/24/opinion/in-america-a-church-destroyed-by-hate.html.

23. Bernard Beck quoted in Teresa Wiltz, "Whose History?" *Chicago Tribune*, January 13, 1997, http://articles.chicagotribune.com/1997-01-13/features/9701130093_1_medgar-evers-beckwith-myrlie-evers.

24. Perhaps reflecting the largely negative public opinion of the Klan in the 1980s, most coverage of the rally focuses on the preempted anti-Klan demonstrations. See "600 March in North Carolina to Protest Klan's Rally Today," *Los Angeles Times*, June 7, 1987, http://articles.latimes.com/1987-06-07/news/mn-1091_1_klan-s-rally-today; William E. Schmidt, "Klan's Carolina March Kindling Fear and Unity," *New York Times*, June 5, 1987, http://www.nytimes.com/1987/06/05/us/klan-s-carolina-march-kindling-fear-and-unity.html.

25. Duke's first unsuccessful run for the Louisiana Senate was in 1975. He ran again in 1979 and was elected in 1989. In 1988, after he lost the Democratic presidential primary, he ran instead for the right-wing Populist party.

26. Walter Goodman, "Medgar Evers and His Tragic End, with Re-enactments," *New York Times*, July 11, 1994, http://www.nytimes.com/1994/07/11/movies/television-review-medgar-evers-and-his-tragic-end-with-re-enactments.html; Jack Mendelsohn, *The Martyrs: Sixteen Who Gave Their Lives for Racial Justice* (New York: Harper & Row, 1966), 83–84.

27. Quoted in Renee C. Romano, *Racial Reckoning: Prosecuting America's Civil Rights Murders* (Cambridge, MA: Harvard University Press, 2014), 132; Amy Dawes, "Making Film Emotional Trip for Rob Reiner," *Sun Sentinel* (South Florida), January 3, 1997, http://articles.sun-sentinel.com/1997-01-03/entertainment/9612310140_1_evers-killer-medgar-evers-myrlie-evers-williams/2.

28. A transcript of the original interview shows that Beckwith's religious preoccupations were indeed central to his worldview. Committed to an idea of "Dixie" as "a white Christian republic," Beckwith denied his role in Evers's murder but admitted, as an Episcopalian, "I was trained from my youth to make war for the enemies of this white Christian republic." Interview with Byron De La Beckwith, April 30, 1990, box 4, folders 27, 40, 18, Bobby DeLaughter Papers, Mississippi Department of Archives and History, Jackson.

29. See Willie Morris, *Ghosts of Medgar Evers: A Tale of Race, Murder, Mississippi, and Hollywood* (New York: Random House, 1998), 144.

30. Ibid., 87. Morris later describes the intricacies of Woods' transformation: "Everything was rubber except his nose, eyeballs, and eyelids. . . . A crew member was assigned to hold an umbrella over him so he would not melt "in the Mississippi sun" (155).

31. Allison Graham, *Framing the South: Hollywood, Television, and Race during the Civil Rights Struggle* (Baltimore: Johns Hopkins University Press, 2003), 5. See also Allison Graham, "'We Ain't Doin' Civil Rights': The Life and Times of a Genre, as Told in *The Help*," *Southern Cultures* 20 (Spring 2014): 51–64.

32. Deson Howe, "Mississippi Burning—at High Noon," *Washington Post*, December 9, 1988, WE51; Parker, quoted in Jack Kroll, "Rerunning the Racial Gauntlet," *Newsweek*, June 6, 1988, 68; Patrick Goldstein, "It's Only a Movie . . ." *Empire*, June 1989, http://www.empireonline.com/features/empire-mississippi-burning. Though *Mississippi Burning* never specifies the town in which it is set, Philadelphia is the seat of Neshoba County

(renamed Jessup County in the film). Chaney, Goodman, and Schwerner were held at the county jail in Philadelphia for an alleged speeding offence before being released, chased, and eventually murdered on the road toward Meridian. For Parker's comments, see Wayne King, "Fact vs. Fiction in Mississippi," *New York Times,* December 4, 1988, http://www.nytimes.com/movie/review?res=940DE2DA1F30F937A35751C1A96E948260.

33. Alan Parker, quoted in Kroll, "Rerunning the Racial Gauntlet," 68.

34. Kelly Baker, *Gospel According to the Klan: The KKK's Appeal to Protestant America, 1915–1930* (Lawrence: University Press of Kansas, 2011), 17–18.

35. Bobby DeLaughter and Lewis Colick, quoted in Morris, *Ghosts of Medgar Evers,* 68, 131.

36. Rob Reiner, quoted in Dawes, "Making Film Emotional Trip"; Bobby DeLaughter, quoted in Morris, *Ghosts of Medgar Evers,* 68; Peter T. Chattaway, "Setting the Record Straight," *Ubyssey,* January 10, 1997, 4, available online at http://www.library.ubc.ca/archives/pdfs/ubyssey/UBYSSEY_1997_01_10.pdf. DeLaughter mentions his role as a deacon in his book *Never Too Late: A Prosecutor's Story of Justice in the Medgar Evers Case* (New York: Lisa Drew, 2001), 103.

37. See Internet Movie Database, *Mississippi Burning,* Full Cast and Crew, accessed November 12, 2016, http://www.imdb.com/title/tt0095647/fullcredits?ref_=tt_cl_sm#cast.

38. Paul Harvey, *Freedom's Coming: Religious Culture and the Shaping of the South from the Civil War through the Civil Rights Era* (Chapel Hill: University of North Carolina Press, 2005), 4.

39. Oral History with Reverend Clay F. Lee, interviewed by Orley B. Caudill, July 1980, Mississippi Oral History Program, University of Southern Mississippi, 17–18, http://digilib.usm.edu/cdm/compoundobject/collection/coh/id/4521.

40. Florence Mars, with the assistance of Lynne Eden, *Witness in Philadelphia* (Baton Rouge: Louisiana State University Press, 1989), 88, 180. See also Lee Oral History: "Two of the men were associated with lumber companies, high up in the lumber companies, family type things. And, really, the success of the whole thing of rebuilding that church depended upon those two men. And before night came [following a visit to the site of the burned church], both of them had been called and told that their mills would be burned down" (23).

41. Mars, *Witness in Philadelphia,* xv, 90.

42. R. Milton Winter, "Division and Reunion in the Presbyterian Church, U.S.: A Mississippi Retrospective, "*Journal of Presbyterian History* 78 (Spring 2000): 70–71.

43. Richard C. Marius, "Ruleville, Reminiscence, Reflection," *Christian Century,* January 23, 1964, reprinted in *Wrestling with God: The Mediations of Richard Marius,* ed. Nancy Grisham Anderson (Knoxville: University of Tennessee Press, 2006), appendix; Dupont, *Mississippi Praying,* 182.

44. David R. Jansson, "'A Geography of Racism': Internal Orientalism and the Construction of American National Identity in the Film *Mississippi Burning,*" *National Identities* 7 (September 2005): 265.

45. Christopher Ames, "Restoring the Black Man's Lethal Weapon: Race and Sexuality in Contemporary Cop Films," *Journal of Popular Film and Television* 20, no. 3

(1992): 52; James D. Williams, "Mississippi Burning Offers Distorted View of History," *Crisis* 96 (April 1989): 27. Anderson's days as a sheriff in his home state ensure that he can understand the local mentality better than his superior, Ward. Unthreatened by the Klan, Anderson ridicules them from the beginning of the movie with his comic rendition of an old rallying song and concludes that the organization was "better with lynchings than with lyrics." For Parker's comments, see "A Conviction in Mississippi, *Times,* June 2005, available online at Alan Parker's Web site, at http://alanparker.com/essay/a-conviction-in-mississippi/ (emphasis Parker's).

46. Sharon Monteith, "The Movie-Made Movement: Civil Rites of Passage," in *Memory and Popular Film,* ed. Paul Grainge (Manchester, UK: Manchester University Press, 2003), 130. *To Kill a Mockingbird,* directed by Robert Mulligan (1962; Universal City, CA: Universal Home Entertainment, 2006), DVD. In the real murder case, crucial evidence was secured from a man the FBI alluded to simply as "Mr X," who was reportedly paid $30,000 for his information. See Jerry Mitchell, "New Details on the FBI paying $30K to solve the *Mississippi Burning* Case," *Jackson Clarion Ledger,* February 15, 2010: http://blogs.clarionledger.com/jmitchell/2010/02/15/did-the-fbi-pay-30k-to-locate-the-bodies-of-the-three-missing-civil-rights-workers/?nclick_check=1. Delmar Dennis, a Methodist minister and Klan chaplain turned FBI informant, testified during the 1967 court proceedings that *Mississippi Burning* avoids altogether. For an account of Dennis's activities during this time see Maryanne Vollers, *Ghosts of Mississippi: The Murder of Medgar Evers, the Trials of Byron De La Beckwith, and the Haunting of the New South* (Boston: Back Bay Books, 1995), 221–22, 227–28. Dennis does appear in *Ghosts of Mississippi,* played by Jim Harley. Having heard Byron De La Beckwith boast in 1965 about murdering NAACP field secretary Medgar Evers two years earlier, Dennis proves vital to Bobby DeLaughter's efforts to finally convict Beckwith, in the 1990s. Jack Ables, the friend who alerted DeLaughter to Dennis's existence, was defending Orion Pictures in a defamation suit brought by members of the Philadelphia, Mississippi, police force following their depiction in *Mississippi Burning.* See DeLaughter, *Never Too Late,* 99.

47. David O. Selznick, quoted in Jenny Woodley, *Art for Equality: The NAACP's Cultural Campaign for Civil Rights* (Lexington: University Press of Kentucky, 2014), 133; Nancy Bishop Dessommes, "Hollywood in Hoods: The Portrayal of the Ku Klux Klan in Popular Film," *Journal of Popular Culture* 32 (Spring 1999): 18; *O Brother, Where Art Thou?* directed by Joel and Ethan Coen (2000; Universal City, CA: Universal Home Entertainment, 2013), DVD; Django Unchained, directed by Quentin Tarantino (2013; Culver City, CA: Sony Pictures Home Entertainment, 2013), DVD; Melvyn Stokes, *American History through Film: From the Revolution to the 1960s* (London: A & C Black, 2013), 120.

48. For the dominant reading of *Mississippi Burning*—white FBI agents responsible for civil rights victories, African Americans as powerless victims—see Henry Bourgeois, "Hollywood and the Civil Rights Movement: The Case of *Mississippi Burning,*" *Howard Journal of Communications* 4, nos. 1–2 (1992): 157–63; and Robert Brent Toplin, *History by Hollywood: The Use and Abuse of the American Past* (Champaign: University of Illinois Press, 1996), 25–44.

49. *Selma*, directed by Ava DuVernay (2014; Los Angeles, CA: 20th Century Fox Home Entertainment, 2015), DVD.

50. In 2015 and 2016, all actors nominated in each of the four Academy Award acting categories were white, sparking a significant social media backlash against perceived racial bias in Hollywood. In 2014, minorities bought 46 percent of movie tickets sold in the United States, despite being just 37 percent of the population. See Motion Picture Association of American (MPAA), "Theatrical Market Statistics 2014," Motion Picture Association of America Web site, http://www.mpaa.org/wp-content/uploads/2015/03/MPAA-Theatrical-Market-Statistics-2014.pdf; Drew Harwell, "Diverse Movies Are a Huge Business. Why Doesn't Hollywood Make More?" *Washington Post*, December 15, 2015, https://www.washingtonpost.com/business/economy/diverse-movies-are-a-huge-business-why-doesnt-hollywood-make-more/2015/12/15/ec002564-9774-11e5-b499-76cbec161973_story.html; Jason Bailey, "'Straight Outta Compton' Is Only a 'Surprise Hit' If You Aren't Paying Attention," *Flavorwire*, August 18, 2015, http://flavorwire.com/533555/straight-outta-compton-is-only-a-surprise-hit-if-you-arent-paying-attention?utm_source=twitter&utm_medium=socialflow&utm_campaign=FlavorwireSocial.

51. Warren Hinckle and David Welsh, "The Five Battles of Selma: 3, Charge of the Bible Brigade," *Ramparts Magazine*, June 1965, 36.

52. Peter Dreier, "Selma's Missing Rabbi," *Huffington Post*, January 17, 2015, http://www.huffingtonpost.com/peter-dreier/selmas-missing-rabbi_b_6491368.html; Susannah Heschel, "What Selma Meant to Jews Like My Father," *Forward*, January 18, 2015, http://forward.com/opinion/212971/what-selma-meant-to-jews-like-my-father/; Taylor, "Jim Crow, Civil Rights, and Southern White Evangelicals"; Morgan Rhodes, interviewed by Alex Cohen and Jacob Margolis, "The Music of 'Selma': Scoring the Civil Rights Movement," *Take Two*, January 9, 2015, http://www.scpr.org/programs/take-two/2015/01/09/41040/the-music-of-selma-scoring-the-civil-rights-moveme/. See also Megan Hunt, "'Men and Women of God and Goodwill Everywhere': *Selma* and the Role of Religion in Civil Rights Drama," in *The Shadow of Selma*, ed. Joe Street and Henry Knight-Lozano (Gainesville: University Press of Florida, 2018), 196–216.

9

Lesbian Invisibility Continued

The "Straight-Washing" of Southern Women in *The Color Purple* and *Fried Green Tomatoes*

Gene Kelly

bell hooks argues that film study helps us to consider major questions regarding diverse lives and experiences, mainly due to film's availability and how it can subversively influence us. We are rarely "resistant spectators," as hooks says—we willingly enter theaters to be entertained and, at the same time, sometimes have our ideas challenged by the experiences on the screen.[1] *The Color Purple* and *Fried Green Tomatoes* were natural selections for this volume; both films depict life in southern states during the 1920s and '30s and situate women as the main protagonists.[2] Studies and portrayals of women's experiences during this time period are relatively rare—but each of these films presents us myriad opportunities to examine not just women's lives but, more specifically, how the depiction of the characters' sexuality supports the cultural expectation of lesbian invisibility. To explore these thoughts, we must begin with a discussion of the theoretical foundations on which this analysis is constructed.

Theoretical Foundations

Feminist Film Theory

Laura Mulvey published a very influential essay regarding feminist film theory, centered around sexual differences advocated by psychoanalytic theory, in 1975. Mulvey argues that major components of psychoanalytic theory that assist in constructing this new viewpoint include the unconscious centering of patriarchy in film form, placing women as "other," and scopophilia (the pleasure derived from looking).[3] Patriarchy places men in the center of power, thus, Jane Gaines suggests, at its core, representation of women within this same patriarchal culture only reinforces it.[4] Using Mulvey's essay as a starting point, Judith Mayne argues that feminist film theory offers us a way to not only understand women's representation in film but also to change those representations that help to challenge the patriarchy.[5] In essence, in order to challenge it, we must center women instead.

Feminist film theory, particularly in its early days, is not without its critiques. The primary criticism is that all of the original theorists were white women, thus, Gaines argues, at its core it is ill-equipped to deal with films that surround racial differences as well as differences in sexuality. She suggests that the focus on film construction for male eyes ignores lesbian viewers and that it supports the male/female dichotomy, which doesn't allow for non–gender binary persons.[6] Lorien Castelle argues that Mulvey's theory was constructed for a heterosexual, white, male audience.[7] Keeping all of this in mind, it is my goal to use a modified feminist theoretical foundation that incorporates two distinct points: first, that representations of women matter in order to change the patriarchal system and second, that lesbian viewers matter and can assist in this deconstruction of patriarchy.

Cultural Studies Model

I made a distinct choice in analyzing the films in this chapter using a critical cultural studies approach, specifically one proposed by Douglas Kellner. Kellner insists that to truly understand the culture produced, we must situate it within a broader analysis of the structural systems that influence us, including reproductions of oppression, like racism, sexism, heterosexism, and classism. Once we are able to do this, Kellner argues, we can recognize these forces and begin resisting dominant paradigms.[8]

In Kellner's model, we are asked to examine three important factors that contribute to the development and understanding of media: political and production economy, audience reaction, and textual analysis. "Political and production economy" refers to the time period, historical setting, and sociological and anthropological influences on creators, actors, and production personnel. Further, it also refers to situating the creation of film within the limitations provided by business practices of the day, how media is distributed (and by which company), and even the format demanded by the consumer.[9]

Audience reaction is relatively straight-forward—how do those who watch films respond to it? The measurement of large-scale audience response though has evolved beyond box office gross receipts. In our instant-gratification culture, popularity is measured more broadly: "likes" and "follows" on social media; tweets and hashtags; trailer streaming counts on YouTube; on-demand, DVR, DVD, and Blu-Ray sales; and even critic and audience response aggregators like RottenTomatoes.com and Flixter.com. In addition to the reaction is the use of the text—how do different groups interpret the messages encoded within the text itself?[10]

Textual analysis investigates what the media is telling us.[11] Dialogue between actors, background music, lighting choice and other cinematographic designs, editing of shots and story, the screenplay itself, the director's interpretation of that text, and nonverbal communication and cues all contribute. Beyond the text itself is *who* is actually doing the talking—the sociological underpinnings of race, class, gender, sexuality, ability, et cetera.

Political Economies: The American South, circa 1920

Beginning with Kellner's political and production economies, the films chosen for this analysis represent the overall theme to this volume, modern depictions of the late nineteenth and early twentieth-century American South.

Genteel Women of the South

McMillen argues that much of women's history in the old South was thought lost due to inadequate recordkeeping; however, she was able to examine multiple experiences related to marriage and family, education, religion, and work for both white and black women. Compared to the North, there were few urban areas in the South, which, while limiting the amount of interaction women had, centered the home as the focal point of their lives. In addition, McMillen helps paint a picture of women as significantly subservient to men.[12]

While the passing and ratification of the Nineteenth Amendment in 1920 provided women with the right to vote, during the ratification process, it was a southern state, Georgia, that was the first to reject it, and proudly so.[13] Women were still expected to keep the home and certainly not engage in any advocacy or civic engagement. Even after ratification, Sarah Wilkerson-Freeman argues, white women were systematically disenfranchised from voting—even with their newly granted rights—because of the poll tax. Economic conditions for most families did not permit multiple parties to pay the tax; the financial sacrifice to vote was greater for two.[14]

Even if white women had some rights, black women certainly did not.

In an amazing qualitative analysis, Anne Valk and Leslie Brown present a number of oral histories from black women who grew up in the South during the Jim Crow era. Many of these women discussed the important balance they had to strike between their own desire for independence and their community's needs. If they didn't conform to the community's standards, they could be shunned, sometimes violently. In addition, black women married early for multiple reasons and rarely finished formal education. Similarly to white women, they had significant burdens to bear—notably childrearing, taking care of the household, and fulfilling their husbands' needs. A significant difference, though, existed; because of the lack of social services available to lower-class blacks in the Jim Crow South, there were strong community ties. Everyone served everyone—women served as midwives, passing on this knowledge to their children, while other women and family members took in children of unmarried girls.[15]

The Closet of Southern Sexuality

While there were scientists researching and theorizing about homosexuality during the 1920s and '30s, it proves quite difficult to research how the old South responded to same-sex interactions between women. Henry Hinton describes this as "the medicalization" era, whereby psychiatrists completed studies of homosexuality, almost exclusively through the use of the case study method and coming from a deviance perspective. In his analysis, Hinton describes how a revolutionary study of "sex deviants" was conducted—secretively, anonymously—including physical examinations, family histories, personality eccentricities, and degrees of masculinity and femininity.[16] Results varied; however, participants indicated that they believed the maladjustment medicalization model employed in various studies of the times did not adequately describe their experiences—they had worked hard to overcome contemporary stigma to develop a more positive self-identity, never mind that all of the variables in the above described study have nothing to do with sexuality.[17]

Vern Bullough and Bonnie Bullough summarized an unfinished series of case studies of a group of lesbian women living in Salt Lake City in the 1920s and '30s. This author, M.B., straddled the divide between the medical model and new models put forward by Magnus Hirschfeld (a biological model) and Havelock Ellis (a non-pathological model), and the results showed this. They indicated that while the women described themselves as happy in their relationships and friendships and not "maladjusted," they knew they had to keep their identities secret for fear of repercussion.[18]

Lillian Faderman's analysis of lesbian lives aligns closely with these two studies, although she describes some greater environmental and cultural influences to a more emerging lesbianism, such as its inclusion in numerous works of literature, women discovering and discussing the pleasures of sex, and various transgressions: traveling and experimenting in Harlem as well as working-class women visiting saloons (which evolved into the establishment of lesbian bars).[19] One major caveat of all of these assessments is necessary though—all of the participants in this study were found in New York City, a "home to the largest and most vibrant lesbian and gay community," where Faderman describes a more "laissez-faire morality," or other urban centers across the country.[20]

Finally, White reminds us of the Hollywood Production Code, called the Hays Code, employed from 1930 to 1968 as it relates to media depictions of lesbians.[21] Written by a Jesuit priest, it prohibited any depiction or discussion of homosexuality as well as graphic violence and miscegenation.[22] Writers worked around this by encoding subversive messages in the films, as Gore Vidal says in the classic documentary *The Celluloid Closet,* with a "wink here, a nudge there."[23] Vito Russo provides a thorough overview of these times in his seminal work *The Celluloid Closet;* a couple of films with these encoded lesbian messages include *Rebecca* (1940) and *Queen Christina* (1933).[24] David M. Lugowski summarizes lesbian depictions during the era as "clad in a mannishly tailored suit . . . her hair slicked back . . . possess[ing] a deep alto voice and a haughty, aggressive attitude toward men, work, or any business at hand."[25]

Race and the Jim Crow Era

Although slavery ended in 1865, change in the American South was excruciatingly slow. During Reconstruction, blacks were subjected to ever-increasing legalized oppression to further disenfranchise them. Laws created separate public facilities, restricted voting participation to those who could afford to pay a tax and pass a literacy test, and kept public schools and libraries for blacks extremely underfunded.

Even without these laws in place, blacks were routinely terrorized. Due to perceived threats to whites' political power, as many as three thousand blacks were lynched.[26] Terrorist groups began to form as well. As many as 5 million white men became members of the second iteration of the Ku Klux Klan, reorganized in Georgia in 1915. This Klan was well-versed in propaganda, well supported by southern political leaders, and inspired to save white civilization.[27]

Media produced and disseminated during this period was extremely influential in spreading and maintaining racist ideas. Katherine Lennard provides us a clear link between the reorganization of the Klan and the production and release of D. W. Griffith's *The Birth of a Nation,* a film that depicted the original Klan as a disciplined, almost fraternal, organization, complete with their white robes and pointed hats.[28] Donald Bogle offers an in-depth analysis of *The Birth of a Nation,* arguing that it completely changed American filmmaking. Because of its oversized spectacle, it was easy for audience members to have their own racist notions confirmed by a director who had his own beliefs about the correct moral order.[29]

Other films that reinforced racist ideas included *Uncle Tom's Cabin* (1927), *Confederate Spy* (1910), and *Ten Pickaninnies* (1908). Bogle argues that these films made possible the greater dissemination of five classic Hollywood stock characters (the Tom, the Coon, the tragic Mulatto, the Mammy, and the black Buck and their white actors, wearing blackface). These characters and others, like the jesters and the servants, served as themes in Hollywood throughout the 1920s and '30s.[30] These stock characters reduce blacks to simply entertainment or servants, not individuals with wants and needs, thus making it easier for whites in power to ignore their plight.

Plot Summaries

The Color Purple, based on Alice Walker's Pulitzer Prize–winning novel, centers around Celie Johnson (Whoopi Goldberg), a poor black woman living outside of Atlanta, Georgia. As the film opens, it is approximately 1908, and the audience is treated to Celie at her happiest—running through a field of purple flowers with her best friend, sister Nettie (Akosua Busia). At only fourteen, Celie is pregnant by her father for the second time. She is treated no better than property, given away as second-best to a widower from the next farm, "Mister" Albert (Danny Glover).

Because their father abuses her, Nettie runs away a short time later, then moves in with Celie and Albert. One abusive situation is replaced by another, however. After Nettie rebuffs Albert's advances, he discards her like trash, dragging her from the house. This heart-wrenching moment creates a small nugget of hope for Celie, however, because Nettie promises to write.

In 1922, on a proverbial "dark and stormy night," we are finally introduced to the mystical Shug Avery (Margaret Avery), a nightclub jazz singer and Albert's real love. She is the "pretty woman in the picture" on his nightstand, described to his son Harpo (Willard E. Pugh) as "the woman who was supposed to be your mammy." After some initial hesitance and sarcasm upon her arrival, including insulting Celie, Shug and Celie develop a strong bond, which fills Celie with hope. Shug writes and performs a new song at Harpo's juke joint, dedicated to Celie: "Miss Celie's Blues." Later that evening, she helps Celie let loose, smile, and feel loved—by kissing her and introducing her to the way her body should feel. Shug eventually leaves, but she returns years later, a married woman.

It is now 1936, and Celie discovers that Albert has kept all of Nettie's letters from her. We learn that Nettie has been living in Africa with a missionary family, which includes Celie's children, Adam and Olivia. In the pivotal climactic moment, Celie finally fights back, pulls a knife on Albert, leaves with Shug and her husband Grady (Bennet Guillory), cursing him.

After her departure, Celie learns an important truth—the man who she thought was her father, who raped and impregnated her twice, wasn't her real father. Once her real father (a local shopkeeper) dies, she inherits his house and farm. She becomes independent, opening a clothing store, where she makes pants. In the meantime, Albert's life has crumbled; however, he ultimately decides to do right by Celie, paying for Nettie, Adam, and Olivia to return to the United States.

The film concludes with an emotional reunion and a series of reconciliations. Celie and Nettie have reunited, and Celie sees her children for the first time since they were infants. The film closes with Celie and Nettie, some forty years after the film begins, recreating their happiness from the beginning of the film.

Fried Green Tomatoes, adapted from Fannie Flagg's novel *Fried Green Tomatoes at the Whistle Stop Café*, centers the audience between the life of Idgie Threadgoode (Mary Stuart Masterson) in Depression-era Alabama and Evelyn Couch (Kathy Bates) in the 1980s. We will be primarily focusing here on Idgie's life, and thus the summary below is of her experiences.

As the film opens, we learn almost immediately that Idgie is a headstrong child—when she refuses to dress in "appropriate" attire for her sister's wedding. Eventually, her best friend, older brother Buddy (Chris O'Donnell), coaxes her to participate, and she is permitted to wear a pair of knickers and a jacket instead of a dress. During the reception, the unthinkable happens; while Buddy is showing off for both Idgie and his sweetheart, Ruth (Mary Louise Parker), his foot gets caught in the railroad tracks and he is killed by an oncoming train.

Due to both Buddy's death and her rejection of the acceptable behavior for a southern woman, as she grows, Idgie withdraws from her family, instead choosing to live on the banks of the river, hanging out at the Riverboat Club with Grady Kilgore (Gary Basaraba) and the boys. The only person who knows where to find her is Big George (Stan Shaw), the Threadgoode family's hired black servant. In an attempt to reconnect, Idgie's mother (Lois Smith) asks Ruth to come visit for the summer. Ruth reaches out to Idgie, helping her realize that she's not the only one who lost Buddy—an intense relationship emerges between the two, culminating in an overt display of affection from Ruth. Ruth then discloses to Idgie that she's to be married to a man, Frank Bennett (Nick Searcy), at the end of the summer.

We learn soon that Ruth is pregnant; however, Frank abuses her, and only upon Ruth's mother's death does she accept help. Idgie, Big George, and Idgie's brother Julian (Haynes Brooke) show up to help Ruth leave, seemingly without issue, until Frank comes home and kicks Ruth down the stairs, which prompts Idgie to threaten his life. They leave without further incident, returning home to Alabama.

The two women create a life together, opening the Whistle Stop Café and jointly raising Ruth's son, Buddy Jr. Frank appears again and is murdered while attempting to kidnap Buddy Jr. Initially, Big George and Idgie are charged with his murder; however, after Reverend Scroggins (Richard Riehle) provides an alibi, albeit a false one, they are found innocent. (We learn later that Big George's mother, Sipsey [Cicely Tyson], killed Frank after she caught him kidnapping Buddy Jr.)

The second challenge Ruth and Idgie face is Ruth's coming death, presumably of cancer. Upon her death, the café closes and the town slowly dies. We never know what happens to Idgie or Buddy Jr. after Ruth's death, only that at the end of the movie, Idgie is still alive. We are clued into the true depth of their feelings when we read Idgie's note, left on Ruth's tombstone beside a jar of freshly harvested honey: "I will always love you. Idgie ~ The Bee Charmer."

Intersectional Themes

Kimberlé Crenshaw contributes a significant theory surrounding examinations of diverse social identities.[31] She suggests that for us to truly understand lived experiences, we must examine them through the viewpoint of the intersections of the identities, rather than individually.

Friends of Convenience or Lesbian Sexuality?

One major theme both these films share is a significant downplaying of the importance of same-sex love. In *The Color Purple,* Celie seems as taken by Shug's beauty as Albert is. She stares, mouth agape, at Shug's picture on the mirror while Albert rushes around to get dressed to watch her perform at a local show. Later, when Shug finally does show up at their house, Celie is extremely concerned with how she looks—she blatantly ignores Albert's request to help him with a passed-out Shug in the back of the wagon (even though she knows what the repercussions could be). The camera shows her rushing up the stairs to their bedroom, face covered in painted-on mud and wearing stained house clothes, trying desperately to make a better first impression. She is awestruck by Shug's presence, telling us through her internal monologue, "I can't move, I can't move. I need to see her eyes. I feel like once I see her eyes then my face can let go of the spot they stuck in."

Over time and after Celie brokers trust with Shug by taking care of her—making her an outstanding meal, bathing her, combing her hair, listening to her pain about her father—we see Shug reciprocate in the way she knows best, performing. Her composition and performance at Harpo's focuses on Celie, whose emotions we see clearly—shyness, bewilderment (that she would be honored so), and a smile that reaches her eyes. This serenade fills Celie with confidence, which she displays by mocking a woman who insulted her earlier in the scene. Notably, the first word of "Miss Celie's Blues" is "sister."

After the performance, Shug dresses Celie in what appears to be the dress she wore to Harpo's, showering her with compliments, coaxing real smiles and laughter from her. During this interaction, Celie discloses that when she has sex with Albert, she just pretends she isn't there, describing it as him "climbin' on top of me and doin' his business." In disbelief, Shug, looking radiant in comparison to our first glimpses of her, recognizes that Celie has very little self-confidence and tells her that she loves her. She then proceeds to help Celie understand herself and her body, telling her that she is beautiful and kissing her on her cheek, forehead, and lips. Celie kisses her back, smiles widely, and laughs, extremely reminiscent of first teenage love. Their interaction is sensual and reciprocal; Shug the only person in her life other than Nettie who has ever really shown Celie love. While the audience is left to wonder if or how their physical interaction continues, during the next scene, Celie (as narrator) says, "Shug like honey and now I's just like a bee. Must follow her everywhere, wanna go where she go. What life like for her, and why she sometime get so sad, so sad just like me." hooks argues that the interaction between Shug and Celie is depicted as "non-exploitative, erotic affirmation" and helps Celie on her journey of self-discovery.[32] She is truly worthy of love.

Further evidence of Celie's love for Shug comes when Albert's father, Old Mister (Adolph Caesar), comes to visit and disparages Shug, calling her "blacker than tar, nappy-headed, with legs like baseball bats . . . a juke joint jezebel." Celie, overhearing this while inside getting the old man some water, spits in his glass and takes great pride in watching him drink it all down, exclaiming to herself, "next time he come I put a little Shug Avery pee in his glass and see how he like that!"

When Shug decides it is time to head out of town, Albert and Celie walk with her. When we last see Shug's coach leaving, Celie collapses on the ground, like a puppet whose strings have been cut, as if all of the life has been sucked out of her. In some ways, it has, because not only does Albert beat her more when Shug isn't around, but the only person who shows her any intimacy has gone. Shug doesn't return to Celie's life for about fourteen years. When she does come back, Albert and Celie's reactions are the same—big smiles, blustering around the room to get dressed—and even more so when they come to the realization that Shug is married: extreme surprise and almost crushing disappointment

We are left wondering if Shug and Celie's relationship continued in any physical sense; however, we are definitely informed that the intimacy hasn't abated. Shug plays an extremely influential role in Celie's life, even beyond introducing her to same-sex love and behavior. During the film's climactic scene, Celie finally confronts Albert about Nettie's letters (which Shug helped her discover) and announces to everyone that she's leaving with Shug and Grady. Celie stands up for herself, cursing Albert loudly, exclaiming with a look of radiant joy as she leaves on the back of Grady's car: "I'm poor, black; I may even be ugly. But dear God! I'm here! I'm here!" Celie undoubtedly would never have been able to do this without Shug's influence. At the conclusion of the film, Shug is still a part of Celie's life, for we see her among the guests at

Celie's house when she meets her children again. There is true love between the two, regardless of the sexual orientation questions.

In *Fried Green Tomatoes,* the director uses gender expression to suggest that Idgie is not heterosexual. She refuses to wear a dress, preferring traditionally "male" attire, climbs trees, has skinned up knees, and acts gruff. Lugowski agrees: because of the links between gender and sexuality a woman only has to dress like a man to "seem queer."[33] In our first view of her, Ruth Jameson, however, is the quintessential southern lady of the era, complete with parasol and a dainty walk.[34] It is clear to the audience who is the "male" and who is the "female" of this relationship. Long before Ruth kisses Idgie on the banks of the river, we are treated to a summer of courtship—Idgie charming bees to give Ruth fresh honey, Idgie helping Ruth let loose from her more conservative upbringing by drinking and gambling at the riverboat club, the two jumping freight cars and redistributing food to those less fortunate, and Ruth helping Idgie express her emotions. The devastation on Idgie's face when Ruth tells her that she's leaving and marrying a man is clear; although she tries to hide it with a return to her gruff exterior, it is heartbreaking. Ruth's departure affects Idgie deeply; she returns to her pre-Ruth ways, staying out all night, choosing to live with Sipsey and Big George and even refusing to attend the wedding (although she does drive to Georgia to see Ruth's "happiness" at being carried across the threshold).

Idgie keeps her torch for Ruth burning, however, and after a few years, she visits her at her new home in Valdosta, Georgia. This is when we are first shown that Frank is abusive—Idgie immediately wants to come to Ruth's rescue, but Ruth tells her that if she really cares for her she should just leave. However, during their brief conversation, Ruth attempts to ascertain whether Idgie has a "fella." Is it just polite conversation between two friends who have lost touch? I believe it's an important plot device—the next scenes show Idgie rejecting Grady's invitation to dance (and to marriage) and Ruth's disguised attempt to ask the Threadgoodes for help. The look on Idgie's face when her mother reads a copy of Ruth's mother's obituary and a passage from the Bible about true family is hopeful.

Idgie returns to Valdosta, running up the steps to "save her woman." The image is shot from behind, with Ruth seated at the window in a long floral dress and heels, hair coiffed, hand demurely laid on the arm of the chair—juxtaposed against Idgie, in a button-down-collared dress shirt with sleeves rolled up, suspenders, and heavy boots (the same outfit Frank wears). During the following heated confrontation, Idgie can't hold her emotions in check.

Ruth and Idgie's intimate relationship is implied. We see them sharing a home and a business, jointly raising Ruth's son. Idgie's gender expression continues to be masculine, and the heteronormative assumption that Idgie is the "man of the relationship" is confirmed not only through her dress but also her mannerisms and lack of emotionality (besides her temper). She is foremost a protector. She steps in to take care of Frank's body and protect Sipsey, vows to protect Ruth and Buddy Jr., and refuses to be intimidated by the Ku Klux Klan members who threaten her about her protection of and friendship with local black people. After the chaste peck on the cheek at the river, the two are never shown sharing any physical intimacy; instead, the audience is treated to a food fight that serves as sexual tension.[35]

Lesbian Invisibility Continued: The 1980s and '90s

Lesbian invisibility is a shared theme in the two films. Castelle provides some important thoughts on the subject of this invisibility, arguing that you can only accurately "fill in the blanks" of the displayed relationships if you've already read the novels. In *The Color Purple,* Walker makes it very clear that Celie and Shug are not heterosexual and are lovers. Flagg's *Fried Green Tomatoes* doesn't even present active homophobia toward Ruth and Idgie's relationship—their families are supportive; the town is supportive.[36] While a background in the novels is helpful, I would argue that members of the LGBT community can infer the relationship statuses because we are quite used to the symbols of semi-hidden sexuality. Most media directed toward our community must also placate the masses.

Part of this invisibility must be contextualized within the political economy of the films' releases. The screenwriters and directors intentionally chose not to include these elements, in direct opposition to the expressed lesbian plots in both novels. Neil Miller argues that many lesbians of the late 1970s and 1980s were *women first,* connected to greater feminist causes such as the anti-porn movement, rape response and prevention, and combating the sexualization of the culture, which includes depictions of sexual activity by women outside of a mainstream, and somewhat sanitized, version.[37]

The mid-1980s and early 1990s was not a particularly visible period for lesbian inclusion in film or culture in general, with the lesbian "boom" not coming until the mid-1990s.[38] Harry Benshoff and Sean Griffin provide some context to this era as well by reviewing how Hollywood depicted gays and lesbians in the early 1980s—as trying to "play to straight viewers." Of the films produced and released nationally between 1989 and 1992, the only one with even some prolonged, implied lesbian content is *Fried Green Tomatoes.* Even if we expand the years, US theatrical releases with LGBT themes between 1980 and 1994 can be combined into the following categories (asterisks denote lesbian-themed films):

- HIV/AIDS-related: *Parting Glances* (1986), *Common Threads: Stories from the Quilt* (1989), *Longtime Companion* (1989), *Philadelphia* (1993), *And the Band Played On* (1993);
- Independent films with limited release: *Go Fish* (1994)*;
- Extremely exploitative or centered LGBT folks as comedic value: *Cruising* (1980), *Partners* (1981), *Tootsie* (1981), *Victor/Victoria* (1981), *Torch Song Trilogy* (1988);
- Box office flops: *Personal Best* (1981)*, *Lianna* (1982)*, *Desert Hearts* (1985)*.

The lone exception to these categories was the film *Making Love* (1981); however, audiences still didn't seem ready for open expression of sexual attraction and desires: "When Zack and Bart [the two main characters in *Making Love*] began undressing, you would think someone yelled 'Fire!' in the audience. There was absolute pandemonium. The audience reacted with such hostility and turned so ugly toward the movie, it became unbearable . . . homophobic catcalls, shocked screams, and conspicuous walkouts were commonplace among straight moviegoers."[39]

Might audiences have reacted differently to suggested lesbian sexual intimacy? I would argue yes, and there is research to support this. While analysis of the General Social Survey (administered by the nonpartisan National Opinion Research Center) indicates that overall attitudes toward homosexuals are getting better, when Gregory Herek asked individuals about their attitudes toward lesbians *or* gay men, their responses indicated that heterosexual men were more likely to accept lesbians than gay men. Herek continues, arguing that those who struggle with sexual prejudice aim it people of their own gender because they want to make sure they are as different from them as possible.[40] Gender expectations that shape masculinity are often connected to the fear of being presumed gay; thus, when men reject gay men is very different than their rejecting lesbians.[41] Finally, Laura Louderback and Bernard Whitley Jr. argue that a major factor influencing this behavior is that men often eroticize lesbians.[42]

Culturally, during the films' release era, there was significant backlash against the AIDS epidemic. Many remained apprehensive and confused about its causes and who, in all honesty, was to blame. Content about the community was quickly shunned, and politicians such as Jesse Helms made it their main point to defund and denounce anything LGBT-related. By 1986, sixteen thousand Americans had died of AIDS-related complications and the Reagan administration hadn't even said the word in public. The religious and political leaders of the time suggested that HIV patients be quarantined—even that gay men had brought this on themselves.[43] This definitely could have played a significant role in the depiction of sexual behavior between lesbians, even if they hadn't been the ones to "bring on the plague." All were guilty by association.

In addition to the hesitance to produce LGBT-related content or even discuss LGBT-related issues in the mainstream, we also must consider that the Hollywood corporate structure, or, as Kellner would say, the production economy, was all male. As of 1985, the six major film companies (20th Century Fox, Warner Bros., Paramount, Columbia, Universal, and the Walt Disney Company) all had men in their CEO and president positions.[44]

Unfortunately for viewers, the "Year of the Lesbian" didn't come until 1993. *Newsweek* and *New York* magazine featured lesbians on their covers, k. d. lang broke the pop charts, Sandra Bernhard appeared on *Roseanne*, and the selection of the first openly lesbian political appointee made national news.[45] Many argue that this led to the film boom of the mid-90s, which featured several LGBT-themed films, all released in 1995: *Boys on the Side*, *The Incredible True Story of Two Girls in Love*, *Jeffrey*, *Serving in Silence: The Margarette Cammermeyer Story*, *Showgirls*, and *To Wong Foo, Thanks for Everything! Julie Newmar.*

Finally, Castelle tells us that the producers of *The Color Purple* were under a great deal of pressure from black civil rights groups to negate the mentions of the relationship between Celie and Shug because "women loving women was considered a social problem, analogous to drug addiction and violence."[46] Hill provided information regarding levels of homophobia within the black community versus the white community, citing evidence from the National Black Survey indicating that African Americans were more likely to report negative attitudes toward homosexuals, even as recently as 2008, when 72 percent of blacks versus 52 percent of whites indicated that "homosexuality was always wrong."[47] This most likely does not translate into structural heterosexism, due to a lack of power afforded to blacks as a group; however, *indi-*

viduals decide to attend movies or concerts, purchase products, change their television stations, or read newspapers or magazines. Jones, disagrees, arguing that while the reduction of Shug and Celie's relationship is problematic, any exploration of black women's homo- (or even bi-) sexuality during this time period was groundbreaking in that it challenged homophobic notions.[48]

Conclusion

Feminist film theory argues that the inclusion of women as a film's main protagonist helps deconstruct patriarchal views of the "women's place." Both of these films accomplish this—Celie, Shug, Idgie, and Ruth are all presented as complex characters, resisting the yoke of patriarchy with the assistance of other females. Where the films struggle is in my second thesis, that lesbians matter and can help deconstruct this patriarchy. Both of the pairs of characters still adhere to a male-female dichotomy, and their chaste relationships (with the exception of a kiss each) help maintain that lesbians should be invisible, almost asexual.

While both films illustrate life in the American South during the 1920s and '30s from a female point of view, their depictions of the intersectional aspects of their lives presents a more detailed, richer picture of the struggles encountered during the era. Women, while still oppressed, were even further affected by the heterosexism sustained throughout the era. True change only occurred after this time through the work of coalitions of individuals across the dividing lines initially created through the power dynamics of race, class, sex, and sexuality.

Notes

1. bell hooks, *Reel to Real: Race, Class, and Sex at the Movies* (New York: Routledge, 1996), 2–4.

2. *The Color Purple,* directed by Steven Spielberg (1985; Burbank, CA: Warner Bros./Warner Home Video, 2011), Blu-Ray; *Fried Green Tomatoes,* directed by Jon Avnet (1991; Universal City, CA, Universal Pictures/Universal Studios Home Entertainment, 2014), Blu-Ray.

2. *The Color Purple,* directed by Steven Spielberg (1985; Burbank, CA: Warner Bros./Warner Home Video, 2011), Blu-Ray; *Fried Green Tomatoes,* directed by Jon Avnet (1991; Universal City, CA, Universal Pictures/Universal Studios Home Entertainment, 2014), Blu-Ray.

3. Laura Mulvey, "Visual Pleasure and Narrative Cinema," in *Film Theory and Crit-*

icism: Introductory Readings, ed. Gerald Mast and Marshall Cohen, 3rd ed. (New York: Oxford University Press, 1985), 804–6.

4. Jane Gaines, "White Privilege and Looking Relations: Race and Gender in Feminist Film Theory," in *Multiple Voices in Feminist Film Criticism,* ed. Diane Carson, Linda Dittmar, and Janice R. Welsch (Minneapolis: University of Minnesota Press, 1994), 178.

5. Judith Mayne, "Feminist Film Theory and Criticism," in Carson, Dittmar, and Welsch, *Multiple Voices in Feminist Film Criticism,* 50.

6. Gaines, "White Privilege and Looking Relations," 176, 177, 179.

7. Lorien Castelle, "Hollywood and Homophobia: Reconstructing Lesbian Identity in Cinema, or Some Questions on Writing about Film," *Phoebe: An Interdisciplinary Journal of Feminist Scholarship, Theory, and Aesthetics,* 8, nos. 1–2, (1996): 126.

8. Douglas Kellner, "Toward a Critical Media/Cultural Studies," in *Media/Cultural Studies: Critical Approaches,* ed. Rhonda Hammer and Douglas Kellner (New York: Peter Lang, 2009), 3, 4.

9. Ibid., 5–9.

10. Ibid., 8.

11. Ibid., 6–7.

12. Sally G. McMillen, *Southern Women: Black and White in the Old South,* 2nd ed. (Wheeling, IL: Harlan Davidson, 2002), 1, 6–7. 10.

13. A. Elizabeth Taylor, "Revival and Development of the Woman Suffrage Movement in Georgia," *Georgia Historical Quarterly* 42, no. 4 (1958): 339.

4. Sarah Wilkerson-Freeman, "The Second Battle for Woman Suffrage: Alabama White Women, the Poll Tax, and V. O. Key's Master Narrative of Southern Politics," *Journal of Southern History* 68, no. 2 (2002): 333, 334.

15. Anne Valk and Leslie Brown, *Living with Jim Crow: African American and Memories of the Segregated South* (London: Palgrave MacMillan, 2010), 53–56.

16. Ibid., 444–45.

17. Henry L. Hinton "Community Empowerment and the Medicalization of Homosexuality: Constructing Sexual Identities in the 1930s," *Journal of the History of Sexuality,* 6, no. 3 (1996): 435, 444–45, 446.

18. Vern Bullough and Bonnie Bullough, "Lesbianism in the 1920s and 1930s: A Newfound Study," *Signs,* 4, no. 2 (1977): 898, 901–3.

19. Lillian Faderman, *Odd Girls and Twilight Lovers: A History of Lesbian Life in Twentieth-Century America* (New York: Penguin, 1991), 76–80.

20. Hinton, "Community Empowerment and the Medicalization of Homosexuality," 446; Faderman, *Odd Girls and Twilight Lovers,* 67.

21. Patricia White. *Uninvited: Classical Hollywood Cinema and Lesbian Representability.* (Bloomington: Indiana University Press, 1999), 1.

22. Harry M. Benshoff and Sean Griffin, *America on Film: Representing Race, Class, Gender, and Sexuality at the Movies,* 2nd ed. (Hoboken, NJ: Wiley-Blackwell, 2009), 36.

23. *The Celluloid Closet,* directed by Rob Epstein and Jeffrey Friedman (1995; Culver City, CA: Sony Pictures Classics, 1996), DVD.

24. Vito Russo, *The Celluloid Closet: Homosexuality in the Movies,* rev. ed. (New York: Harper Perennial, 1987), 64, 103.

25. David M. Lugowski, "Queering the (New) Deal: Lesbian and Gay Representation and the Depression-Era Cultural Politics of Hollywood's Production Code," *Cinema Journal* 38 (Winter 1999): 4.

26. E. M. Beck and Stewart E. Tolnay, "The Killing Fields of the Deep South: The Market for Cotton and the Lynching of Blacks, 1882–1930," *American Sociological Review* 55, no. 4 (1990): 526.

27. Nancy MacLean, *Behind the Mask of Chivalry: The Making of the Second Ku Klux Klan* (New York: Oxford University Press, 1994): xi–xii, 126–30.

28. Katherine Lennard, "Old Purpose, 'New Body": *The Birth of a Nation* and the Revival of the Ku Klux Klan," *Journal of the Gilded Age and Progressive Era* 14 (2015): 618–19.

29. Donald Bogle, *Toms, Coons, Mulattos, Mammies, and Bucks: An Interpretive History of Blacks in American Films* (New York: Continuum, 1992), 10.

30. Ibid., 3–10, 19, 35.

31. Kimberlé Crenshaw, "Mapping the Margins: Intersectionality, Identity Politics, and Violence against Women of Color," in *The Public Nature of Private Violence,* ed. Martha Albertson Fineman and Rixanne Mykitiuk (New York: Routledge, 1994), 93–118.

32. hooks, *Reel to Real,* 300.

33. Lugowski, "Queering the (New) Deal," 7.

34. Pamela Tyler, "The Ideal Rural Southern Woman, as Seen by *Progressive Farmer* in the 1930s," *Southern Studies* 2, nos. 3–4 (1991): 316.

35. Castelle, "Hollywood and Homophobia," 126.

36. Ibid., 124, 125.

37. Neil Miller. *Out of the Past: Gay and Lesbian History from 1869 to the Present* (New York: Alyson Books, 206), 436.

38. Kelly Kessler, "Temporarily *Kissing Jessica Stein* (2001): Negotiating (and Negating) Lesbian Sexuality in Popular Film," in *Feminism at the Movies: Understanding Gender in Contemporary Popular Cinema,* ed. Hilary Radner and Rebecca Stringer (New York: Routledge, 2011), 215.

39. Harry M. Benshoff and Sean Griffin, *Queer Images: A History of Gay and Lesbian Film in America* (Washington, DC: Rowman & Littlefield, 2006): 186, 188.

40. NORC at the University of Chicago, "Same Sex Marriage and Gay Rights: A Shift in Americans' Attitudes," 2013, Associated Press–NORC Center for Public Affairs Research, available online at the AP–NORC Web site, www.apnporc.org/projects/Pages/same-sex-marriage-and-gay-rights-a-shift-in-americans-attutydes.aspx; Gregory M. Herek, "Sexual Prejudice and Gender: Do Heterosexuals' Attitudes toward Lesbians and Gay Men Differ?" *Journal of Social Issues* 56, no. 2 (2000): 252, 254.

41. Michael S. Kimmel, "Masculinity as Homophobia: Fear, Shame, and Silence in the Construction of Gender Identity," in *College Men and Masculinities: Theory, Research, and Implications for Practice,* ed. Shaun R. Harper and Frank Harris III (San Francisco: Jossey-Bass, 2010), 24.

42. Laura A. Louderback and Bernard E. Whitney Jr., "Perceived Erotic Value of Homosexuality and Sex-Role Attitudes as Mediators of Sex Differences in Heterosexual College Students' Attitudes toward Lesbians and Gay Men," *Journal of Sex Research* 34, no. 2 (1997): 179.

43. David Artavia and Diane Anderson-Minshall, "Art, Activism, and AIDS: These Decades Were Filled with LGBT Change, but the Impact of AIDS Was the Biggest," *Advocate,* June–July 2017, 87.

44, Aljean Harmetz, "Columbia Pictures Chiefs Reportedly Resigning," *New York Times,* October 7, 1983, http://www.nytimes.com/1983/10/07/arts/columbia-pictures-chief-reportedly-resigning.html?mcubz=0; "Disney History," Official Disney Fan Club Web site, https://d23.com/disney-history/; "Frank Price Biography," IMDb, http://www.imdb.com/name/nm0696895/bio; "Warner Bros. Studio History," Warner Brothers Web site, https://www.warnerbros.com/studio/about-studio/company-history.

45. Miller, *Out of the Past,* 520.

46. Castelle, "Hollywood and Homophobia," 185.

47. Marjorie J. Hill, "Is the Black Community More Homophobic? Reflections on the Intersectionality of Race, Class, Gender, Culture, and Religiosity of the Perception of Homophobia in the Black Community," *Journal of Gay and Lesbian Mental Health* 17, no. 2 (2013): 211–12.

48. Sharon L. Jones, "From Margin to Centre? Images of African-American Women in Film," *Social Alternatives* 17 (October 1998): 37.

10

Intergenerational Struggle and Racial Progress in *The Help* and *The Butler*

Tatiana Prorokova

> Oh, we have paid for our children's place in the world again, and again
> —Sherley Anne Williams, *Dessa Rose*

In its numerous fictional and documentary stories about slavery in the United States, film not only successfully constructs, creates, and recreates southern history, but it also addresses the problem of racism as a social issue. A number of cinematic examples, however, introduce this matter not only by means of contrasting the lives of people of different social statuses and races, that is, enslavers and the enslaved, or, simply, whites and blacks, but also through the depiction of the relationship between people of different ages, who visibly belong to different generations.[1]

Perhaps one of the most vivid early examples that addresses the problem of slavery from the perspective of age is the film adaptation of Margaret Mitchell's novel *Gone with the Wind* (1936) released in 1939. Specifically, the film includes various scenes that depict the relationship between the famous slave character Mammy (Hattie McDaniel) with the spoiled daughter of her enslavers—Scarlett (Vivien Leigh). Through these scenes, the audience perceives the hard work of black house servants and witnesses how those servants could become closer to certain members of their enslavers' families, particularly to children, for whom they were responsible, usually from the children's birth until they reached adulthood, and to a certain extent, substituting for their parents. In this respect, children frequently grew up treating the enslaved as integral parts of their family; yet those "family members" were obliged to serve. Enslaved people could never become socially equal to their owners and thus were never considered part of the family, despite that they were sometimes literally *family* to their enslavers—for men owned their children and siblings through rape and coercion—but were not acknowledged as such. Yet the enslaved remained devoted to their white enslavers and especially to their children. Hence, in *Gone with the Wind*, although Scarlett is no longer a little girl, Mammy continues to take care of her as if she were.[2]

Recent films, including Lee Tate Taylor's *The Help* (2011) and Lee Daniels's *The Butler* (2013) continue to explore issues of intergenerational relations to deconstruct the problem of racism and celebrate the concept of intergenerational struggle as a key element of racial progress.[3] Whether focusing on the relations between whites and blacks or only on life within the black community, these films attempt to reveal the sacrifices various generations of black people had to make in their fight for racial equality. The films gradually and persuasively make the viewer aware of the conflicts and misunderstandings that existed within the black community among people of different generations. To celebrate the role of every black person, regardless of age, in the fight for racial equality and to reveal the losses each black person has experienced, these cinematic examples try to reconstruct the complex social surroundings that African Americans existed in during the times of slavery as well as in the twentieth century when preparing the ground for the civil rights movement. Both *The Help* and *The Butler* reconsider the concept of racial progress through the prism of intergenerational fight, ultimately shaping the history of racial struggle as an intergenerational one.

Age and Interracial Relations in *The Help*

The notion of the "generation gap" attempts to explain the conflicts that might emerge between people of different ages. Undoubtedly, while some of these can be considered minor, a number of issues provoke disagreement. A problem as sociopolitically complex as racial struggle, and the means by which this equality can be achieved, can provoke disagreements among different generations. As *The Help* and *The Butler* attempt to convey, each black person in the United States who shaped the history of racial struggle employed different means to fight for equality.

While *The Butler* is visually a more progressive example, *The Help* is an important cinematic contribution, which, perhaps in a more veiled manner, also tackles the problem of racial struggle through intergenerational relationship. It provides insight in the life of black female workers whom mid-twentieth-century white families employed, *before* the civil rights era. The film discusses the racial struggle of the South through multiple perspectives, including that of age.

It zeroes in on the fact that after the abolition of slavery black women continued working (for low pay) as maids in the houses of white folks, doing household chores and bringing up white babies. Although the Association of Black Women Historians characterizes *The Help* as "ahistorical," claiming it is "an [in]accurate or [un]realistic portrayal of black people or the time period" because it "reduces systematic, violent racism, sexism and labor exploitation to a cat fight," the film brilliantly comments on the "reality of African American women taking care of white children in American culture."[4] Two of the film's main storylines focus on black maids bringing up white children. In the first, first Aibileen Clark (Viola Davis) takes care of Mae Mobley (Eleanor and Emma Henry). The audience learns that in her life, Aibileen, not having an opportunity to raise her own son, has brought up seventeen white children. In this way, she is "established as a black mother who belongs to white children—the cornerstone of the complex and longstanding Black Mammy stereotype."[5] The second storyline focuses on a young white woman, Skeeter Phelan (Emma Stone), who was brought up by her black maid, Constantine (Cicely Tyson). The hard work of bringing up white babies and the inability to find time for one's own children echoes black women's roles during slavery, when they were forced to serve their white enslavers and were literally deprived of their own private lives. Although Aibileen earns a salary, however small, for this work, she has no choice but to offer herself as a maid in a white people's house. It is obvious that if she had had a chance to get a better job and have more time for her own son, she would have undoubtedly taken it. Thus, it is clear the role of a black woman as mammy—which was born during slavery—persisted in the United States even in the 1960s, when the film is set.

The use of the image of a black woman as mammy in the 2010s, when the film was made, arguably helps to significantly transform the stereotypes that surrounded mammy and black motherhood in the Jim Crow era. While the culturally constructed image of mammy was rather positive, if condescendingly so—"rotund and handkerchiefed, Mammy was both the perfect mother and the perfect slave"—slave owners never perceived the black mothers as such in relation to their own children. To specify, in Dorothy Roberts's words, "whites described Black women as bad mothers not only because of immorality but also because of incompetence." According to Roberts, such "scapegoating" began during slavery, when slave owners considered the deaths of black children the fault of their mothers.[6] Thus was created a perverse image of a black woman: while as mammy, she was a perfect mother to the children of her enslavers, she was an absolute failure as a mother to her own children. Such a distortion obviously illustrates the racism that surrounded black mothers. The twentieth-century return to the portrayal of the mammy, as in *The Help*, therefore, can be viewed as an attempt to rehabilitate the image of a black woman as a mother and reveal her bleak situation in a racist society. More than that, the image of mammy serves as a reminder of black people's struggle against racism and toward racial progress that had to take place with black mothers being away from their children. Today, the image of mammy not only illustrates the role of the older generation in the fight against racism but it also celebrates black womanhood and motherhood.

Through the portrayal of black woman as mammy, the film raises two significant issues related to the problem of racial progress as the result of an intergenerational struggle. On the one hand, by presenting black nannies who appear to live for their white charges, it overtly comments on the problem of younger generations of black people being left out of American society—by the whites, indeed, but also, more importantly, by their own mothers. Excluding Aibileen's son from the story and explicitly suggesting that such was common, the film draws the viewer's attention to younger generations of black people's dim prospects, being rejected both by their families and by society in general. Racial progress thus stagnates as the older generation, forced by life circumstances, reinforces the insignificance of the lives of black children, who grow up "orphans" while their mothers raise white children. On the other hand, through this portrayal, *The Help* complements the idea of intergenerational struggle, accentuating the sacrifices black families made to provide their children with better futures. It is apparent that these black women leave their children not because they want to but rather because systemic inequality does not allow them to combine motherhood with work. Crucially, they choose work, *prioritizing* their children, for having no money is death to them and their offspring. They largely exceed regular working hours to earn the paltry incomes that would help provide the maximum a black person could have in the mid-twentieth century.

To illustrate that older generations of blacks inhibited racial progress, it is worth examining the relationship between the black nanny Aibileen and the white baby Mae. Aibileen's feelings toward the girl are sincere. She "strongly identifie[s]" with Mae, despite that Mae is white.[7] In this context, black women are vividly contrasted with racist white women. Mae's pretentious mother clearly neglects her, never even takes the little girl in her arms. Aibileen sees this and, like a real mother, teaches Mae: "You is kind, you is smart, you is important." The girl seems mature enough to understand that her mother, unlike the black maid, does not pay any attention to her. Thus, the love the girl is ready to share with her mother is directed at not her white, biological mother but rather her black nanny, who becomes her real parent. This substitution the film underscores through Aibileen's son's invisibility and Mae's constant presence not only hints at the exclusion of the younger generations of blacks, but it also suggests a more dangerous problem—the vanishing of blacks (metaphorical at a minimum) from American society. White children, even when unloved by their own mothers, survive because they have black nannies who mother them. Black children are portrayed as unnecessary on multiple levels.

The film also tells the story of the relationship between Skeeter Phelan—now a young woman—and her maid, Constantine. In several flashbacks, the audience learns about the tight bond Constantine and Skeeter shared when the latter was a child. Yet when Constantine leaves the family for good, Skeeter simply accepts it. Valerie Smith comments that Skeeter "undoubtedly feels a deep attachment to Constantine, the African American woman who raised her, but Skeeter has never understood the circumstances that caused her sudden departure from her household. . . . Her lack of knowledge about her beloved Constantine's life suggests the asymmetry in the relationship between the black maids and the families for which they worked. The maids attended to the most intimate details of the lives of the families that employed them, yet even the children who believe they love them knew next to nothing about their private lives."[8]

The relationship between Constantine and Skeeter and their ultimate separation also contribute to an understanding of racial progress as an intergenerational struggle. While Constantine sacrifices her own family to raise Skeeter, she never replaces Skeeter's mother; a black maid never becomes a mother of white children by abandoning her own. Skeeter's reaction to Constantine's absence only reinforces this idea. For many years, unaware that Constantine was unjustly fired, Skeeter seems to accept her departure. Indeed, she views Constantine as just a maid—no matter how tight their bond. Black nannies did not raise their own children, yet the new generation of white Americans that they helped raise ultimately rejects them.

Moreover, Skeeter's endeavor to write a book about the lives of black maids based on their own words, which can make her appear a fighter against racism, only reinforces her lack of knowledge about the maids' lives. To borrow from Kimberly Wallace-Sanders, Skeeter "plays a surprising role in both establishing and affirming the racial superiority of white children."[9] Her eventual indifference to Constantine's life, indeed, corroborates her role as a racist white woman. Her desire to openly speak about the problems that black maids experience working for white people only proves that she is, as Smith puts it, "unaware of the dangerous racial environment in which they live."[10] Finally, her writing the book because she wants equality for black people is problematic, too. While working on her project, she gets closer to a group of black maids who eventually reveal to her the emotional and physical hardships of working in white people's homes. Although Skeeter seems sympathetic and even expresses her condemnation of racial inequality, she does nothing to help the maids. It is crucial that the book is published anonymously; its characters and their actions, based on real people and events, are never acknowledged as such. Skeeter's book could perhaps have made white Americans realize racial inequality's drastic ramifications for black women, but that the author remains anonymous reveals Skeeter's cowardice to act against the system and become a social outcast in a predominantly racist society (although she certainly does so also to protect her sources). The book is a means only of building her own career, not to fight for racial equality in the South. As her project is a success, she easily leaves Jackson, Mississippi, and moves to New York to pursue a writing career, whereas the maids either lose their jobs or continue working in white people's homes.

Despite its depressing tone, as it interprets black nannies' job as diminishing to their own race, especially to the younger generation, *The Help* also celebrates black women as, first of all, mothers ready to sacrifice for their children's future. The film lingers especially on the scenes in which the black characters look at the pictures of their children, think about them with the aching hearts, and realize that, trapped within the circumstances of racism, abandoning their own children is the best they can do for them.

The Generation Gap: Age, Discrepancies in Views, and the 1960s' Black Family in *The Butler*

Analyzing the issue of racial progress in the United States in the middle of the twentieth century through the prism of an intergenerational struggle, one inevitably comes across the generation gap that existed within the black community. Most actively and successfully fighting for their civil rights and equality in the mid-twentieth century, black people among different age groups were, apparently, strongly divided. While *The Help* rather peacefully hints at the complex problem of racial progress (and its obvious lack) through the lens of intergenerational relationship, *The Butler* actively engages with the racial protests and fights in American society during the civil rights movement.

Through the story of Cecil Gaines (Forest Whitaker), which encompasses his years as a hand in a cotton field, a household servant, and butler in the White House, as well as in his retirement, *The Butler* considers racial segregation as an everlasting problem for the black population of the United States. Showing Cecil at different ages, the film aims to display the hard life of black people, who even in the twentieth century did not have freedom of choice. Cecil's tale is obviously one of a very lucky black man, since a position in the White House was the most prestigious one a black servant could dream of. Thus, Cecil's "happy" story does not illustrate the general experience of blacks. At the same time, this story is not really a happy one: if he had had a choice, likely he would have had a better job.

President Barack Obama expressed a similar reaction: "I teared up thinking about not just the butlers who worked here in the White House, but an entire generation of people who were talented and skilled. But because of Jim Crow and because of discrimination, they could only go so far. And yet with dignity and tenacity, they got up and worked every single day and put up with a whole lot of mess because they hoped for something better for their kids."[11] He foregrounds the problem I articulated in the discussion of *The Help*: the perpetual (non)silent fight of blacks for their rights and, even more significantly, for the rights of their children, the next generation. While *The Help* underscores black mothers' role in racial progress, *The Butler* examines black fathers, who also contributed to better lives for their children.

Cecil is happy to get the job in the White House because it clearly pays more than his previous positions did, and thus he can secure financial stability for his family—his wife, Gloria (Oprah Winfrey), and their two sons. However, while Cecil and his wife are proud of his promotion, their son Louis (David Oyelowo) believes that being a servant does not differ much from being a slave. The young man overtly underscores that his father, as well as millions of other blacks, does not have freedom of choice. While Cecil continues working diligently as a butler, his son enrolls at a university, where he soon joins a group of other black students fighting against inequality. One of the most important scenes in the film shows the students, after long preparation, going into a diner to boycott segregation. The scene when students enter the diner and walk to the whites-only section quickly moves to the one in the White House, where a posh dinner is being prepared for US political elite. While Louis politely tells the waitress, "We would like to be served, please" and gets an expected refusal, his father carefully puts the flatware on the table in the White House. The students' boycott continues until the evening, as the White House event starts. The audience observes nervous but prepared butlers, and then the well-dressed white guests. At the same time, a group of white people comes to the diner to "take care" of the boycotters. They enter, assaulting the black students with words like "monkey" and "nigger" and then starting to pummel them. At this moment, the film cuts to the White House again: white people stay at the richly served table, clapping their hands, while classical music plays in the background. The butlers stand firmly nearby, ready to serve. The scene changes to the one in the diner, where the humiliation of the students continues, as the whites throw ketchup at and spit into the faces of the boycotting group. They finally push the students from their chairs; at the same moment as in the White House, black butlers move chairs to help the white guests sit comfortably at the table. As one of the whites in the diner pours hot coffee into Louis's face and the young man starts screaming in pain, his father is shown continuing with his duty in the White House. The scene finishes with the boycotting students being arrested by the police, while in the White House the servants, including Cecil, celebrate the success of the dinner with champagne. Clinking their glasses, they say: "To serving our country."

The scene is, indeed, symbolic. First of all, it demonstrates that Cecil and his son—representatives of two different generations—live in two different realities. Cecil, having witnessed, as a child, the savage murder of his plantation worker father and the rape of his mother on a field, understands that the position of a butler guarantees him physical security and a stable income—something his ancestors have never had. Louis, knowing about the times his father lived in only as part of history, not having experienced those hardships himself, cannot understand his father's positive attitude toward being a servant and considers it passivity or inaction. He believes that if people like his father remain satisfied with what they have, there will be no changes.

The two different viewpoints clearly illustrate the conflict between the two generations. Neither is completely wrong nor completely right. Louis is specifically wrong about his father's passivity: when considering Cecil's hard life, one realizes that the man is, indeed, a fighter who achieved the most he could at a specific historic time. Louis, however, lives in a different time—he has more possibilities than Cecil did in his youth, although, crucially, not because society has given these to him but because his father earns enough to support his children. Louis lives in a time of radical, historical changes. When he was younger, Cecil, along with others in his generation, clearly could not make such changes.

Filming the events in the White House and in the diner in such a way, the director seems, however, to suggest that Louis is right about his father. While Cecil serves whites—a job Louis finds deeply humiliating—his son and other young blacks are shown disrespect, humiliated, and beaten by whites who refuse to eat at the same place with blacks. It is symbolic that while Cecil is proud of serving white men, a white waitress in the diner refuses to serve the black students. Looking at the same problem through the eyes of the men from two different generations, the director, Lee Daniels, thus, not only attempts to reveal how black people of different ages viewed the problem of racial segregation specifically in the 1960s, but he also tries to look at the broader history of racism, juxtaposing the attitudes of the son and the father to demonstrate that the father witnessed more of the radical racial changes in the United States—the country that started with the brutal enslavement of Africans and in the twenty-first century elected the first black president. Those changes, however, would be impossible without the hard work of people like his son Louis who, risking their lives, struggled to achieve equality for blacks.

Throughout the film, the audience witnesses the very complicated relationship between Cecil and Louis. The relationship is difficult mostly for the reasons enumerated above but also because Louis eventually decides to join the Black Panthers, which Cecil largely disapproves of. Cecil believes that violence will not help black people achieve racial equality, whereas Louis and his comrades from the Black Panthers consider "self-defense" an appropriate response to the beatings whites carry out to suppress and even mute blacks. The clash of the two generations is particularly apparent in the scene when Louis, his girlfriend, brother, and parents have dinner. An innocent talk turns into an argument between father and son: Cecil realizes that many in the younger generation consider aggression the most effective tool with which to fight racism. Disagreeing and censuring Louis's behavior, Cecil tells his son to get out of the house. He notices that the Black Panthers' politics have irrevocably changed his son, who now overtly blames Cecil for being a submissive servant, a butler, instead of a real fighter. Louis's mother, who usually tries to maintain peace in the house, takes Cecil's side, slapping her son and saying to him with bitterness: "Everything you are and everything you have is 'cause he's a butler." Toward the end of the film, Cecil realizes that because of their disagreement, he has simply lost his son. Disappointed with President Reagan's racist policy toward the situation in South Africa, Cecil leaves his job. He eventually attends one of the protests organized by Louis and his comrades, to stand with them, join their activism, and be part of the noble African American history happening in the second half of the twentieth century.

By depicting African Americans of different generations, the film comments extensively on the problem of racial segregation. It is significant that Cecil's now large family—which includes his wife, children, and grandchildren—celebrates Barack Obama's run for the presidency. Thus, no matter how much the film extols the impact and actions of the people who fought for civil rights in the 1960s, it eventually demonstrates that such an achievement took place thanks to *all* black people, who were slowly coming to the day of their freedom, literally from the times of enslavement. In this respect, it is symbolic that the film concludes with Obama's famous quote: "Yes we can!" Finally, as Obama becomes the president of the United States, Cecil and Louis listen to his speech on TV together, as tears run down Cecil's face. This moment proves that despite all their differences, the son and the father are both part of that history. They both contributed to a black man's eventually becoming the head of this country. Racial progress is thus celebrated as, indeed, a collaborative effort, an intergenerational struggle.

Conclusion

The problem of racism in the Deep South has been widely reflected in film. From D. W. Griffith's *The Birth of a Nation* (1915) to Alan Parker's *Mississippi Burning* (1988) to Steve McQueen's *12 Years a Slave* (2013), it has been dealing with issues of slavery, racial segregation, and injustice.

While *The Help* and *The Butler* investigate the problem of racism in the South, they do so through the prism of age, commenting on of racial progress as the result of an intergenerational struggle. Although initially foregrounding the generation gap, these films celebrate the unity of black people as well as the collective power that after long years of suffering and humiliation has brought them freedom.

Analyzing the problem of racism in the South through the depiction of people of various ages, these films celebrate blacks as people who worked for their paltry incomes, in Obama's words, "with dignity and tenacity."[12] They reveal that young or old, those people did everything to secure better lives for their children, slowly but steadily achieving success. Racial progress, as *The Help* and *The Butler* contend, was, is, and will be feasible only through a collective effort of different generations.

Notes

1. Epigraph from Sherley Anne Williams, *Dessa Rose* (New York, Harper Perennial, 1986).

2. *Gone with the Wind*, directed by Victor Fleming, George Cukor, and Sam Wood (1939; New York: Loew's Inc., 2005), DVD.

3. *The Help*, directed by Tate Taylor (2011; Burbank, CA: Walt Disney Studios Motion Pictures, 2012), DVD; *The Butler*, directed by Lee Daniels (2013, New York City: Weinstein Company, 2014), DVD.

4. Ruth Feldstein, "Women's Bodies and the Myth of the 'Post-Racial,'" *Reviews in American History* 41, no. 1 (2013): 150; Suzanne W. Jones, "The Divided Reception of *The Help*," *Southern Cultures* 20, no. 1 (2014): 12; Melissa Harris-Perry, qtd. in Feldstein, "Women's Bodies," 150; Kimberly Wallace-Sanders, "Every Child Left Behind: The Many Invisible Children in *The Help*," *Southern Cultures* 20, no. 1 (2014): 65.

5. Wallace-Sanders, "Every Child Left Behind," 66.

6. Dorothy Roberts, *Killing the Black Body: Race, Reproduction, and the Meaning of Liberty* (New York: Vintage, 2016), 13, 14

7. Wallace-Sanders, "Every Child Left Behind," 67.

8. Valerie Smith, "Black Women's Memories and *The Help*," *Southern Cultures* 20, no. 1 (2014): 29–30.

9. Wallace-Sanders, "Every Child Left Behind," 68.

10. Smith, "Black Women's Memories," 29.

11. Quoted in Ben Child, "Barack Obama 'Teared up' Watching Oscar-Tipped Drama *The Butler*," *Guardian*, August 28, 2013, https://www.theguardian.com/film/2013/aug/28/barack-obama-oscar-tipped-drama-butler.

12. Ibid.

Acknowledgments

This volume, a long time in the making, is a product of the faith shown by Leila Salisbury, who first suggested a book on the topic. I appreciate her foresight, flexibility, and patience in getting this project to completion. Working with the staff at the University Press of Kentucky was a joy; they quickly answered every question. I thank Tasha Huber for being particularly helpful and Erin Holman for her careful copyediting. The peer reviewers made insightful suggestions and improved the book. A compilation like this is impossible without a passionate group of contributors. The contributors to this volume, whether advanced in their academic careers or at the beginning of their scholarly lives, were always completely professional. They met deadlines, were open to suggestion and revision, and offered insights far beyond my own. I thank them all and hope they are proud of the finished work. I also thank my colleagues in the historical studies department at Southern Illinois University–Edwardsville. We have great freedom to go where our interests lead us, and I appreciate the opportunity to both teach classes and write about the intersections between film, history, race, and the South. The members of the department writing group were very generous in offering their suggestions and critiques as this project took shape. I would also like to thank the SIUE College of Arts and Sciences for supporting this project financially. Friends and family were encouraging as this work moved from a hazy idea to a finished product, and my students continue to motivate me with their energy. Finally, I thank my wife, Jenny Deyto, for her love and support in everything I do.

Bryan Jack
Saint Louis, Missouri
2018

Contributors

Erik B. Alexander is assistant professor of historical studies at Southern Illinois University–Edwardsville. He earned his PhD at the University of Virginia. Alexander was the assistant editor of *The Papers of Andrew Jackson*, volume 9: *1831* (2013). He is currently completing a book manuscript, "Revolution Forestalled: Northern Democrats and the Politics of Reconstruction, 1865–1877."

Kwakiutl Dreher is associate professor of English at the University of Nebraska–Lincoln. She earned her PhD at the University of California–Riverside. Dreher is the author of *Dancing on the White Page: Black Women Entertainers Writing Autobiography* (2008). Her articles have appeared in *Film Criticism* and *The Popular Culture Review.*

Daniel Farrell is currently adjunct professor at William Patterson University. He earned his MA in history from East Stroudsburg University. He has published numerous encyclopedia entries and book reviews. His dissertation research focus is US military policy toward civilian prisoners of war during the American Civil War.

Oliver Gruner is senior lecturer at the University of Portsmouth. He earned his PhD at the University of East Anglia. Gruner is the author of *Screening the Sixties: Hollywood Cinema and the Politics of Memory* (2016). He has contributed essays to several film studies collections, and his articles have appeared in *Rethinking History* and the *Historical Journal of Film, Radio, and Television.*

Megan Hunt is a PhD candidate in American Studies at Northumbria University, UK. Her research highlights the ways in southern religious stereotypes intersect with the racial and class-based distinctions that have been used to indicate the region in Hollywood film. Hunt has contributed chapters to forthcoming edited collections on *The Help* and *Selma*. She also sits on the executive committee of HOTCUS (Historians of the Twentieth Century United States).

Bryan M. Jack is associate professor of historical studies at Southern Illinois University–Edwardsville. He earned his PhD from Saint Louis University. He is the author of *The Saint Louis African American Community and the Exodusters* (2007). He has contributed chapters and articles to edited volumes and journals and is currently completing research on historical memory and race in St. Louis, Missouri.

Gene Kelly holds faculty appointments in the student affairs in higher education program at Kutztown University of Pennsylvania and in the psychology departments at both East Stroudsburg University of Pennsylvania and Marywood University. He also serves as a consultant and trainer on diversity and social justice. Kelly holds a doctorate in human development from Marywood. He has published chapters on race, masculinity, and homophobia in Tyler Perry films; new sexual scripts for gay male youth in the television show *Glee;* and intersectional identities in doctoral students.

Tatiana Prorokova holds a PhD in American studies from the University of Marburg, Germany. Prorokova is an academic editor at Pod Academy, United Kingdom. Her research interests include war studies, ecocriticism, gender studies, and race studies. She is a coeditor of *Cultures of War in Graphic Novels: Violence, Trauma, and Memory* (2018). She is currently working on her second book, which examines representations of the environment and climate change in fiction since the Industrial Revolution.

Caroline Schroeter is a PhD student in English and film and screen media at University College Cork (UCC) and a recipient of the University College Cork Celtic Studies, Arts, and Social Studies PhD Excellency Scholarship. She is the editor in chief of *Aigne Journal* and an editorial board member of *Alphaville: Journal of Film and Screen Media*. Her research focuses on North American literature and film, cinematic education, African American representation, audience reception, race, gender, and identity.

Todd Simpson is assistant professor of library science at York College, City University of New York. He received an MLIS from Long Island University, and an MA from King's College, London. His research interests include organization, access, and preservation of performing arts resources. His current scholarship includes research on LeVar Burton and Ellen Gould Harmon White.

Index

Pages numbers in *italics* refer to illustrations or material contained in their captions.